Liberations

New Essays on the Humanities in Revolution

John Cage

Daniel Stern

Michael Wolff

Hayden White

Louis Mink

Frank Kermode

David Daiches

Harold Rosenberg

Richard Poirier

Leslie A. Fiedler

Ihab Hassan

R. Buckminster Fuller

LIBERATIONS

New Essays on the

Humanities in Revolution

Edited by IHAB HASSAN

WESLEYAN UNIVERSITY PRESS

Middletown, Connecticut

Acknowledgement is gratefully made to the following persons and companies: Big Sky Music and Pryor, Braun, Cashman & Sherman for permission to quote from the lyrics of Bob Dylan's "Lay, Lady, Lay" (Copyright © 1969 by Big Sky Music; all rights reserved); The Bobbs-Merrill Company for permission to quote from LeRoi Jones's poem "T. T. Jackson Sings;" Doubleday and Company for permission to quote from Edgar Paiwonsky's poem "Icons," which was first published in the anthology *Quickly Aging Here,* edited by Geof Hewitt; Giulio Einaudi Editore for permission to quote from Cesar Pavese's poem; Harper & Row, Publishers, for permission to quote from John Cheever's *Some People, Places and Things That Will Not Appear in My Next Novel;* Houghton Mifflin Company for permission to quote from J. R. R. Tolkien's *The Lord of the Rings;* Kirshner Entertainment Corporation for permission to quote from John Lennon and Paul McCartney's "A Hard Day's Night" (Copyright © 1964 by Northern Songs, Limited; all rights reserved); Random House for permission to quote from W. H. Auden's "Prologue" to *On This Island;* Elliot Roberts & Associates for permission to quote the lyrics of Joni Mitchell's "Both Sides Now;" Charles Scribner's Sons for permission to quote from Robert Creeley's "Ballad of the Despairing Husband;" Suhrkamp Verlag for permission to quote from the lyrics of Bertolt Brecht's "Alabama Song" (Copyright © 1967 by Suhrkamp Verlag); Charlie Vermont for permission to quote from his poem "My Father's Retirement Dinner," which was first published in issue 49 of *The Paris Review;* R. W. Worthy for permission to quote from the computer poem "Steaks" (Copyright © 1962 by R. W. Worthy).

ISBN: 0-8195-4034-x

Library of Congress catalog card number: 77-142729

Manufactured in the United States of America

FIRST EDITION

For
Adam and Eve,
perhaps.

Contents

Thanks

to the administration of Wesleyan University for its unwavering support of the Center for the Humanities; and to the staff of the Center, Tania Senff, Joan Farrell, and Linda Thompson, for their sustained courtesy and help.

Preface

I

The authors of these new essays were associated with the Wesleyan Center for the Humanities in 1969–1970. They came as Fellows or Visiting Fellows — I served as Director — to search a central theme: the Humanities in Revolution. For more than a century now, the Humanities have suffered from a certain piety which even Revolution does not escape. True liberations engage some deeper energy, quiddity, or humor of life; and this is what the present authors, I think, wish to engage.

Our time is the time we have; we are always in the middle of things. Is Yeats, among so many moderns, right about a Second Coming? The center may hold forever or break down tomorrow; but we need to experience ourselves in images, and Apocalypse has become a figure of our speech. In the Humanities, in America, in the World, every crisis implicates itself in the first and last things. Ecology and technology, politics and economics, our common sanity, tell us that the end is truly possible though it may not be near.

Let us give Apocalypse a rest. We do not need it to tell us that our ways must mend, or that our business suffers from daily outrages. Pick up an issue of *Time, Daedalus,* or *College English;* purchase the latest radical reader or anti-text. The discomforts of the academy are already too much in the public eye. Yet how many see, I wonder, that we now strike past the college administrator and campus guard, past the curriculum, past scholarship itself, at an older idea of man? The famous drawing of Leonardo, arms spread and legs apart, giving the human measure to circle, square, and universe, no longer takes our breath away. A post-humanism is in the making. What will be its shape?

II

The authors of *Liberations* do not summon from the future a complete shape. But they speak deeply of certain issues and concerns. More, these authors qualify, challenge, instigate. Always, they apprehend their theme concretely, in terms of their intellectual passion or personal experience. As reader of this work, as auditor of colloquia that made its oral counterpart, I take from it some impressions, some judgments and hopes. I sense foremost that much is at stake. I find in it some queries about the Humanities that I should also note:

1. Distinctions, relations, connections, the ways the humanistic mind itself tries to make wholes, are under strain. Everything is a part of everything else; yet discontinuities prevail. How can we discover new methods, metaphors, conjunctions in various disciplines, and for what use?

2. The form of humanistic statement invites attention. Some choose the mode of lecture or essay; others want to improvise on different forms. What, then, is the nature of argument, exposition, or performance in the Humanities? What does the humanist really want to render? How?

3. Some humanists also have a new sense of their audience; it may share few of their assumptions, bring to them unexpected demands. Is the audience younger, angrier, more strange or uneasy than we know? Who is out there?

4. Certain discriminations about the arts, the central "content" of the Humanities, seem now in doubt. The line between art and non-art shifts, fades, hardens suddenly when least we expect it. What do we mean by "art"?

5. There is a strong reaction against history, against the uses, values, and definitions of the past. Resting traditionally on historical method, the Humanities now face a challenge to their way of conceiving knowledge, ordering it, sustaining its worth.

6. Resting traditionally on an ethical ideal, the Humanities face another challenge to their effectiveness, even their sincerity, in upholding a vision of man. Some ask: What, precisely, can the Humanities do to enhance the moral possibilities of our life?

7. Technology demonstrates every day its benign or notorious powers; and science develops marvelous models of consciousness or the universe. How can the Humanities engage these powers or reveal their own without cant?

8. Power is also the means and end of politics — power or terror. The modern world knows this only too well. What are the politics of modern

humanistic systems? How do these systems relate to class, race, nation, in our global setting, in peace or strife? Can the Humanities define and issue into an act?

9. The Humanities have been active in the academy. Their politics have been pedagogical, most immediately felt in class. What, then, are the implications of the Humanities to the new curriculum? So far, the revolution in educational theory — see George Leonard or Charles Silberman — has preceded changes in scholarly fields.

10. The languages of the Humanities, not merely their terms, may be in process of change. Their discursive and analytical character may yield, under pressure of other languages, to less partial expression. Can the Humanities contribute to a language fluent, rich, and "silent"?

No doubt, these themes, these queries, reflect my own concerns as much as those of the authors of this work. The authors speak far better for themselves. They will not speak in a common voice. In background, training, and sensibility, they bring variety to their single statement. Their respective views, their senses of the moment, meet in the mind's seriousness which is also its play.

III

The volume opens with statements of the artist. John Cage puts the immense generosity of creation in the random form to which it is entitled. It is all there, humor, love, and poetry. Cage invokes Buckminster Fuller, who is the visible and invisible presence behind several of these essays, to share the resources of "spaceship Earth" with his fellow men. Not power but utilities in service of all; not willful progress alone, but delight and attention wherever they may lead. Cage silently teaches. Daniel Stern also speaks in a personal form, at once narrative and dramatic, fencing with his "imaginary friend" or fiend through the corridors of fiction. Ironic, oblique, wise, and funny in old Chassidic ways, he exposes the temptations of the contemporary novelist near the end of his untethered fancy.

The following section examines the Humanities in the perspectives of history, philosophy, and criticism. Michael Wolff discovers the Industrial Revolution of Victorian England within the "Long Revolution" of modern times, focusing on the history of urbanization. He valiantly deduces a practical end for the Humanities, an end to human indifference, scarcity, and pain. Hayden White, after delineating the history of the Humanities and deftly identifying the concept of cultural autonomy that came to dominate their disciplines, shows the threat that avant-garde movements now present. (He does not believe that the threat can be made to vanish by turning our glances backwards toward the past.) His analysis of Gombrich, Auerbach, and Popper suggests that the collision between artistic avant-gardes and humanistic diciplines derives from certain notions of realism which the latter assume. Louis Mink describes the spent revolution in modern aesthetics — the disappearance, for instance, of the concept of beauty — and the still current revolution in "art without artists" that a new aesthetics must begin to comprehend. Taking his cue from the expression theory of art of Cassirer, Collingwood, Wollheim, and Susanne Langer, he begins that task himself. As a critic of modernist literature, as a witness to earlier radical movements in art and politics, Frank Kermode wants to redress the balance between the judgments of the generations. His modesty lends dignity to "mistakes" of the elders: he now recognizes Dada and technologism, forgotten in earlier accounts, and with few admonitions to the young, recommends patience, pluralism, and absorptiveness, without abdication, to his peers.

The third section of this volume explores, in greater detail, the vexed politics of the imagination and their influence on culture. David Daiches probes the relation between art and social order; modernist art, he concludes, is "Janus-faced," looking toward both reaction and revolution. His learning permits him to contain the ironies, the paradoxes, of his subject; and the humanist in him compels him to limit "political truth." Harold Rosenberg, making original use of Marx's *The Eighteenth Brumaire of Louis Bonaparte*, illumines the "theatrics of revolutionary revivals" on our political stages. History, repeating itself as farce, now takes the form of spurious events made by "pseudo-personages"; thus the politics of illusionism prevail. Richard Poirier, concerned in another way with politics and performance, argues that the generation gap is itself a metaphor of larger issues and mysteries in ourselves, in our culture. His polemic engages three works — an article in *Rolling Stone*, John Aldridge's *In the Country of the Young*, and Magaret Mead's *Culture and Commitment* — that seem to him to conceal "pressures waiting" from us. There is urgency behind his style and also undue harshness.

The final section of *Liberations* makes explicit a concern of nearly all its authors: the future. In one projection, Leslie Fiedler anticipates a revolution in poetry that popular culture has always concealed. Taking risks with the canons of High Art, he proposes an alternative line of verse, harking back to Longfellow and Foster, closer to the ungoverned soul of men. Adept as usual and outrageous, Fiedler reveals the myth within the sentimental clichés of Pop. In another projection, I comment on current fiction as it moves toward forms of self-subversion or self-transcendence and invoke the dream that the Humanities may help one day to incarnate. I experiment with a kind of writing that I have elsewhere called Paracriticism. (Unlike the other essays in this volume, which were based on lectures delivered at the Wesleyan Center for the Humanities, mine was read at the Michigan State Conference on Modern Literature, April, 1970.)

It is fitting that as this volume begins with the contribution of John Cage, it should end with one from Buckminster Fuller: both make original statements on the future of the Humanities. In his essay, Fuller takes us as far into human destiny as science and vision can take us now. He places man in the large context of creation where man belongs. It is unwise to summarize his ideas. They have scope, poetry, and enormous hope.

IV

Neither the Humanities nor Revolution can always escape the subtle or harsh reassurances that humankind requires. Where, then, does the value of this work lie? And if not comfort, what conclusion does it offer?

The reader, no doubt, will wish to decide. In deciding, he may consider that each writer of this work writes not only to demonstrate his mastery of a topic but also to acknowledge forces shaping the survival of men. Moreover, each author gives of himself, putting before us forms of his loyalty or mistrust and thus offering paradigms of existence within the Humanities. Finally, each declares himself open to contingencies of the mind, searching where research may serve only to close the issues.

Speaking for myself, I look, beyond comfort or criticism, for some natural wisdom lost in dreams that may guide cultural and biological evolution. Dreams and mutabilities — we shun them both — do they not amount to a broken definition of man? Liberations come from some strange region where the imagination meets change. Perhaps the Humanities can discover part of that region and return to tell the tale. Perhaps our consciousness will then change, hearing that tale and fashioning from it new tales. Humanists may not agree; nor do they often agree with one another, and therein may lie a condition of freedom or vitality. Yet one thing now seems clear to me: we need to re-imagine change itself, else we labor to confirm all our errors. How many of us, radical in politics, morality, or art, seem only repetitious there where life cries to remake itself!

Centers of one kind of knowledge or another spread across this planet. But centering itself is a metaphor of creation and mortality that we seldom permit to take hold as we dispense knowledge or receive it, or share the curious inquiry of man with others. But there is perhaps a limit to liberations that even the best of scholars can achieve, writing alone and talking together. Let us not ask from them here more than their generosity proffers.

I. Statement of the Artist

JOHN CAGE

1.

DIARY: How to Improve the World (You Will Only Make Matters Worse) Continued 1969 (Part V)

CXIX.   No need to move the camera.
(Pictures come to it.)   Gather, Fuller
advises, facts regarding human needs and
world resources.   Place in computer
memory bank.   Update continuously.
Join team of programmers, competing
to find speediest peaceful means for
giving each world inhabitant what's needed
for his kind of living.   Videoize
solution on football-field-sized geodesic
world map, so fact continuously
changing intelligent solution of world
game exists becomes via TV household
knowledge.   A study was made with
computer to find out where in the world
wealthy Americans prefer to **retire.**
They retire, computer tells us, to
Cuernavaca in Mexico, a hilltown near
Nairobi in Kenya, and some place or
other in Nepal.   CXX.   The goal is
not to have a goal.   The new universe
city will have no limits.   It will

not be in any special place.   Having
returned, as Fuller puts it, to his
studies, teacher will be flying all
over the world and even out into
space.   **Questions I might have learned
to ask him can no longer be
answered.**   Waiting in the hotel in
Rio de Janeiro to hear whether or not I
was to meet with the people who were
studying anarchy (they had come in their
studies to Thoreau and, having heard
that I was enjoying Thoreau's
Journal, had asked me to share with them
my thoughts) : telephone didn't ring.
      CXXI.   Act of sharing is a community
act.   Think of people outside the
community.   What do we **share with them?**
Teacher played hooky.   Sent message:
      "Receiving instruction.   Enjoying
myself thoroughly.   See you next week."
      **Lejaren Hiller's computer music
project: "fantastic orchestra."
Each sound to** be a plurality of
vibratory circumstances known or not
known in nature.   Impossible made
possible.   Fuller: Nothing's
artificial.   It exists?   It is natural.
How d'you manage to live with **just one**
shirt?   Before going to bed, I take a
shower with my shirt still on.
      Afterwards I scrub the cuffs and
collar with my electric toothbrush.   Then
      I turn on the TV, hang my shirt on it.
Best place I've found to dry it.   CXXII.
      Years ago zoological gardens began to get

rid of wire fences, substituting
means that decreased the sense of
separation between animal and man.
Coming back from The Junior Museum
of Natural History in Sacramento,
Billie Berton told me children now
make applications for checking animals
out.   It took six weeks to teach the
computer how to toss three coins six
times.   Somewhat worried, I tossed coins
manually to discover from the
I Ching how **I Ching felt about being
programmed.   It was delighted.
I Ching promised quantitative
increase of benefits for culture.   What
we've already done conspires against
what we have now to do.   CXXIII.   Advice
to Brazilian anarchists: Improve
telephone system.   Without telephone,
merely starting revolution'll be
impossible.   Pinkville.   Charles Peck.
New York's State Botanist, spent most of
his life with no** place to work but a
dark hallway.   Just **before he died
the Government gave him a room with a
window.**   Cadaqués: up around nine or
ten; coffee; off by boat to a cove
where no others are; white wine,
almonds, olives; chess, swimming,
dominoes; back in town by one or two
for lunch with him.   (He had not been
with us.)   Feared plan'd fail (no one
wanted to get **deeply involved**).
**However, it worked.   When disaster
was imminent, people rose to**

5 : *Diary: How to Improve the World*

occasion, did whatever was necessary
to keep the thing going.   (Reminder,
not a revelation.)   He'd have preferred
silence to applause at the end (**art
instead of slap in the face.**)   CXXIV.
Whispered truths.   **Looking for
something irrelevant, I found I
couldn't find it.**   "Wild as if we
lived on . . . marrow of antelopes
devoured raw."   (Thoreau.)   Wanting
to make some easy money, he took to
cracking safes, was caught, put in
penitentiary.   While ill in the prison
hospital, he had an affair wth middle-aged
nurse.   When he was released from
penitentiary, nurse introduced him to a
beautiful young girl whom he married.
His bride immediately **inherited three
million dollars.**   College: two hundred
people reading same book.   An obvious
mistake.   Two hundred people can
read two hundred books.   Clothes I wear
for mushroom hunting are rarely sent
to the cleaner.   They constitute a
collection of odors I produce and
gather while rambling in the woods.   I
notice not only dogs (cats, too) are
delighted (they love to smell me).   CXXV.
Vacaville.   Spent the evening with a
murderer.   I asked him why he drank so
much coffee.   He said, "There's
nothing else to do."   **University, which
now embraces studies formerly excluded
from it such as home economics,
music, and physical education, has**

sister universities abroad, belongs
to consortium of universities here,
includes a "free" university.   What's
adumbrated's indistinct from society
itself.   Not a community of scholars
living like monks, but society
which works for any kind of living,
any kind of attention-placement, any
activity.   Something seems
beautiful?   Wittgenstein: You mean
it clicks?   When things don't click,
take clicker from your pocket and
click it. **CXXVI.   Death.**   Process
involving Christmas trees takes place
each year.   Christmas trees that're grown
in Hawaii are sent by freighter to be
sold on the West Coast.   Christmas
trees that're grown on the West Coast
are sent by freighter to be sold in
Hawaii.   Ready or not, we are being
readied.   Complete checkup.   I was more
examined than ever before.   Doctor's
report: You're very well except for your
illnesses.   John **McHale:** "It has taken
the history of mankind to produce the
articles we have around us (the match,
the computer); it is essential to see
one sector of population isn't servicing
another; we are all using the same
materials simultaneously; information
storage never depletes; ability to
reuse materials makes us, after all
these centuries, quite skillful."
CXXVII.   Impatience.   Why do you have
one TV set on top of the other?

7 : *Diary: How to Improve the World*

The bottom one doesn't work.   There
were fifty-two tapes.   We had to
combine them for a single recording.
We went to a studio where they
could record eight at a time.   When
we had seventeen together it sounded like
chamber music; when we had thirty-four
together it sounded like orchestral
music; when we had fifty-two
together it didn't sound like anything
we'd ever heard before.   Milarepa.
London publisher sent blank ("Fill out.")
so I'd be included in survey of
contemporary poets of the English
language.   Threw it out.   Week later
urgent request plus duplicate blank
arrived.   "Please return with a
glossy photo."   Complied.   July, August,
September.   Publisher then sent
letter saying it'd been decided I'm
not significant poet after all: if I
were, everyone else'd be too.   CXXVIII.
Used to say "never the twain shall
meet."   Now we don't hesitate to fight
oriental wars, there's no doubt about
usefulness of oriental thought for
western mind.   Same's true for
Utopia.   Its impracticality is no longer
to be assumed.   Everything's changed.
Develop facilities that remove need
for middlemen.   Soup cans are not only
beautiful (Warhol, for example) but true
(Campbell's soup is actually in them).
They're also constant reminders of
spiritual presence.   "I am with you

always." Function fulfilled by images of the Virgin Mary along a path is now also fulfilled by the public telephone. Instead of lighting a candle, we insert a dime and dial. **CXXIX. Computer mistake in grade-giving resulted in academic failure of several brilliant students. After some years the** mistake was discovered. Letter was then sent to each student inviting him to resume his studies. Each replied he was getting along very well without education. Buddha reclines on his right side. So does the lion. How thorough he is! He told me his secrets. Town is very small, well-organized. Nothing can be found in it. An idea was given to them because they didn't have one. The Seychelles. Cloth calendars for kitchen walls designed by Lois Long are sold throughout the USA. Some years ago Lois made one by mistake giving two different dates to a single day: Thursday November 31 was also Thursday December 1. **The calendar was very successful. CXXX. Discipline (Disciple). Giving up one's country, all that's dear to one's country: "Leave thy father and mother. . . ." Yoga (Yoke). Taming** of the globe (Open: In and Out). Einstein wrote to Freud to say men should stop having wars. Freud wrote back to say if you get rid of war you'll also get rid of love. Freud was

wrong.   What permits us to love one
another and the earth we inhabit is that
            we and it are impermanent.   We
obsolesce.   Life's everlasting.
                Individuals aren't.   A mushroom
lasts for only a very short time.   Often I
go in the woods thinking after all these
years I ought finally to be bored with
            fungi.   But coming upon just any
mushroom in good condition, I lose my
mind all over again.   Supreme good
fortune: we're both alive!   CXXXI.   Things
governments wish to divide between us
            belong to all of us: the land, for
            instance, beneath the oceans.
            People speak of literacy.   But I, for
one, can't read or write any computer
                language.   Only numbers I know are
those based on ten.   I'm uneducated.
Home in Wayzata, Minnesota's very much
            like a home near Sitges (just south of
            Barcelona).   Now we're itinerant there's
no reason to go on, for instance, picking
            fruit.   Since we live longer, Margaret
            Mead says, we can change what we do.   We
                can stop whatever it was we promised
we'd always do and do something else.
CXXXII.   He is one of my closest friends.
                He asked me for help.   I gave it.
He couldn't use it.   TV Guide tells what's
going on, doesn't tell what we're
                obliged to look at.   Where you are
            limits what channels you can receive.
            (Hearing sounds before they're
audible is not the way to hear them.)
                Imitate the telephones of your

homes'n'highways.   (Their
indifference.)   They aren't
displeased when the person speaking
is black.   They aren't pleased when
the person speaking is black.   When lady
in charge of university concerts asked
what music day was to be called, I
replied *Godamusicday.*   She was
delighted.   Her husband, also
affiliated with university (but in
its legal aspects) wasn't.   "Profanity
is forbidden.   Nothing can be printed
that might come to the Governor's
notice."   Duchamp, asked whether he
believed in God: No.   God is Man's
stupidest idea.   CXXXIII.   Traveling
from one place to another we confine
ourselves to the roads.   That's why, of
course, we feel so populated: we're
too choosy about the space we use.
**Guests had left.   Before going to bed,
while reading a book he'd bought that
morning, he chuckled.   Ten minutes later,
brushing his teeth, he died.   Whole**
Earth.   We connect Satie with Thoreau.
Eleventh thunderclap?   **1928.   Walter
loved the Chinese, hated Communists.
He** couldn't bear the Japanese.
Fortunately for Uncle, he died before
the tables turned.   Mushroom?   Leaf?
Backs ache.   If we had immortal life
(but we don't), it'd be reasonable to do
as we do now: spend our time killing one
another.   CXXXIV.   Chadwick, gardener at
Santa Cruz.   Nobby'd said, "You must
meet **our wizard."**   (Chadwick's back,

11 : *Diary: How to Improve the World*

Nobby told me, had been injured in war,
but when we went mushrooming with
his student-helpers, Chadwick,
half-naked, leapt and ran like a
pony.   Catching up with him, it was
joy and poetry I heard him speak.   But
while I listened he noticed some distant
goal across and down the fields and.

shouting something I couldn't
understand because he'd already turned
away, he was gone.)   Students had defected
from the university or had come
especially from afar to work with him
like slaves.   They slept unsheltered
in the woods.   After the morning's hunt
with him and them, I thought: These
people live; others haven't even been
born.   CXXXV.   It was not quite
midnight.   Duchamp was waiting for us in
the street.   He looked for all the
world like a handsome young man.   Want
list of communes (places where Americans
live who've given up dependence on
power and possessions) ?   Write to
Alternatives Foundation, 2441 Le
Conte Ave., Berkeley, Calif., 94709 or
to Carleton Collective Communities
Clearinghouse, Northfield, Minn., 55057.
Future's no longer a secret.   Murderer
asked, "What time is it?"   "Nine
o'clock."   Five minutes later he
repeated his question, "What time is it?"
"Five minutes after nine."   Ten.   She had
problem children.   Their grades were so
poor they couldn't enter college.   I

told her to stop worrying about them.
She did.   They've turned out
beautifully.   One married a Californian,
has two fine sons, paints beautifully.
Tucker's automobile expertise is in demand.
CXXXVI.   Talked about fact writing's less
and less attractive.   Picking up
the pen, one knows idea's already
entertained in other minds.   Pen becomes
absent.   Sword'll follow suit.   Flower
Sermon.   In the plane ready for last leg
of flight to Yucatan (he'd flown from
Berkeley, I from Palermo in
Sicily).   Grounded by fog we remained in
Mexican plane three hours, which with
subsequent flight gave me time to
read Stent's typescript of his book, *The
Coming of the Golden Age.*   When
questions came to mind, I simply put
them to the author!   Completely
satisfied.   How do you propose, Fuller was
asked, to accomplish this without
involvement in political action?   His
answer: The World Game provides an
apolitical option, a solution no one's
forced to accept.   When, however,
you want it, you'll be able, since you know
it exists, to use it.   **CXXXVII.**   Puppy
was eating his vomit.   "That's one
thing," his mistress said, "we don't
do."   Picked him up; put him outside;
resumed her conversation.   No one
cleaned up the mess.   (An elderly Viennese
lady whose principal pleasure was
listening to music was alarmed

13 : *Diary: How to Improve the World*

because she thought she was losing
her hearing.   She went to the doctor.
He discovered her ears were full of wax.
He removed it very easily.)   Man
living in the Ojai knew how to manage
unsheltered.   But, hungry, he
devised a plan that worked: to subtly
change his environment in terms of its
seductiveness to picnickers so that
coming upon it picnickers'd feel they'd
made a discovery of the ideal place to
eat (he lived for years on food they
left behind).   CXXXVIII.   Busy
signal in the telephone system
sometimes means person one's calling's
talking to someone else.   Sometimes busy
signal means someone else's trying to
reach very same person you're trying
to reach.   This creates a problem.
Solution: two different types of busy
signals.   If at some moment person
we're trying to reach (being called
before by someone else) answers,
genuine busy signal rings.
Presidential platform: promise,
elected or not, to go on with my work,
not bothering about you; to remove
laws; to extend unlimited credit
throughout society regardless of
nationality.   Observing distinctions
(race distinctions), side with underdog,
learning from him who was oppressed
to live outside the law not committing
crimes.   Become slave to all there
is.   (No need to become King.)   Siding
with noises, musicians discovered

**duration's impartiality.   What
corresponds in society to sound's
parameter of duration?**   CXXXIX.
Vacation.   This is ours.   Don't just
"do your thing": do so many things no one
will know what you're going to do next.
**Add video screen to telephone.   Give
each subscriber a thousand sheets of
recordable erasable material so
anytime, anywhere, anyone'd have**
access to a thousand sheets of *something*
(drawings, books, music, whatever).
You'd just dial.   If you dialed the
wrong number, instead of uselessly
disturbing another subscriber, you'd
just get surprising information,
something unexpected.   CXL.
Statement by Stulman, manufacturer/
distributor of lumber products, founder/
President of the World Institute: The
question before us is whether we will so
organize the processes for gathering
and applying knowledge that the
creative powers of all men can be
catalyzed for growth toward
wholeness, or whether we will
persist in our egocentric,
ethnocentric, fact-accumulating,
thing-oriented, power-amassing ways
that are leading us to destruction.
Looking out the window into the forest,
illuminated surfaces in the house
(that aren't in the forest) are
seen in the forest, 3-D in color.   Hand
that's placed on TV is placed at the
same time outside on the tree.   CXLI.   The

15 : *Diary: How to Improve the World*

shower's in the room, not confined to a
cubicle.   On the opposite wall's a
            mirror.   Steam from the hot water
        produces the slow disappearance of
one's image.   Pleasure of having a body.
            "Waiting for the gift from me to me
of death."   Assassination of Martin
Luther King.   **Apocalypse.**   They have
homes but they don't have the idea. Keep
        Out.   Languages separate people.
    Images (TV, highway signs, trademarks,
            film) bring them together.   Going
    to the moon, we speak in numbers.   A
    year has passed.   We pretend we can get
    along without him.   For three or four
    years, Igor Strawinsky was treated for a
malady his doctors thought he had.   When,
    at death's door, Strawinsky's hands
    turned black, the doctors concluded a
            mistake had been made.   CXLII.
    That that's unknown brings mushroom
and leaf together.   "Ego dethroned."   **In**
    the course of being provided with
    false teeth, Thoreau took ether.   "You
        are," he wrote, "told that it will
    make you unconscious, but no one can
    imagine what it is to be unconscious
    until he has experienced it.   If you
        have an inclination to travel,
        take," he advised, "the ether.   You go
    beyond the farthest star."   We know from
            a variety of experiences that if we
    have a sufficiently large number of
things, some or even many of them can be
    bad but the sum-total is good for the
            simple reason, say, that not all of

the things in it are good.   CXLIII.
Found, page 74, in a book by Cassirer: it
is speech itself which prepares the way
whereby it is itself transcended.
        From navigation to aviation.   Fuller:
Renounce water as sanitation-means;
        adopt compressed air (following
lead of dentists).   Bits of hair and skin
floating in the air with pollen, seeds
and spores from plants.   Out of water into
        air and back to earth.   I asked
        Xenakis what's wrong with USA.   He
was quiet for a moment and then said,
"Too much power."   Put 'em who threaten
possessions and power together with 'em who
        offend our tastes in sex and dope.
Those who're touched, put 'em in
        asylums.   Pack off old ones to
"senior communities," nursing homes.   Our
children?   Keep'em prisoner,
baby-sitter as warden.   School?   Good for
        fifteen to twenty years.   Army
afterward.   Liberated, we live in prison.
No this, no that.   Kill us before we
        die!   CXLIV.   We have no icons: we
believe what we do.   (Telephone
conversation turned toward politics.
        Mrs. Emmons said she was certain
        what the government was doing was
        right.   Beverly said, "How do you
        figure that?"   Her mother replied,
"Well!   This is a Christian country.")   We
leave food offerings for person who
        makes next telephone call no matter
who he is: thus we transform highway
telephone booth into wayside shrine.   I

don't believe, Duchamp said, in the
verb, to be.   "I do not believe that I
        am."   Commune problem: communes're
filled with gurus, needing (not having)
others "to guru."   But teaching's
part'n'parcel of divisive society we're
    leaving.   Thoreau: "My seniors have
        told me nothing . . . , probably can tell
me nothing to the purpose."   Davis: don't
    know what we're studying; don't know
        how we'll do it.   Studied map.
Should have taken road not on it (went
    off to the left).   CXLV.
    Reprogramming.   Jack McKenzie's
proposal: Set up alternative university
        program freeing a student from all
curriculum responsibilities.   Let him
        elect his studies.   When he leaves,
    give him, instead of degree,
certificate telling what he did while
    in school.   Looking at the sunset,
Brown noticed part of its beauty is
caused by air pollution.   Day after the
        assassination.   Human being sitting
    at the table next to mine.   Wanted to
    speak to him.   Didn't.   Didn't have
the right.   As we left the valley to
    enter the desert, I gave up all
    thought of finding mushrooms.   But for
        some reason we stopped along the
road.   There underneath the pepper trees I
    found *Tricholoma personatum*,
        excellent, in quantity.   CXXLVI.
The poor?   Where do *they* go to retire?
    Takilma, Oregon (America's third poorest
        town).   Nothing to do: Free jam,

peanut butter, staples.   Have two
children?   Government'll give you two
hundred and forty dollars a month.   Money
comes through the mail.   Slight
irritations ("make life sufficiently
interesting to live") are provided by
visits of welfare worker whose
assignment is Takilma.   Takilma's
beautiful.   Problem in Takilma: Boredom.
People often together sitting around
talking.   Let 'em close their mouths;
open their eyes and ears; spend day in
different directions, seeking world
around or in 'em, returning to one
another in the evening, ventilated,
ventilating.   Provision for changes
in schedule.   CXLVII.   She brought him
food.   Clairvoyant, he knew it was
poisonous.   Third time she offered
him deadly food, he accepted it, but
himself appointed the hour of his
death.   Religious tract David Tudor gave
me: "Christ International."   Train is
made up of engine, coal car, caboose.
Engine is fact.   Coal car's faith.
Caboose is feeling.   Train can run with
or without feeling.   Caboose can't make
train run.   After breakfast he offered her
a cigarette.   She said, "No, thank
you."   He said, "What's wrong?   Have
you stopped smoking?"   She said,
"Yes."   Next day he stopped too.
That was Nobby and Beth ten years
ago.   CXLVIII.   I've learned to say No
to those I don't know.   Learned to
say No to some of those I know.

(Example of underdevelopment of
religious spirit.)   Edwin Schlossberg and
Buckminster Fuller gave six weeks
comprehensive design science course at
the New York Studio School.   (I was
invited to the last meeting.   There were
about twenty-two students.   The first
         thing Bucky said was that the young
         people sitting around the table had
sufficient intelligence to run the world,
to solve all of world problems.   Glancing
         at the students, I was skeptical.
   They looked like a bunch of hippies
with some older oddballs thrown in.)
CXLIX.   (But while they spoke, did as I do
at the movies when it's clear
everything'll turn out all right.   I wept.
Fuller would've said, "You sleep too
      much.")   All God's religions and all His
      servants (Lawmakers, Philosopher-Kings,
Saints, Artists) have not been able to put
Mankind back together again.   "You can
   lead a horse to water but you can't make
      him drink."   We've got the
automobile.   No sense in leading horses
around.   Let 'em go where they will.   Fix
      it so if they're thirsty there's
something for'em to drink.   Earth's the
   Way to Heaven.   There's no mystery
      about it.   Don't change Man (Fuller):
change his environment.   Humanities?
   Save them for your spare time.
      Concentrate on the Utilities.   CL.
      In anything experienced nowadays
      there is much that is true, much
         that is false.   Proofreading.

Chadwick described magnetic effect of
moon on tides, on germination of seeds.
"Moon inclining draws mushrooms out of
Earth."   We talked of current
disturbance of ecology, agreed man's
works no matter how great are pygmy
compared with those of nature.
Nature, pressed, will respond with
grand and shocking adjustment of
creation.   **Out of ourselves with a
little o, into ourselves with a big O.**
Reunion.   Received month's check.   Paid
bills.   Went to Farmer's Market
(economy).   Returned at six having
spent last penny on turkey and all
the trimmings.   Friends arrived at
midnight for Thanksgiving in the Spring.
Cared for us, day in, day out, rest
of the month.

2.

The Mysterious New Novel

I am a writer of fictions. I am not a scholar; rather, a teller of stories, of untruths. In approaching the situation of the modern novel — and even the mysterious post-modern novel — I will do it from the inside out. The truths will have to fall, as they may, between the fictions.

When I was six years old, I had an imaginary friend. He changed shapes, faces and names so often my mother grew absolutely bewildered. But I didn't. I knew he was both real and imaginary. I knew, too, that he often asked me questions, kept me on my toes, looking for the answers. Now that I'm grown up, or at least grown older, I have chosen to address this essay to a friend I have imagined. He has the face of all the problems I face as a novelist. And he has the names of all the movements and styles of thought and work that characterize our time. He is a good and tough-minded companion, and it is to him that I will direct my remarks.

You are my good friend, although I have, in a sense, created you. Sometimes you are twenty or thirty years older than I, more often younger by ten or fifteen years. Still, you share my concerns: art, love and getting through the day as a human being. We share, too, the sense of living very much at the end and very much at the beginning of something. You're better educated than I am — thus you know more than I do — but, as some mad old cat once said, I am what you know. I and all the books I've read and the music I've played — and if I'm lucky, perhaps a book or two that I've written.

AUTHOR'S NOTE: Material on page 32 is, in part, taken from Donald Barthelme's "Paraguay." And the Chassidic tales quoted throughout the essay are told in the subtly transmuted form created by Elie Wiesel. The line between the tale and the commentary grows thinner every day.

Of course, your face and identity keep changing. Sometimes you're a kind of anonymous young fellow — the intense one who asks me a tough question at a party. Other times you become an historically real person: the young Nietzsche, for example, long before he went mad, cajoling me, with hidden threats, into new ways — or perhaps the final ego, Nabokov, laughing at me, and at all of us, from his imaginary Switzerland.

At other times you wear my own face, tormenting me with the death of all I have believed in: with the death of Humanism, the by-now-banal death of God, with the death of the novel . . . searching me out behind my typewriter, or at three in the morning, when the spirit is vulnerable to the sense of futility, and convincing me that there is no place to go, nothing to say that is meaningful, and questioning the very notion of meaning as it has been thought of until now.

You have been known, like the Devil, to wear most pleasant disguises. Sometimes you are the exciting young revolutionary of the Arts, filling my ears full of the possibilities of new experiments, anti-literature, superexplosive pop-novels, mixed-media, non-linear superdenials of dense-character fiction that may blow the mind — and yet chill, or at least cool, the heart and the imagination at the same time. But more often than not, it is bad news that you bring: signposts all pointing to the dead-ends of Western Culture and in particular to my corner of it: the novel. There are times when I'm moved to respond like the Chassidic Jew who lost his way in the forest on the Day of Atonement without a prayer book and who, in desperation, unable to read his prayers, at last simply turned his face upwards and recited the alphabet, adding: "I give up, God. You take the letters and make words and prayers out of them. You know how. I don't."

Sometimes, particularly when I'm working, you come to remind me that Rimbaud, at the last, chose Silence. You come to remind me that Freud labored like a Titan to free the ego (where Id was, there shall Ego be) and then Artaud came along and said: "It is by revolt against the ego and the self that I disburden myself of all the evil incarnations of the Word." Well, I reply to you, Artaud was a madman. Inspired — but still mad. And you reply that Artaud's children are everywhere, striving to lose their egos on clouds of Mexico Gold — or even stranger lands. Eighteen-year-old De Quinceys, Indians of the Middle Class. Rimbaud merely wanted to deepen his writing by deranging the senses. Today, a whole generation — or a deeply sentient part of it — cannot get through its life without some of that sense of derangement. During the French Revolution of 1968 someone wrote on a wall: *Unless your experience seems strange to you — it is false.* And one thing these young people have in common with the new writers — whom I'm told they don't read much — is a sense of the apocalyptic. This, my friend never tires of telling me, is the time of technological man — the man who is at home with doomsday — because he understands Doomsday Machines. He is post-humanist. He understands the truth that man is irrelevant, thanks to the uses of the computer. And he has qualified this sense of irrelevance into general theory. (If relevance itself is irrelevant, it must hurt considerably less to *be* irrelevant. Out of the pain of feeling superfluous, a philosophy of detachment is born.)

Thus, your attacks upon me as a 'humanist' . . . in the name of anti-art: your midnight incantations to me, from your Irish God Beckett, writing in French from a Paris apartment: *The expression that there is nothing to express, nothing with which to express, no power to express, no desire to express, together with an obligation to express. . . .*

If this is, in some measure, the shifting ground on which we stand, let me put together a little collage — a culture-collage of origins which may have brought us here — and thus may help us understand a little better where we go from here. It is a free-form collage; a culture-dream, if you will.

Remembering that the Marquise went out at five o'clock, I, too, went strolling at five and found an old Jewish beggar on the street corner. The beggar told me an ancient Talmudic riddle:

"Why was Man created on the last day?"

"I don't know," I replied.

"So that he can be told, when pride takes hold of him: God created even the Gnat before thee."

When I asked him why he had told me this riddle, the beggar said: "To remind you that anti-humanism is nothing new — nor is it, necessarily, anti-human."

I moved along, past a Rock group called Jimmy Joyce and the Jesuits, singing their latest hit: For Every Taling There's a Telling and That's the He and She of It . . . and I ran into a fellow who looked familiar. When I asked him who he was he said: "I am, in a sense, Jacob Horner." When I tried to question him he vanished. And I walked along thinking of the letter I'd received that morning from my friend in St. Petersburg, who, having gambled away the advance royalties of his unwritten novel, wrote in despair: "My dear friend: If one could but tell, categorically, all that we Russians have gone through during the last ten years in the way of spiritual development, all the realists would shriek that it was pure fantasy. And yet it would be the one true deep realism." Which last ten years, I wondered — and wondered, too, about that last ten American years. . . .

Passing by the open door of a Church I heard the tag end of a sermon going on. . . . "The courage to be is rooted in the God who appears when God has disappeared in the anguish of doubt." Such talk made me want a drink, fast, so I stopped into a nearby Spanish Café where I had a quick brandy, only to hear the old Spanish waiter murmuring: "Our Nada which art in Nada, hallowed be thy Nada. . . ." And I understood, more than ever, the truth stated by the old perfectionist, writing the same sentence over and over again for days, weeks and months: "The less one feels a thing, the more fit one is to express it in its true nature." And I thought: for myself, I want only to be such a poet, forever, who sacrifices himself in the Kabbala of self for the immaculate conception of things. . . .

And I found myself, at the last, at the outskirts of the city, which was, as it turned out at that moment, Paris of the early twentieth century. That city so beloved by visiting, tormented German poets — and I saw just such a one leaving the city, and he left an epitaph of his visit: "What did they know of him? He was now so terribly difficult to love, and he felt that One alone was able for the task. But that One was not yet willing." And I called out to him: *God has no riches of his own. He gives to one what he takes from another.* . . .

These then were the persons of my dream-culture-collage: Dostoyevsky, Rilke, Artaud, Joyce, Valéry, Gide, Hemingway. . . . Included in their legacy: nihilism, doubt, indeterminacy and dehumanization.

But those were days you could tell the devils from the angels without a scorecard. And they were on the side of the angels. The role they played in the spiritual life of their time — and in ours — can be illustrated in this tale from the great sage Rabbi Nachman of Bratislav: There was, in ancient times, a gifted seer who divined that when the grain crop was harvested and made into bread and eaten, everyone who ate of it would go mad. How long this madness would last, no one could tell. Knowing this, the King decreed that his Prime Minister must take upon himself the loneliest task in the world. He, alone, would *not* eat of the grain or the bread. But when everyone else had eaten and gone mad, his task would be to go from house to house and tell the people, *Remember, you are mad.*

25 : *The Mysterious New Novel*

This was the role of the great writers who arrived after World War One and founded the Modern movement on the bones of The Wasteland. Cautionary and moral beneath their magnificent aesthetic experiments, their job was to remind us when we were mad; that is, when we were jeopardizing our essential humanity. This was a humanist vision, a humanist action. And their art, so apparently revolutionary and incomprehensible at the time, is now seen to be profoundly humanistic in its texture.

The differences between them and my imaginary friend to whom I speak tonight are interesting. They grappled with spiritual hopelessness. He takes it with his morning coffee; he's never known anything else. They — Joyce, Pound, Eliot and the others — were concerned with the absence of usable values; he questions the very use of consecutive thought and language with which to couch either the loss of old values or the creation of new ones.

Despair? One feels in his longings an impatience with despair. Not that despair may be only a fashion — and it is, of course, an always returning one — but even if it is authentic, it is no longer satisfying enough. If Camus, a spiritual child of these forbears, speaks of the existential desert of thought, he speaks of it in hopes of finding or creating oases.

But my friend is a Bedouin of thought. The desert does not frighten him. He's known nothing else. He learns nihilism in grammar school, along with the new math. He trusts no illusions of Western society. When he was a child, Nietzsche took him aside and warned him not to believe what strangers told him. All ideas are, to him, received ideas. Eastern thought has a suspect seductiveness for him, perhaps because it is anti-thought, anti-linear. If its idea of metaphysical applause is the sound of one hand clapping, this brings to him a soothing concept: silence. Instead of going from house to house saying: remember, you are mad, he plays at madman himself, stoning his mind in a longing for sacred Highs. Remember, he says, everyone else is falsely mad. *Our* madness is sanity. This is quite another matter. And in his zeal he leads me to the British psychiatrist R. D. Laing, who is founding a school that believes what we call madness to be only a spiritual state we're unwilling or unable to cope with. And when I confess myself unable to quite follow Laing into his psychotic world of formless forms, he smiles bitterly. He smiles, too, at my die-hard desire to write works that recapture a sense of wholeness in a torn world. Instead he urges me toward randomness and chance — urges me to reject the entire idea of form as Western culture has known it. And in my moments of weakness, which are many, I give him some, but never all, credence. Thomas Aquinas said that three things are needed for Beauty: wholeness, harmony and radiance. Our times' answer to Aquinas is both terrifying and banal. Our wholeness was fragmented at Hiroshima. Our vision of harmony died in a gas chamber at Auschwitz. And our sense of radiance, whose source was the notion of a God shining with love, has been obscured by a black cloud of doubt. As for borrowing some of that badly needed radiance from Man — it gets harder all the time . . . as the Beatles sang: "I heard the news today, O boy. . . ."

And if I insist, in some of my classical moods — which are many — that the artistic prospect and the situation of language are better than my imaginary friend allows, he chooses one of his many voices and this is what he replies:

The Problem of Language: In the larger stores, Silence is sold in paper sacks like cement. The softening of language usually lamented as a falling off from former practice is, in fact, a clear response to the proliferation of surfaces and stimuli. Imprecise sentences lessen the strain of close tolerances. Silence is also available in the form of white noise. The extension of white noise to the home by means of leased wire from a central generating point has been useful.

The Problems of Art: New artists have been obtained. These do not object to the rationalization process. Production is up. Quality-control devices have been installed at those points where the interests of artists and audience intersect. Shipping and distribution have been improved. The rationalized art is dispatched from art dumps to regional art dumps, and from there into the life stream of cities. Each citizen is given as much art as his system can tolerate. Each artist's product is translated into a statement in symbolic logic. The statement is then "minimized" by various clever methods and translated back into the design of a simpler circuit. Formed by a number of techniques, the art is then run through heavy steel rollers. Sheet art is generally dried in smoke and is dark brown in color. Bulk art is air-dried and changes color in particular historical epochs.

Well, the color of our particular historical epoch is quite clear: as totalitarian as the preceeding passage indicates. The encroachments of absolute controls are everywhere in it — as they are everywhere in our lives. It's no wonder that writers, critics and philosophers are eager to write an ending to The Book of Man — which is what the novel has been since its beginnings.

In America, the brief age of the transcendental Romance of Melville and Hawthorne gave way to the great period of the American novel — Howells,

Mark Twain and Henry James. Significantly, all three of these had parents to whom religion was vital. And all three rejected religion as a force for their inner lives or their art. They went on to create the modern American novel: social in its texture, humanistic in its concern. Their offspring continued the tradition. Wolfe, Fitzgerald, Hemingway, Faulkner and Steinbeck — these all wrote the Book of Man. That is, as long as Man was seen in some solid relation to his humanity.

But two events I mentioned earlier have had some of the effect I understand the famous earthquake of Lisbon, in the eighteenth century, had on the people of Europe, including such tough customers as Voltaire. If God could treat His children so, what *kind* of God was He, really? When Hiroshima and Auschwitz were implanted in our consciousness — in all their foul and radiant details — the question again arose: Who is Man, really?

Of course, natural disaster had happened long before the Lisbon earthquake. And unspeakable cruelties had been practiced long before Auschwitz and Hiroshima. The key difference in our time was: the total technology with which the total evil could be practiced. What kind of man could practice such *complete* evil?

The resulting answer, seen in our art, has had the effect of a terrible and apparently permanent diminution of the stature of Man. Who is this Man? He is the cremator, incinerator, computerized terrorizer and total controller of other men — that's who he is! In short, the word *man* is not as distinct from the word *madman* as it used to be. The very assimilation of the notion of the Absurd into our daily consciousness, leaping from Waiting For Godot into our daily newspapers, tells us that new definitions of madness and sanity will affect our definition of what Man is.

All right, my friend says, with a grin borrowed from the Marquis de Sade, revised by William Burroughs, go ahead, write novels with such men as your heroes — or victims. The game is over. Bulk art will be dried, shipped and consumed. But don't fool yourself. The novel you call The Book of Man will either be The Book of the Apocalypse or The Book of Trivia. It has, of course, been, of late, largely the former. We live in a world James or Mark Twain would not recognize. Out of the despair of man has come, I believe, the beginnings of a new sense of ourselves. Our most interesting writers have tamed, or at least assimilated, madness. The Prime Minister has eaten of the same tainted grain as the rest of us. There is no one to say: remember, you are mad. Instead, we hear: listen — those who attempt such absolute control of you are mad.

Let us resort to our two secret weapons: the body and the will.

It is, I think, pretty clear that there has been a revival of our sense of the body. One doesn't need movies with scenes of sexual intercourse, or nudity on the stage, to sense in the air a feeling for the flesh different in earlier times. Norman O. Brown urges us back to the most primitive, undifferentiated sense of the flesh — the polymorphous perverse. In the works of William Burroughs and Genet the body and the will join in a subversive pact to defeat the forces of a deadening society. They know something D. H. Lawrence knew: when the world is too much with us, the body ransoms us.

Hanging over all of these is a sense of the metaphysical. Ultimate concerns stand behind the silliest of actions. The words *sacred* and *holy* are used in everyday discourse as the words *personality* and *emotion* used to be used. *Magic* is a word no longer confined to theaters.

It's too easy to believe that this trend is Pompeian — that we are living in the last days of our Lord the Mushroom Cloud and a sense of doom turns our thoughts to the eternal mysteries, to orgiastic ceremonies of the flesh, as holds on a vanishing reality. It is, I think, at once more complex and simpler than that. Reality has, for a great many people, turned more mysterious than ever before. This may be because the number of people whose felt life is experienced as out of their control, rationally, realistically, is greater than ever before. The separation between traditionally sacred mysteries and banal everyday things grows dimmer. Which is more mysterious, the Hydrogen Bomb or Immortality? A computer or a poem by Robert Lowell? They are all mysterious; only some are more threatening than others.

The brief, magical time when Camus invoked the concept of measure, the Mediterranean sense of limits, and the tanned, mortal body under a warming sun as a defense against the terrors of totalitarian Man and an indifferent or vanished God, seems now an enchanted, exhausted, historical moment. His sense of the body and the will may have been a final Humanism. More extreme enterprises are afoot today. At their heart is a will towards what may be called 'usable mysteries.' And it is the exploration of these mysteries that gives me hope for my own corner of work: the novel.

How many figures does it take to make a trend — how many for a genuine renaissance? I'll just take a few. Samuel Beckett, Jorge Luis Borges, Iris Murdoch, Norman Mailer, Vladimir Nabokov, Jerzy Kosinski, Donald Barthelme, John Barth, Elie Wiesel. . . .

If some of these names are unfamiliar, it may simply prove that the term *post-modern* is justified in this case. I am not proposing any kind of a movement. Just an undercurrent, but an important one. I could name a number of even newer writers: like Leonard Michaels, Rudolph Wurlitzer, Leonard Cohen and others who are exploring extreme situations with artistic courage.

But what interests me in all of the writers I've named is a sense of the mysterious possibilities in the body or the will — against an increasingly totalitarian life — and the relationship of these possibilities to the religious sense. A good case in point is our special inspired lunatic of American literature: Norman Mailer. In a book I did not like when I first read it, *An American Dream,* and about which I still have serious reservations, Mailer proposed a kind of demonology of the body.

The way people use their bodies sexually is constantly related to a whiff of hell or of heaven. In one chapter the hero, Stephen Rojack, murders his wife and buggers her maid and, in a virtuoso performance, almost makes us believe that supernatural forces are involved in both acts — that God and the Devil lurk behind various bodily orifices; that our spiritual gestures can destroy our bodies and our bodily mistakes can murder our spirit. This last seems to me undeniably true even though Mailer's self-indulgent handling of this theme in his own obsessive way often fails to convince me. In a world where the old signs no longer direct us clearly along the roads, Mailer's attempt to invent a new system of metaphysical maps is an exciting adventure. Still, we do not quite know what to do with him. The nineteenth-century Russians understood that their great writers were always operating on the knife edge of events, either before or after the fact. Turgenev's *On the Eve* caused his partial exile and it also is credited with hastening the emancipation of the serfs. Dostoyevsky was deeply involved in the political madness of his day: *The Possessed* was both his political and metaphysical truth. The British critic A. Alvarez has said: "Mailer's strength as a novelist has always been his sense of which issues are erupting into the American consciousness. *An American Dream* was begun in September, 1963. Two months later the private bedroom violence he described was given overwhelming political expression when Kennedy was assassinated."

Many writers today see Politics in a metaphysical light. Alvarez's insight might be hard to prove. But there is a sense in which private life became political forever, and vice versa, after the two major events of our day: atomic destruction and genocide. Jerzy Kosinski's two books, *The Painted Bird* and *Steps,* are startling literary demonstrations of this notion. In *The Painted Bird* a child on the run in Nazi Europe is subjected to such mindless and desperate indignities that the book is almost too painful to read. In *Steps* that child has grown up and come to America. Here his searching out of the will to survive has resulted in an ethic of cruelty so extreme as to touch a corner of madness. Yet it is placed in context of a contemporary sexual experimentation that is recognizable and of the role of the criminal and political Mafia in our lives that rings true. So that, finally, though the mind wants to reject it, it presents itself as an authentic vision.

Elie Wiesel, the Hungarian novelist who writes in French, is the most significant of these fugitives from the land of the Dead. (Not enough is understood yet as to the effect these survivors of the ultimate outrage of the modern European experience are having on American writing.) But Wiesel's approach towards the rebellion of will has been to include the cruel God in his metaphysics — and to engage in a bitter dialogue with Him. In one of his books he quotes Dostoyevsky: "I have a plan — to go mad." But Wiesel's plan fails in each one of his extraordinary books. He goes to the edge, but always the cruel God refuses him the gift of madness, of oblivion. The dialogue goes on: Wiesel as the tormented Jew accuses God of ultimate cruelty. God replies with still more cruelty: silence. And, as Lawrence Durrell has said in the lingering question that ends *Justine:* "Does not everything depend on our interpretation of the silence around us?" Wiesel is a prophet of silence — but like Beckett, he cannot stop his voice.

Samuel Beckett buries the body while it is still alive and exerts his will — a massive will — on behalf of the Word. In Beckett the Word as a World is reaffirmed with each hopeless book, with each decaying character: Malone dying, Molloy meandering through past and present, the Unnamable going on even though he cannot go on. This magnificent retreat from an unbearable life into an unbearable ironic art has opened up possibilities which have yet to be fully realized. It is Beckett's plays that have made the great general impact. But his novels are a profound and seminal achievement — and the results are just beginning to be felt. I mentioned earlier a young man named Rudolph Wurlitzer who wrote a novel called *Nog*, published last year. The hand of Beckett in this time-paralyzed novel-poem is perhaps too obvious. But it is a genuine and valid influence. And not the last one we will see.

In a sense the work of Donald Barthelme could not be what it is without Beckett. The spinning out of parody-language which tells us, by implication, of the exhaustion of straight statements of our situation recalls Beckett's endless and beautiful last grasps. Barthelme is funny — as Beckett is funny. Like many modern parodists, art is one of his targets. But behind the attack is always the metaphysical mystery. Often, he attacks it head on. In one story he opens: "Henry Mackie, Edward Asher and Howard Ettle braved a rainstorm to demonstrate against the human condition on Wednesday, April 26. . . . They began at St. John the Precursor on 69th Street at 1:30 P.M. picketing with signs bearing the slogans MAN DIES! / THE BODY IS DISGUST! / COGITO ERGO NOTHING! / ABANDON LOVE! . . . ." And when a clergyman argues with this concern over the perishability of the human body, saying: "The body is simply the temple wherein the soul dwells," Henry Mackie replies with his famous question *"Why does it have to be that way?"*

Why indeed? Mailer, Beckett, Kosinski — Genet — Nabokov — our writers are treating the body as if it were as much of a mystery as the unseen spirit. Here again, the totalitarian control which covers so much of our daily lives may be forcing us back upon ourselves. Camus said: I want to see if I can live only with what I know. Post-existential man seems to be saying: I want to see if I can live only with what I am: my body, my spirit, my will.

I deal with this institutionalization of ultimates and the retreat from it in my novel *The Suicide Academy.* By proposing an Academy where people may go for one day in order to decide whether or not to end their lives, and by making the Academy entirely indifferent as to that choice, I tried to raise the issue of choices: of the will when the back is to the wall, at the moment when the mystery of the body — its pleasure, pain and survival — is heightened to an absolute value. Choice under such circumstances takes on shades that neither psychiatrists nor clergymen can handle. When total control touches our rock-bottom choices: life, death (and, of course, this has taken place not only in concentration camps), then a qualitative change has taken place — and perhaps a revolution in our sense of our own humanity is in the making or should be.

In the midst of such a revolution, the point at which the interests of artists and audience intersect, to quote my friend, may be just this question of human suffering — of pain.

How do you make a revolution in one's sense of humanity — and of reality in a suffering world growing increasingly strange and out of our control? I offer two anecdotes, each of which implies a different road. The first involves the modern prophet of Silence, John Cage. The other is from an older prophet, one of my favorite miracle Rabbis. Some years ago I went to a concert with John Cage and some other friends. We were to hear a new piece by the modern composer Stefan Wolpe. Wolpe, a classic revolutionary and humanist, had subtitled his work: *There's so much suffering in the world.* After the concert, Cage and I went backstage, where he walked up to the composer and said: "But Stefan, there's exactly the right amount."

The other story — to counterbalance the first one — is told of the great Polish madman-Rabbi, Reb Mendel of Kotzk. Reb Mendel had a disciple who came to him one day and said: "Rabbi, I have something terrible to confess."

The Rabbi said: "What is it?"

And the disciple said: "I am angry at God. I think the God we serve has made a terrible world — full of pain and suffering."

The Rabbi towered over the young man and boomed down at him: "What! and do you think you could make a better world?"

The young man looked up shyly and nervously said: "That's just it, Rabbi. I think I could."

At this, Rabbi Mendel grabbed the young man by the shoulders, shook him back and forth in violent, ecstatic spasms and shouted at him: *"Then begin!"*

Well, we are all beginning — all the time. And the beginnings being made by the mysterious new fiction in an attempt to deal with — and perhaps even to help create — a new sensibility are varied. For one thing, the differences between fact and invention seems to be blurring. And thus, the differences between fiction and the essay, as well. The guidelines are down. Mailer calls *Armies of the Night* "History As A Novel, The Novel As History." Rather too ambitiously, I think. But I know what he means. Facts are much too unstable and mysterious today. They don't have the density they had some years back. And the imagination is so dense and so real today — and not just via drugs — that a mix is taking place. The Argentinian, Jorge Luis Borges, writes little essays which are actually fiction, packed with erudition though they are. Between him and Mailer lies a vast, new territory that holds the possibility of a new sense of reality. It will have to be explored by our writers.

Finally, to reply to my imaginary friend, I must speak in fiction. One of my own beginnings. It is both essay and fiction — more and less than each. It is called:

I am glad that everyone is going to have more than one mother from now on. I write this because the first snow came yesterday to inaugurate the last month of the year. Inevitably, it reminded me of my mother surrounded as she was, at the end, by snow and cold. But here at the Society of Art Students the New Year is awaited with excitement; there is much to distract me. It is fortunate that there will be a contest and exhibit to close out the year because I have naturally been tempted to turn to the medium of elegiac prose. But the death of the novel was announced only a week after my mother's death and that, apparently, is that!

I don't want to be a Pollyanna about the situation here at the Society. There is at least one secret dissenter besides myself (and I am only a potential rebel). His name is Boris and he is entirely bald, which itself is suspicious. I'm sure I've been watched because of my association with him. If that wasn't enough, I've formed a life class in which the model is fully dressed and everyone is painting her nude. I'm working on even more drastic ways to stimulate the flaccid imaginations I sense all around me.

It was sort of luck that I was assigned to the Art Society after the death of the novel became official, permanent. Other writers were assigned as sculptors, designers, film cutters (that's the most popular one of all these days). It was all done with computers, and I'm not sure precisely what part luck plays in the way they work. It wasn't a bad place to do my double mourning. A little shabby in the decor department. Musty red velvet drapes full of shadows and dust; aluminum lockers that hadn't been cleaned in years; a reception room with blue plastic flowers in a cut-glass bowl. You know, the kind of place whose style speaks of good intentions, good faith and bad art. Which, by the way, was not always the result. One Japanese girl was doing some beautiful portrait work in pulverized pebbles; and several young men were shaping and reshaping canvases to handsome effect.

Of course the jumping spots before my eyes — which I've had for years — inhibit my ability to experience the visual arts. I complained about this to the admissions office when I first arrived. They were unimpressed.

"A lot of our students complain about that," one officer said. "Especially the writers."

"Oh?"

"I know what those spots are," he grinned wisely.

"What are they?" I genuinely wanted to know.

"You'll see."

All through this chilly autumn of the death of the novel I waited to see. Then two nights ago everything started to clarify and — at the same time — to come apart. I had been to Town Hall to hear the report on multiple mothers. I had a basic interest, since I was one of the signers of the original petition that finally forced the action, even though I had always been cynical about the movement. I have never shared the hostility of my generation towards mothers. Mine was a dark-eyed, gentle lady who laughed as often as she spoke. Thus, the idea of curing the mother-son dilemma by having a group of mothers assigned at birth seemed ridiculous to me. But shortly after my mother's death I woke up in the grip of an impossible grief one morning — and the idea took hold. The logic was perfect, inevitable. The one way to eradicate such grief was to have multiples. The arithmetic was undeniable. Grief, like anything else, must be less when divided. It was too late to help me or my generation. But, as the Moderator said at the Town Hall meeting, "There are millions being born right at this moment who can be spared the agony of mother-loss."

I strolled back to the Society after the meeting, feeling purged of one death, left now with the death of the novel, for which no solution came to mind. Fat flakes of snow softened my path, and the wind slipped past my cheek whispering, "Borisssss. . . . "

He was waiting for me in the corridor which led to the dormitories — a bald, conspiratorial Russian emigré with cloudless, blue eyes. "Ive been wating," he said.

"I have to check the drawings I finished today."

"Why?"

"I'm going to win that year's-end prize, that's why," I said with a mock boastfulness.

"Listen," he said nervously, "I dreamt about Charles Darnay and Stephen Dedalus last night."

"I'm sick of those dreams of yours," I said. I should get married quickly, I thought. Men marry quickly after a parent dies. But I wanted to hear what Boris had to say, and he knew it.

"Literatures are revealed to us," he said, smug as ever, "which indicate an ongoing panorama and do not inflict an arbitrary pattern upon life for all eternity."

"If somebody hears you talking like that, we'll both be in a lot of trouble," I said.

He ignored me. "That pattern does well for small nations and races whose conventions have hardened into a mold, England, Denmark and possibly provincial France, but it is not suitable for a polyglot America any more than it is, or ever was, for Russia."

I felt anger shorten my breath like asthma. Turning away, I tried to distract myself by lining up a series of drawings in the order I would submit them to the contest. But there was no stopping Boris. After all, I was the only person he could talk to.

"It's quite possible," he continued, "that Russia, with her *Dead Souls* and various lengthy novels of family life in the process of decay due to a social order, has more to say to Americans than the so-called classic tradition derived from Greece by way of English literature."

"Shut up, Boris," I said. As my eyes moved from left to right, the ragged little spots trailed along after them.

"In our time Proust, Joyce, Dorothy Richardson . . . "

"I'm warning you," I said. And I knew he was finished because he would not stop and I was too furious now to let him continue.

" . . . Dos Passos, Jules Romains and others have departed from the 'classic' formula (as, indeed, did Cervantes) . . . "

As soon as my hands touched his throat, he was silent, as if he'd expected this all along. But I could not stop. "You idiot," he croaked out, "I was quoting . . . " And then he was dead; or at least silent — I never found out which. Because I gathered my drawings all vinegary with fixative and ran to my room. When I returned the next day, there was no Boris, dead or alive.

The admissions officer who had called me in for a conference was friendly enough.

"I wanted to ask you a few simple questions: for one, didn't you feel a sense of relief when you heard that the death of the novel was final?"

"No!" Actually, I had, but it's best not to give them an inch. They try to degrade you — like making you testify against yourself. How could I not have felt relieved of that burden? But if only they'd left me alone to find something new — the way it is after someone you love dies.

"You're sure?" he asked.

"Absolutely!"

He seemed at the same time suspicious and relieved. Apparently none of this had to do with Boris. I was at the same time suspicious and relieved.

"Congratulations," he said.

"For what?"

"You've won the prize for your drawings."

On New Year's Eve, in the shabby ballroom lined with red velvet drapes and dusty aluminum lockers, I stepped up to the dais to receive my award: blue plastic flowers in a cut-glass bowl. I was also privileged to make a speech. It would have to be short. The snow outside was falling so quietly, and Boris had been, finally, so silent. It was only just to keep the words down. But then, staring out into the amorphous face crowds become when seen from above, my eyes moved from left to right, and I saw the ragged little spots and knew what they were letters: G — B — Z — R —. They were stuck in my vision like cataracts. Fragmented alphabet, language, always between me and what I saw. And without having planned to, I said: "Listen, we've seen the elegant junk sculpture — we've applauded the award given for the best scratched color film, and, in truth, there has been much that is beautiful here tonight." I halted the applause with a gesture. "But something else has to be said. I am, like you, one of the last men ever to have only one mother. And I swear to you, by that mother whom I loved: language lives . . . the novel is dead and that's why it may be alive somewhere . . . there *is* a life after the novel . . . if there are any out there who are like me, living secret lives, I am asking you — tell the tale, start where it seems to begin and stop where it seems to end, and in between it may be true and in between it may be beautiful. . . . "

Oh, I thought, as the silence in the ballroom grew cold and menacing as snow, if ever I needed more than one mother, it's now!

37 : *The Mysterious New Novel*

II. History, Theory, and Perspective

MICHAEL WOLFF

3.

Understanding the Revolution:
The Arena of Victorian Britain

I

Whatever the humanities are, whether they are the province of the Muses or a chunk of a college catalog, and whatever revolutions they may figure in, no one denies that their present condition raises problems. For many people more engaged with the contemporary creative arts than with criticism or teaching, the condition of the humanities has become little more than a reflection of the condition of the arts, perhaps especially the verbal arts, so that for them the discussion revolves around "The Arts in Revolution." For others, the revolutionary context in which they find themselves has evoked a feeling that conventional ways of knowing and experiencing oneself are exhausted and must somehow be replaced. For these people, a cultural revolution has already occurred which threatens to dissolve the very concept of "humanities," and any discussion of a "revolution" in them is either derivative or obsolete.

I think, however, that "The Humanities in Revolution" can still be usefully and specifically interpreted — and I also think that there are important ways of "doing" the humanities even in the course of a revolution, and that finding such ways and following them may well be the most important thing a professional humanist can do in these days.

It is true that the very idea of the humanities is time-committed — that it is

AUTHOR'S NOTE: Parts of this paper were originally prepared as Taft Lectures at the University of Cincinnati and as a lecture sponsored by the Department of English and the Office of Urban Studies and Programs at Yale University.

almost impossible to conceive of a version of the humanities which is not aware of survival and change and which does not depend on recognizing the pastness of some of its materials. It is also true that many people working in ways conventionally thought of as part of the humanities are making a significant effort to free themselves from this sort of time-commitment — to free themselves, that is, from history. To these people any appeal to history is off-target. But my claim is that to reject history is not only to reject the past; it is also to reject the future. For the way we describe the past is the way we determine where we actually have come from, and it is undeniable that where we move to will be seriously affected by the way in which we describe where we have come from. All history is a history of the future.

In some ideal sense, the past is perfectly and uniformly describable. But in practice we select what we describe, and that selection ought to be acknowledged as a matter of choice. Technical questions of availability of surviving evidence, fruitfulness of methods of interpretation, and so on, are part of such choices. But more to the point is the matter of the emphasis which accompanies a chosen approach. This part of the choice makes the tacit claim that the road to the present has been discovered. The claim, overt or not, develops a momentum that gives meaning to the phrase "history is the study of ancestors": I mean that the student, by selecting what aspects of the past to study, chooses to be in the line of descent from what he studies. The result is that he no longer has a directionless or dimensionless relationship to the future. He places himself in a given line of force precisely because of the way in which he chooses to account for a particular present in terms of a selected and particular past. He propels himself towards his preferred future by attaching himself to a version of the past already moving in that direction. I believe this to be an intellectually respectable and radical alternative, both to antiquarianism and a discredited historical objectivity on the one hand, and on the other to a complete present-mindedness indifferent to change and to the problems of continuity and responsibility.

Most of the discussion at the Center this year has been narrowly current or broadly timeless. I have persisted in seeing the situation in the context of the last hundred and fifty years, and I shall try here to provide historical underpinning for what is often seen as exclusively and even rootlessly modern and post-modern. In effect, I argue the need for an historical treatment of what is often billed as a post-historical situation. What follows, then, is an experiment in cultural history which claims to identify the revolution in humanities. It also asserts that the humanities as now practiced are essentially strangers to that revolution. And it recommends that they should become more intimately acquainted with it.

II

It may seem grandiose to say so, but it is increasingly clear that within historical times one change in human affairs has been so significant and pervasive that almost everything public can be usefully considered as a consequence of that change. This change is the coincidence of two events which are themselves complicated beyond description but which can nevertheless be conveniently summarized as the Industrial Revolution and the French Revolution. What was unprecedentedly significant about these revolutions was the propositions they put effectively before mankind: first, that all human beings are equal and should so treat each other; and second, that there is no meaningful limit to the material resources available for human use. This twofold possibility — that there could be enough to go around and that it could be shared equitably among all people on the globe — is the ideological hope that informs the process of democratization and industrialization which began at the end of the eighteenth century and which is still spreading fitfully and erratically into all cultures and societies.

This process is the Long Revolution (Raymond Williams' phrase). Its end is the humanization of the human race. If it is not thwarted, it will relieve people of the absorbing need to provide against the threat of scarcity; it will enable them to avoid avoidable suffering; and it will thus, in principle, make available to everyone the full use of his own life. Such a goal is obviously Utopian and such a process obviously global and revolutionary, as Buckminster Fuller constantly shows.

It is my belief that this revolution started in Victorian Britain, that we are now very much in the middle of it, and that whether we move towards Utopia or Armageddon is at the moment a guess. It was in Britain during the lifetime of Queen Victoria that the Industrial Revolution first gathered some sort of self-sustaining momentum. And, because the impact of the French and American Revolutions was intensely felt throughout Britain, Victorian society was the first to experience the dynamic of the modern world. What emerged in outline in Victorian Britain was a conflict between two socio-psychological states — not quite Matthew Arnold's "two worlds, one dead, / The other powerless to be born," nor yet C.P. Snow's literary and scientific cultures, although they are both related to my pair. The conflict was, rather, between two ways of looking at things. The first was based on traditions of hierarchy and order and nourished by an intellectual and spiritual heritage that seemed at the time to have behind it all the authority of history and civilization and revealed truth. The second was founded on the subliminal but spreading recognition that scarcity and the struggle for survival and the consumption of most human lives in the business of animal subsistence were no longer the necessary conditions of life. These positions were not and are not easily separated; they can both be present at the same time in any given class, in any geographic group, even in any individual.

Victorian Britain was the first arena for this conflict because it was the first modernizing society. A major ingredient in modernization and a defining feature of the Long Revolution is the emergence of more and more people — or at least of a greater proportion of the people living at a given time. The effect in Victorian Britain amounted to a revolution in the quantity and the potential quality of humanity. It was the beginning of the long and frighteningly uncertain transition from a world without prospect of change, where life for most people was nasty, brutish, and short, to a world where the humanization of mankind had become imaginable. Most of the defining characteristics of modern society, with their attendant tensions, were present in Victorian Britain: the rapid increase in population, the developing machine technology, and, above all, the beginning of the process of urbanization. Connected with these forces were new opportunities for communication, literacy, social unrest, and mobility, and the occasion for new institutions such as factories, trade unions, state schools, political parties, large-circulation newspapers, and national budgets. All these tended towards the grand effects of modernization: increasing egalitarianism in human relationships and the steady growth of relativism and pluralism in ideas and attitudes.

The simple increase in numbers of people was important — the rate of increase in population had indeed doubled during the eighteenth century and trebled in the early nineteenth century. Though such a rapid increase might well have gone unnoticed, the fact is that the growth in population caused a special awareness of itself, several factors converging to ensure a widespread recognition that there were more people around. The concentration of the increase of population in towns and cities meant a steep and visible rise in density. The movement from the cottage to the factory and from the countryside to the city meant that, for each laboring man, the number of fellow workers within his radius of contacts increased significantly. In turn, a growing sense of new sympathies and solidarities, even of new deprivations, foreshadowed a genuine working-class self-consciousness. The working classes therefore had a new sense of themselves.

As for the upper and middle classes, such new means of transportation and communication as railways and the telegraph enormously increased the ability of people and information to move around. There was also a new sensitivity, engendered by the French Revolution, to the potentially threatening presence of large numbers of unsettled and dissatisfied people. The ruling classes had a new sense of those they ruled. Moreover, economic expansion meant that large numbers of people were for the first time able to call for a say in their own affairs. Spreading literacy meant that more and more people could receive political messages and become the instruments, even the agents, of political change.

For the pre-Victorians, society had had an apparent permanence based ultimately on the acceptance of absolute authorities. It thought of itself as stable and orderly — part of some divine plan and at least as natural as the landscape. The Long Revolution challenged all this. There was a sudden and continuing growth of forces openly antagonistic to these norms. Science dissolved natural fixities, money dissolved social fixities, radicals threatened political fixities, essayists and philosophers attacked spiritual fixities. A society that had thought of itself as dependent on an order provided by King, Church, and Country began to be conscious of living under the shadow of some sort of catastrophe, often quite precisely defined as economic disaster or political upheaval. The basic condition of Victorian Britain, then, was that of a society deeply imbued with a sense of its own permanence but having to adapt to circumstances in which the only permanent factor seemed to be change itself. Moreover, to rich and respectable people, the conflict was not simply a manageable one between permanence and change. It was a conflict that threatened to get out of hand because the stakes were too high, and the choice was between order and disorder, civilization and chaos, culture and anarchy.

The Victorians were the first moderns. They had not yet accustomed themselves to the dangerous life called for when values shift, when the scale of things grows almost unimaginably, when machines, money, and the mob seem poised to destroy the fabric of civilization. To the people who had had Britain in their charge before the French and Industrial Revolutions, the mass of other people had constituted an anonymous herd, for all intents and purposes animal. If an individual member of that herd became differentiable, say as a servant or a tenant, he or she emerged as a kind of grown-up child or a favored domestic animal, rather than as a fellow adult. All this began to change, gradually and painfully, in the nineteenth century. Whatever there was on the lower and darker side of respectability had been perceived as nothing more than a vast shadow. Now, illuminated by the flickerings of the Long Revolution, it became a huge crowd of real people, characteristically thought of as brutal and drunk and potentially riotous and convulsive. Consciously or not, the Victorian gentleman felt threatened by the lower elements not only in society but also in himself. As a father and husband and as a member of a propertied class, he had to guarantee that the higher elements (reason and the respectable classes) maintained their control over the lower (passion and the mob). This obligation was responsible for most of the surface sobriety of Victorian Britain and much of its underlying tension.

The modern analogue, in the United States particularly, is obvious enough. The dominant culture is faced by new groups of people previously thought of as beneath, or beyond, consideration. That the abstract knowledge of black and poor and young America, and of African and Latin American and Asian peoples, has recently become so inescapably concrete derives from various factors, all of them familiar to students of Victorian Britain. It derives from the continuing revolution in means of communication, from the effects of economic expansion and the rippling outwards of viable standards of living, from the increasing impact of political and social egalitarianism upon those who hear the idea but do not see the thing — perhaps above all from the new self-awareness that for the first time gives emerging people their own collective sense of the possiblilities in the phrase "life, liberty, and the pursuit of happiness." From this perspective, the special characteristic of our time is the presence of emerging people and the cultural shock which occurs when a modernizing society inexorably but almost despite itself stirs into awareness groups within itself, or stirs other societies previously excluded from the benefits of modernization. Whether to resist or to accommodate or to yield to emerging people is the problem which the Long Revolution forces on every modern society, and it is the current urgency of that problem that gives Victorian Britain its peculiar relevance.

Let me offer a simple illustration. One of the things we find hardest to understand and forgive about Victorian Britain is its treatment of Victorian Ireland. The attitude of the Government and of the governing classes throughout the period seems, with few exceptions, callous beyond comprehension. This callousness was never more apparent than during the Great Famine of 1845–49, when half a million people died of disease and starvation and a million more were forced into emigration. Governmental relief operations during the Famine were hopelessly ineffective and were hampered by great ignorance of local conditions and by general administrative inefficiency and inexperience. Certain key officials had an intense commitment to an ideology of self-help that set strict limits on what could be done by way, for example, of public contributions of food not worked for by the starving recipients. Also present in these officials' minds was a Malthusianism which was convinced that there were probably too many Irish in Ireland in any event and that the extent of the disaster was nature's ruthlessness, not man's. Behind this was a pervasive prejudice in British public opinion against the Irish in general, which combined xenophobia with an intense and long-seated anti-Catholic feeling. The Irish indeed were characteristically portrayed as even more apelike and degraded than the native poor. The upshot of all this, according to some historians, is that more or less unconscious genocide was at work in British policy towards Ireland, especially at the time of the Famine.

If we train ourselves to see Victorian Britain as a part of our own time and place, we can easily see that the judgment of future history may not forgive North America and Western Europe, in the decades after World War II, their treatment of the rest of the world. Comparative figures of food consumption, infant mortality, and disease rates will indicate that the "Haves," in permitting such gross discrepancies, showed an almost incomprehensible callousness towards the "Have-nots." At times of the greatest crisis, as in the Congo or in Indochina, accusations of genocide do not seem beside the point. And efforts to relieve Biafran famine and Indian epidemic, to do something for the millions who lead a subhuman life on the streets of Calcutta, in the *favelas* of Rio de Janiero, or in the shacks of Hong Kong, will seem to future historians hopelessly incompetent and pitifully inhibited by national prejudices, economic ideology, and administrative inexperience.

There are two related points to such a comparison. First, the parallel deepens our sense of the Victorian situation by helping us see the height of the administrative and psychological barriers which prevent people from exercising their humanity across geographical and cultural boundaries, and the likelihood that their barriers were as high to them as ours are to us. Second and more importantly, our indignation with the Victorians shows us how impermanent these barriers can be and how relative the values they enshrine. If we try to excuse ourselves by saying that Ireland was a direct national responsibility of Britain whereas the underdeveloped world is not the direct national responsibility of the United States, we should answer ourselves by saying that the idea of nationality can no longer be used to set the limits of human interdependence.

To use the past in that way is to make a choice. To take the Anglo-Irish experience as an event among other events, accounted for because it is in the textbooks, is one choice. It distances the suffering and in no way commits the modern student against its repetition. To see it as a symptomatic item in the Long Revolution, with equivalent modern symptoms, is to offer the student of the past a role in that revolution. It permits him through his vision of the past to insist on and work for his vision of the future.

III

This historical perspective, with its claim that society, national and global, is most usefully seen as struggling with a revolution to Utopia, makes intrinsic claims about the humanities. It says that the condition of man which the humanities have mourned and celebrated and analyzed and enshrined has so changed that they must undergo some nearly equivalent change if they are to survive. The tremendous ethical and psychical achievements of Western art, religion, and metaphysics are the slowly and proudly evolved responses of generations of men to the facts of suffering and death. They depend on the omnipresence of these facts. They have been necessary ways of coping with a condition which is otherwise thought to be intolerable. Their task has been to reconcile men to an apparently unbearable situation by making sense of suffering and death. Their primary efforts have gone into explaining and elevating imperfection and introducing the idea that perfection is not altogether unattainable. They assert the existence of heaven, of ecstasy, of infinity, of absolutes outside of space and time and the body and, therefore, beyond suffering and necessity. No metaphysic or aesthetic, no system of theology or ethics, which is based on reconciling people to pain by consoling them with some hidden or momentary good can now suffice. If modern society is caught in a revolutionary dynamic which could either destroy it or lead it to Utopia, then it requires from the humanities, both in the university and in the wider community, something new, if only in emphasis. A new version of the humanities must try to see events and persons, even great ones, not in relation to traditions and heritages but to the incomplete humanity of large numbers of human beings.

People engaged in the humanities as teachers, scholars, or critics must, therefore, consider some radical internal adjustments corresponding to the Long Revolution. What human needs can the humanities serve? And what will help that service to reach all who need it? What is needed, I think, is first an applied or practical humanities, and second and closely related, a nonhierarchic or egalitarian humanities. These ideas will seem to many either self-contradictory or distasteful. The suggestion of human or social engineering in applied humanities can seem in its very nature inimical to the combination of disinterested intellect and sensitive judgment supposed to characterize excellence in the humanities. The very idea of the first-rate and the classic, with its inclination to absolute values, seems to be swept away by a call for an egalitarian and therefore unordered humanities. Nevertheless, if the humanities are to function in a democracy undergoing a Long Revolution, then someone must attend to some version of them bent on solving, as well as comprehending, immediate problems. At the same time, given our political and social condition, someone must also explore a version of the humanities which addresses itself directly to people in general, rather than to a specially trained or selected group. What I look for, then, is a humanistic equivalent of technology, both to satisfy needs brought into being by the material success of that technology and to fill the gap in human affairs which is now often blamed on technology but which is the responsibility of a modern humanities.

There must surely be a sense in which material changes which permit people to lead more human lives must provoke corresponding changes in the humanities. In the Middle Ages the humanities described what differentiated man from the beast. Now they claim guardianship of the human in opposition not to the beast but to the machine, to technology and the threat of dehumanization. But the very word *dehumanization* presupposes that a state of humanization has been reached, and this is not yet true for many men. The humanities, in continuing to address themselves mainly to those who are by and large satisfied with the humaneness of their material situation, have not yet learned how to ally themselves with the process of helping all men move up from the beast.

IV

Two of the defining properties of modern times, I have said, are technology and urbanization. And two of the major informal boasts of the modern humanities, conventionally understood, are that they are anti-urban and anti-technological. Both the city and the machine are instruments of equalization. They tend, that is, to make no distinctions among people, to treat them equally. But the way of the humanities, through judgment and discrimination, seems to be inequality — the selection and protection of masterpieces, the rejection of the second-rate. Thus the anti-urban and anti-technological mode of the humanities seems intrinsic. But is it really? And if it isn't, should it in any event be perpetuated?

I have already suggested that the high culture of Victorian Britain effectively retained its pre-modern and pre-urban quality. It hardly needs arguing here that Victorian literature is at best uncomfortable with, but more generally actually hostile to, the city. I shall not spend time on a catalog of examples of Victorian literary anti-urbanism. But I am interested in the quality of anti-urbanism and in the general relation of literature and the humanities to the city. Victorian writers, like other respectable Victorians, were frightened by the city as they were by the machine because it had no respect for them. The city, like the machine, did not recognize them or their respectability. It took away the identifying space that surrounded them, and it threatened to render them anonymous and nondescript. The Victorian city was a great force, leveling and equalizing its inhabitants.

But if the city levels men and, in so doing, appears to blur and smudge their particularity, literature tries to give them identity, to be precise about them, and to differentiate them. The Victorian novel, with its large cast, tries to provide a way of personalizing anonymity. It gives names and traits to what it claims are representatives of large numbers of unknown and otherwise unknowable people. It tries, in short, to familiarize the urban crowd, to make a family of it. Moreover, literature, in its creation but especially in its reception, is familial and domestic. It makes the space it engages private, even in a park or the reading room of a library. The popular, bardic literature of the great Victorian writers can be seen as an effort to make a sort of superfamily out of the literate nation, especially its unruly children, its immature or unassimilated members. The great authors were a type of uncles and aunts reinforcing the parental roles of Queen, Church, and Ministerial Government. They tried, I suppose with little prospect of success, to reach into the streets, to go where the squire and the justice of the peace no longer could and where the parson and even the policeman had great difficulty in going, and to exhort and reassure, to embrace and admonish their anonymous inhabitants, to provide the salvageable city-dweller with an avenue of escape.

I think there are three humanistic visions of alternatives to, or modifiers of, the real city and its corruptions. They are all paradises and versions of pastoral. The first is the countryside, usually not the wilderness but the tamed nature of rural England. The second is a sort of personal and internal translation of the country, namely, the family. The third is the spiritual and intellectual Paradise, the seat of purity and order — the Good City, the City of God, Jerusalem. Of course the similarities between these three are extensive. Each is a place of harmony and escape from turbulence and disorder; each is a temple and a sanctuary; each (including the countryside in its idealized, feudal aspect) is presided over by a beneficent father whose wisdom and experience are unblemished by anxiety and whose dependents find protection and love in unquestioning obedience to him. And these visions are sound defenses against the actual city, for they do establish real obstacles to the extension of its power. They each represent an intuitionist value-system built upon authority, upon absolutes, upon a hierarchically structured way of life. And they seem to those who need them to represent, not just a choice among ethical alternatives, but the quintessentially human and humane.

In *Middlemarch,* when Dorothea tells Celia of her plan to marry Ladislaw and to go to London, Celia petulantly asks Dorothea, "How can you always live in a street?" And when it becomes clear that the Bulstrodes will have to leave town, Mrs. Vincy's sympathy for her sister, Mrs. Bulstrode, takes the form of a lament that Mrs. Bulstrode will have thenceforth to live among people who don't know her and whom she doesn't know. The anonymity of a numbered house in a row of houses and the fear of losing identity, which is tantamount to the fear of losing being, are the threats that accompany moving to the city. It is not too much to project from these fears to the apparently appalling character of actual city-dwellers, anonymous, without identity, practically without being. The great city is a collectivity not merely of numbers and statistics but of actual nonpersons. The first horror of impersonal contacts is, imaginatively speaking, the contrast between one's own reality and the nonreality of those (apparently real) with whom one must mingle. The second horror is that one might oneself become what one will appear to be from the street — an unreal, identityless figure, a number, no better than a cipher.

Henry Thomas Buckle, who represents naive scientism and shallow optimism in most Victorian intellectual histories, wrote in his *History of Civilization in England:* "The more men congregate in great cities . . . the less attention they will pay to the peculiarities of nature, which are a fertile source of superstition." George Eliot read this and commented: "I am very far behind Mr. Buckle's millennial prospect, which is, that men will be more and more congregated in cities and occupied with human affairs, so as to be less and less under the influence of Nature, i.e., the sky, the hills, and the plains; whereby superstition will vanish and statistics will reign for ever and ever." This exchange summarizes the Victorian difficulty. George Eliot seems to contrast human affairs and nature and to feel forced to choose between them. She chooses nature; human affairs, if they are to be mediated by the unnatural city, must become themselves denatured and reduced to statistics.

The antagonism has very serious implications. The literature of the city, in sum, always suggests that the city is a sort of hell. What is the corresponding heaven? What salvation either for themselves or for their readers do writers pretend to rescue from this indictment? The city may indeed lend itself to such a perception — but consider that the countryside is also hell, however much its hellishness may be mitigated by nonhuman nature, by spaces whose forms and rhythms traditionally speak of beneficence and refreshment. Is not this benign country a pastoral fraud, a self-deception in which we claim that intimations of Eden are still with us? Nature disguises suffering, makes it natural, offers consolation for it by arguing that it is a small and inevitable price for all her wonders. If rural suffering intrudes on rural delight, it is a secular reminder that the torment of the damned is part of the joy of the blessed.

It is an act of choice, a rather desperate humanistic habit, that makes the city the special locale of human misery. It may well be that it takes the compression — the compactness and crowdedness — of the city to force the quotient of hellishness in the human condition to the surface, where it can be observed and realized. But I think that the anti-urban man of letters is standing on nothing; the emptiness and sterility, the void he sees in the city, is under him too. To confine deadliness to the city, even to do so without gloating, is to claim a false escape from responsibility, and, by saying that some places are better than others, to avoid drawing attention to the problem of alleviating needless suffering. To inveigh against the City of Dreadful Night is to make excuses, to condone misery by refusing affirmation. Anti-urbanism is one facet of the traditional role of literature and humanities whereby what is thought to be inevitable human suffering is made tolerable by being shown to be either deserved or, more frequently, part of the scheme of things.

Perhaps the most likely point of collaboration between urban and Victorian specialists will be found whenever we encounter the urban version of the problem of self-consciousness — the difference, for example, between what sociologists call external indexes of social position and hypotheses about the way particular groups of people felt about their social positions. Can a body of usable qualitative material be established? Can we learn to speak with some authority about individual or collective emotional states in the Victorian city? I think it is not enough simply to ask for a well-educated and intelligent reading of documents. It is also necessary to call upon the specific skills of imaginative history and literary criticism and to extricate and render intelligible the deep structural and psychological meanings of works of literature and art, so that other historians and social critics can use them to understand the cultural setting which gave rise to them and of which we are the heirs.

One of the critical tasks of the humanist in education may be precisely that of helping a now nearly completely urbanized population to make city-dwelling intelligible and humane. People are spatially urbanized or suburbanized, but there seems yet to be little understanding, let alone mastery, of any set of urban roles which would be psychologically constructive and mutually supportive. It seems an obvious challenge to the humanities that they try to provide some humane equivalent to the technology of material urbanization. Applied science has created the means of modernization; but there is no applied humanities to enable people to take advantage of these means without the accompanying "dehumanization." It would be a version of professional suicide if humanists were to continue to preach that the choice is between abundance and spiritual health, between technological civilization and so-called "real" civilization, between quantity of life (standard of living and life expectancy) and quality of life; in short, to insist on the opposition of the city, with all it stands for and all it promises, to positive ethical, intellectual, and aesthetic values. It would surely be a moral disaster if such a preaching and such an insistence were to succeed.

It is true that urbanization, as we have seen, poses a great threat. But one way to meet that threat is to try to reverse it. The city deprives people of the consolations of their heritage and takes away from them the securities of *Gemeinschaft*. In a way, it *has* removed them from a place in a great chain of being that somehow made sense of the multifariousness of values and things and movements and people of all sorts and degrees. The city has enormous moral and psychological power, but it is not necessarily a destructive power. The city could, if it were acknowledged, strip people bare in the same way that they were once stripped bare in the presence of God. All acquired attributes, all of what Carlyle called "vesture," become beside the point. Moreover, the inhabitant of the city would render his account to himself alone — not to God or the church — and he would do it by his capacity to cope with the city and to enjoy it. What he must enjoy, it turns out, is the freedom of being himself and only himself, not a name or a description, not someone within a case labeled for other people's recognition. He is offered a kind of total existentialism which is at the same time the impersonality of statistics and the full personality of egalitarianism. He must be willing to be self-sufficient, to be free of the status conferred by birth or wealth or talent. He must also exercise that new freedom within the so-called dehumanization that the tradition tells us must accompany computer technology and utilitarian hedonism.

V

The great scandal, as Fuller knows, is the continuation of scarcity and unnecessary suffering in the midst of plenty — the gross differences, around the world, of standards of living, infant mortality rates, and life expectancy. The humanities do not sufficiently address themselves to this state of affairs. They continue, rather, to train us to accept and be reconciled to widespread human misery as the inescapable lot of most people. As now taught, the humanities encourage us to rise above suffering, to conquer it by the transcendence of history or of tragedy, or of one or another of the cultural devices that arrange the elements of a wretched world so that they are aesthetically pleasing and orderly.

In a world where poverty and scarcity could not be alleviated, this was doubtless a merciful and necessary task. But now it seems only to condone that poverty and scarcity. One might even say that the traditional humanities need the continuation of suffering. If that is true, we must reject, or at least modify, that aspect of the tradition. What the humanities should do now is learn ways to diminish scarcity and poverty and thereby teach the scandal of unnecessary suffering. The humanities should train all people to lead human lives and, more especially and immediately, train those who have enough to find ways of enjoying their abundance and sharing it. It is time that all human misery became intolerable.

4.

The Culture of Criticism

The disciplines that constitute the central core of the humanities — history, literary and art criticism, and philosophy — are as old as the subject matter they investigate. But the humanities conceived as a distinct area of study, with their unique aims, methods, and cultural function, have existed only since the Renaissance. At that time the humanities became disengaged from what might be called the divinities, just as various forms of social practice, such as politics and economic activity, became liberated from the religious restraints formerly placed upon them during the Middle Ages. It was only after the Renaissance that scholars could openly give themselves over to the study of cultural artifacts as specifically *human* creations and suppress the impulse, as old as thought itself, to view everything in the world as a mere epiphenomenon of more basic metaphysical and religious realities. The residues of the original religious loyalties lingered on far into the modern period, but by the middle of the nineteenth century, the theoretical bases for the complete demystification of the world had been worked out, and sufficient reasons had been articulated for belief in the human origins of everything in the world that was not a part of the natural order. History, criticism, and philosophy could therefore proceed to the task of secularizing culture in a radical way, that is to say, by finding the root of every cultural artifact in human reason, will, or imagination alone, without having to postulate the existence of any noumenal ground by reference to which every putatively "spiritual" creation was to be "explained."

The humanities played a crucial role in the global process of demystification of culture which culminated in the foundation, at the end of the nineteenth century, of the social sciences. But their participation in this process obscured the essentially conservative nature of their characteristic operations. For although the humanities shared with the embryonic social sciences a common a- or anti-religious attitude, so too were they anti-utopian in their inherent political orientation. As students of the products of human thought, reason, and will, humanists were deeply suspicious of the utopian visions that often underlay and authorized a given artist's or thinker's impulse to bring under question the world as given in the current social dispensation. It was this opposition to the dream in the name of which men dared to demand something better than the hand dealt them by genetic or social forces that appeared in the humanists' claim to stand as mediators between the powers engaged in the social and cultural drama. Humanists defined their cultural roles as custodial and critical; their task, as they saw it, was to mediate between the old and the new, between "life" and "thought," between the "imagination" and "reality," between the producers of culture on the one side and the consumers of culture on the other — in a word, between genius and the publics that genius sought to order, direct, and fashion after its own utopian visions.

By the end of the nineteenth century, the humanists had blocked out a special preserve of their own, located somewhere between the position occupied by religious rebels like Luther and Savonarola and that held by radical secularists like Machiavelli and Hobbes. Their patron saint was of course Erasmus, and after him Montaigne, men whose personal integrity was assured by the attitude of irony which allowed them to see all sides of every question but in the end to bow to authority in the public sphere as the sole alternative to anarchy. This ironic attitude was elevated into a value under the name of "detachment," which dissolved the tensions created by a sense of membership in the common humanity on the one side and a sense of belonging to an elite group on the other. This ideal of detachment was then, in turn, retrospectively justified by the pretended discovery of an indissoluble tension between the realm of culture and that of society. Thus the humanists characteristically took their stand on a middle ground between "art" and "life," between *ethos* and *kratos,* and took refuge in their own utopian dream, which they called by the name "autonomy of culture." Thus, for example, that late Erasmian and master of irony, Northrop Frye, draws a distinction between two kinds of criticism — one "historical," which always "related culture only to the past," and the other "ethical," which "relates only to the future" — only to dissolve their differences in commitment to that "liberty" which must begin with "an immediate and present guarantee of the autonomy of culture."

As I see it, the so-called crisis in the humanities about which we hear so much these days stems from the realization on the part of humanists that this "autonomy of culture" is under attack, not only from the political Left and the political Right, but also from within culture itself, from those artists and thinkers whose creative activity supposedly requires that autonomy as its necessary precondition. From both the extreme Left and the extreme Right of the political spectrum come recurrent demands for an art, science, and philosophy that are engaged, relevant, or, more generally, "socially responsible." The conventional claim to detachment in scholarship, the ideal of an intelligentsia that is "free-floating," the concept of the "disinterested" scientist, and the idea of an art for art's sake — all these have lately been criticized as mere means of defending privileges of specific social groups. Much of modern art is created precisely out of a need to destroy the distinction between art and life, just as much of modern social thought is directed at the dissolution of the distinction, formerly believed to be inevitable and ineluctable, between social thought and social practice. The rise of a mass audience for both art and thought, an audience that is greater in numbers and power than anything previously known to historical experience, an audience created by mass education and sustained by mass media, has created a demand for a new kind of culture. The consumers of this new culture deny the claim to extraordinary authority in the determination of what may count as legitimate art or thought; they question the necessity of a special group of scholars whose specific task is to exercise custodial and critical functions for an audience which views its own opinions as authoritative in matters of thought and expression, no less than in matters of social practice.

Call this new public whatever you wish: pop, youth, body, drug, or nonlinear — the fact is that it constitutes a large, rich, and increasingly powerful constituency which shares with the avant-garde artist a distrust of the very category of the artistic and with the utopian radical thinker an indifference to the benefits of historical consciousness as we have cultivated it up to now. This means that by virtue of this new public's dedication to the cult of the casual, the immediate, the transitory, the unstructured, and the aleatory, the avant-garde has an important new ally in its traditional attack upon the critical and custodial operations of the humanities. Thus the sense of crisis, the sense of being in a revolutionary situation, in the humanities is more than justified: humanists have to face the prospect of a foreclosure on their most highly valued operations. Small wonder that, in spite of all the evidence to the contrary, humanists should suddenly appear as the most eloquent defenders of the notion that, not only is a real revolution in culture and society undesirable, it is impossible as well.

The humanities are divided today, among themselves as well as between themselves and the avant-garde in art and thought, over whether the cultural upheaval we are witnessing throughout the world is revolutionary or not, and if it is, whether the revolution represents a progressive or retrogressive force in civilization. Creative artists and social radicals have no doubt about the desirability of a revolution and are convinced that whatever comes out of it will be better than what is replaced. Some sociologists regard pop culture as a revolutionary movement, the first genuinely mass cultural movement in human history, with potentialities for creative development every bit as strong as its potentialities for destruction. Marshall McLuhan has given popularity to the idea, setting pop culture within the larger context of a dialectic between culture and electronic technology, and supporting the belief that the revolution in culture heralds the advent of a new kind of consciousness necessary to the creation of a new kind of community. And even within the humanities there are avant-gardists, or at least liberals, who, in their devotion to the principle of creativity, are willing to encourage both the avant-garde and its pop audience in their work of clearing the boards of traditional forms — not because they believe the boards can actually be cleared and a true nonformalist cultural convention can be realized, but because they recognize that the avant-garde, from the early nineteenth century at least, has always declared itself against art and literature as a preparation for the articulation of its own vision, which can always be seen, after the fact, as a further development of, rather than a radical break with, what had come before.

But in general these liberal critics do not constitute a majority in the humanities, and their ranks have dwindled as the revolution has intensified, or at least as it has moved out of the coffeehouses into the universities. The liberal critics have tended to join the larger group of traditionalists in the humanities, who have stood firm against the contemporary avant-garde and, even while continuing to study them, have consistently denied that the current radicalism in art and social thought can have anything but a harmful effect on civilization.

An impressive tradition of criticism has thus taken shape during the last generation, inspired as much by its experience and fear of totalitarianism as by its dedication to traditional humanistic culture; the representatives of this critical tradition are E. H. Gombrich in art theory, Erich Auerbach in literary history and criticism, and Karl R. Popper in what I shall call scientific criticism. They do not constitute a formal school, but their influence is pervasive throughout the humanities, and anyone working in any of the fields they have tilled cannot avoid coming to terms with them. They represent the best work of the last generation on that ground between cultural and social criticism which, it seems to me, the humanities are indentured to occupy in the times in which we live.

This tradition of criticism and historical analysis represents an attempt to provide a definitive defense of naturalistic realism in Western art and literature and to maintain the vital historical link between realistic art, liberal-humanitarian social principles, and humanistic ethics. Its defense of realism as an artistic and literary equivalent of those values that have made progressive development possible in Western culture, in contrast to the stagnancy of non-Western archaic cultures, is so well argued and so oppressively documented that consideration of it may help to illuminate the specific nature of the current avant-garde's revolutionary posture and the nature of the resistance to that revolution which is contributing to the sense of crisis in the humanities at the present time. For the defenders of realism see, as the avant-garde itself sees, that much more is involved in the current cultural revolution than an assault upon tradition, or perception, or reason, or even book culture. The revolution includes such an assault, but it goes much deeper than this. For it also includes an attack upon what is increasingly recognized as the idea that binds realism in the arts to liberalism in society and to progressive developments in science — that is to say, the idea of fictive truth, the notion of a twilight realm between absolute conceptual certitude on the one side and the chaos of unprocessed sense data on the other, that sense of provisional certitude that makes the *orderly* and *incremental* development of our knowledge of reality possible. What the avant-garde in art and the radical utopians' social thought bring under attack is the concept of the fictitious; and it is this aspect of their attack that makes them so much more radical than avant-gardes and revolutionaries in times past.

The avant-garde is not simply opposing traditional forms, whether the emphasis is placed on the word *traditional* or on the word *forms*. The avant-gardists themselves say they represent, not a revision of the old — and they insist that they will not be assimilated to it — but a radically new kind of cultural and social experience, one that permits them to believe that the gap between the possible and the real, the gap where fiction has thrived heretofore, can at last be closed. This utopian dream they justify by appeal to a material situation in which the condition of scarcity, which has hitherto driven artists and visionaries back finally to some compromise with the notion of a fractured humanity, no longer has to be viewed as an inevitable condition for mankind and hence is no longer an ineluctable limitation on cultural creativity and innovation.

This sense of a new material ground for culture and society is reflected in the language of rebellion against both culture and society itself, not in their present incarnations only, but as specific forms of human relationship. Radical writers speak of a literature directed at the dissolution of language; their painters create self-destructive art objects; their dramatists dream of a theater without dialogue; their choreographers envisage a dance without gestures; their composers conceive of a music without sound; and their social commentators speak of the possibility at last of a genuine transcendence of historical existence and the advent of apocalypse, the dissolution of society in the interest of community. Everywhere we find the advocacy of the worth of the casual over the contrived, the bodily over the mental; the triumph of the gestural, the graphic, the random, the aleatory, as against the verbal and structural; and so on.

The will to formlessness. Does it also herald the advent of chaos? Is it — as Buckminster Fuller puts it — an earnest of utopia or an intimation of Armaggedon? The old guard in the humanities know that more is involved in the avant-garde's attack upon form than a simple artistic or intellectual experiment; for them what is involved is the fate of progressive civilization itself. They are inclined to see the recognized pioneers of contemporary art and thought, from Picasso to Rauschenberg, Schoenberg to Cage, Artaud to Resnais, Joyce to Nathalie Sarraute, Yeats to Ginsberg, Freud to N. O. Brown, and Max Weber to Marcuse, as repudiating the very principle that has made progress in society, art, and thought possible in modern civilization. The new avant-garde represents to them an attack upon the world view which produced a culture that was both scientific (hence orderly) and humanistic (hence liberating) — the culture that was created by the of a music without sound; and their social commentators speak of the possibility at last of a genuine transcendence of historical existence and the advent of apocalypse, Greek transcendence of the anxiety-ridden world of the savage on the one side and the oppressive mythic formalism of archaic higher civilizations, such as the ancient Egyptian and Mesopotamian on the other.

According to Gombrich, Popper, and Auerbach, modern, enlightened, and progressive civilization is sustained by a set of moral and intellectual commitments, first envisaged by the Greeks, which have their characteristic expressive forms in the traditions of humanistic realism. All three believe that this set of commitments arose from a genuine revolution in sensibility, a revolution which Gombrich calls "the Greek miracle," which was opposed during the Middle Ages but was taken up once more and was elaborated and refined, between the fifteenth and nineteenth centuries in Western Europe, in such a way as to make any further revolutions in sensibility either impossible or undesirable — impossible because the realistic tradition appears to possess powers of resistance to radical transformation, and undesirable since, if any radical transformation were to occur, it would lead, because of the very nature of consciousness itself, to a regression to earlier, infantile, savage, or archaic forms of imaginative oppression.

In Gombrich's influential *Art and Illusion*, the Greek miracle is presented as having consisted above all in the discovery of the possibility of provisional truths, of fictive possibilities, of approximative realities. The discovery of the realm of fictive reality created a kind of distinctively human psychic space, between the rigidifying strategies of the mythic imagination, of the sort that led to Egyptian king-worship and the closed society of the slave-subject, and the terrifying world of uncontrolled imagination that presumably imprisoned man originally in a savage condition.

Gombrich links this discovery of fictive possibility to the notion of a narratively structured time, which permitted the conception of *the significant moment,* on which the artist — whether painter, sculptor, or writer — could center his attention for the purpose of determining the possible relations obtaining between objects caught in that moment, without appeal to universal explanatory principles or absolute conceptions of causal relationship. That is to say, realistic art, from the Greeks onward to the end of the nineteenth century, contents itself with the careful and progressive matching of hypotheses about what might actually occupy a defined field of perception to that ground on which the field has been constructed, by appeal to the authority of perceptions on the one side and to areas already secured by prior mapping operations, as recorded by tradition, on the other. This ability to bracket a temporal moment, in turn, leads to the creation of a specifically historical consciousness by its implicit suggestion of the moments preceding and the moments following it. In the arts, it ultimately leads to the conquest of a perspectivally structured, or autonomous, space — a space whose reality is confirmed by the sensed internal consistency of the empirically discoverable relations between objects occupying it, and not by appeal to some sustaining transcendental principle, such as eternity or infinite being, as the mythic imagination requires. These two conquests, that of narrative time and that of perspectival space, together with historical consciousness, liberated the imagination from the mythic search for eternal and absolute truths and committed it to the much more mundane, but humanly more profitable, task of controlled information-gathering. At the same time, it led to the search for a principle of rational entailment by which new bodies of information could be assimilated to the older, secured ones contained in tradition.

But there was more to this miracle. The triumph of realism depended upon a mastery and cultivation of the techniques of illusionism, the discovery of a way of using fictions to mediate between what men desired or hoped might be the case about reality and the way things actually were or are in fact. It was the use of fictions in literature, of controlled illusions in art, of provisional schemata (or hypotheses) in science — the use of the notion of the provisional or merely possible, in place of the necessary or merely inevitable — which has permitted every new structuring of reality by each successive generation of artists, thinkers, and scientists to develop toward an ever more precise understanding of the *true* nature of the external world and which has led, in modern Western civilization, to the attainment of whatever control men now have over it.

The dialectical interplay between (1) traditional wisdom or lore, (2) fiction, hypothesis, or provisional schema, and (3) perception broke that tyranny of thought and imagination over sense which consigned men to a servitude to their own illusions in the archaic civilizations of the ancient world and, at the same time, dissolved the power that sense exercised over thought in primitive culture. And Gombrich rightly discerns that the avant-garde art of our time is a threat to humanistic-scientific or realistic civilization precisely because it denies, at one and the same time, the authority of tradition, of thought, and of sensory perception in such a way as to destroy the mediative role that the "fiction" has played in the promotion of a humanistic cultural endowment. For him this threefold denial, however noble the utopian impulses behind it, however motivated by an understandable urge to know reality directly — this attempt to take reality by storm, to seize it immediate and pure, and to liberate it from the constraints of merely fictive truths and provisional generalizations — all this *is* an attack upon civilization. It can lead, in his view, only to a regression into myth and to the creation of the kind of totalitarian society that arises whenever myth takes command, as in Germany during Nazism.

So too for Auerbach. In his magisterial *Mimesis,* he shows that the principal achievement of Western literature has been the full development of the potentialities of *mimesis,* the realistic representation, or verbal imitation, of an action. This achievement Auerbach regards as a product of the progressive liberation of literature, both from the tyranny of unprocessed sense data and from that overprocessing of it, to the point of its near extinction, in mythic thought. He grants a more important role to Christian ideas in the development of literary realism than Gombrich is inclined to do with respect to pictorial realism. But the conclusion with respect to the most important achievements of Western literature is much the same: historical realism results from the controlled interplay of human consciousness with a shifting social and natural milieu. It alone, of all literary traditions, has promoted the progressive charting of the elements in that milieu through the testing of different stylistic fictions, concepts of reality, and paradigms for dictating the nature of relationships that might bind objects together to constitute them as a comprehensible domain. The history of literary realism has been a story, in Auerbach's view, of the gradual elimination of mythical powers as explanatory concepts in social and psychological matters and the cultivation of social, natural, and psychological forces as rationally comprehensible intrahistorical forces in their own right. All of which adds up, in his view, to the gradual discovery of the realm of history as the temporal domain in which man has his proper habitat, just as he has his proper spatial habitat in nature and his proper spiritual habitat in an internally differentiated society. Abandon the historical frame — as Joyce does — and you court disaster.

And so too, finally, for Popper, who has labored long and arduously to demonstrate that science provides no absolute truths, neither for nature nor for society — to show that true science is inductive in method, that its tactic is to generate *disposable* hypotheses, and that it aims legitimately only at the construction of an expanding, yet ever more elegant and comprehensive, set of probability statements about the "true" nature of reality. For him, Western science, like Gombrich's Western art and Auerbach's Western literature, triumphs by giving up the hope for final truths and absolute knowledge in its investigation both of nature and society, while still carrying forward the careful and controlled charting of reality in an evolutionary, or piecemeal, way. It is this willingness to supress the desire for absolute certitude that protects Western culture, Popper believes, from totalitarianism. Totalitarianism always follows close upon the dissolution of belief in the *ultimately* provisional nature of every generalization. It is the inability to live with provisional truth that generated the fallacies of philosophy of history in Marx and Toynbee and which inspired or justified the tyrannies of Nazism and Communism in the interwar period.

For these great critics, then, realism in thought and art is intimately tied in with the open society; and the abandonment of realism, which has characterized so much of avant-garde thought and art of this century, leads inevitably, in their view, to the dissolution of the one cultural protocol capable of promoting orderly development, safe evolution, and expanding control by man of his world, both natural and social. For this reason the avant-gardists appear, to these three authorities as well as to most other humanists, to be indulging in a luxury that is either insane in its motivation or criminal in its intent. Popper, in fact, in *The Poverty of Historicism* and *The Open Society and Its Enemies,* looks upon every radical social theory as both a mistake and a crime. He views even the social-scientific attempt to predict future courses of social change as an error; to him all this is nothing but prophecy masquerading as science. He views all philosophy of history — all metahistorical generalization — as nothing more than personal whim passing for wisdom. Since the best we can hope for in the way of social knowledge is *provisional* truth, the best we have a right to demand of society is *gradual* transformation. He concludes that liberal, piecemeal planning, or what is now called "fine tuning" of the social mechanism, is the only scientifically responsible political program imaginable and that every form of utopian dreaming is a threat to civilization.

And so too, for critics like Gombrich and Auerbach, with respect to the arts. Neither of them can make much sense of anything that has happened in painting since Cezanne or in literature since Proust. Gombrich disapproves of the Cubists because they tried to frustrate perception rather than refine it. Auerbach finds Joyce and Kafka disturbing because, for them, the mapping of external reality had given way to interior psychic probes. Now perception is subordinated to and made captive of the psyche, and the psyche itself is released from the control of tradition, which has always ultimately exercised some direction in previous literary movements, however much they were committed to the justification of the claims of the imagination against both sense and reason. The surfaces of the external world, so laboriously charted over the last three thousand years, suddenly explode; perception loses its power as a restraint on imagination; the fictive sense dissolves — and modern man teeters on the verge of the abyss of subjective longing, which, Auerbach implies, must lead him finally to an enslavement once more by myth.

Of course I am not suggesting that the humanities are dominated by all or any of these three great critics. But attitudes like theirs predominate in them. Gombrich, Auerbach, and Popper are merely somewhat more philosophically self-conscious than many of their colleagues, and they have been — as a result of their experience of Nazism — driven to articulate their understanding of the relations between the humanities and a particular form of society more self-consciously. Whatever their differences with their colleagues on specific points of fact or theory, they share with most critics and scholars in the humanities certain ground assumptions which are now falling under attack by both the avant-garde and the new public. One assumption is that only evolution, not genuine revolution, in the arts is possible. A corollary of this is their belief in the authority of tradition as a control on what will be permitted to count as a creative advance in thought and art. For all three, received tradition serves both as a source of new hypotheses about the nature of reality and as a determinant of the mental set of the individual artist or thinker who wants to make something other than a simple cry or grunt.

This is not to say that they are reactionaries, either in their cultural or their social attitudes. In fact, as I have tried to indicate, they know and appreciate the importance of experimentation and the desirability of innovation in both culture and society. As I said, they take it as self-evident that Western civilization is unique in its capacity to change without falling into anarchy and to resist precipitous change without hardening into totalitarianism. But this means for them, as it does for most humanists, that what might count as a permissible world view in both art and thought has to be, finally, reconcilable with that knowledge of reality contained in the previously secured strategies of realistic representation; that is to say, what could count as art, science, or social theory for them has to be in principle assimilable to the lore of the realistic tradition by something like logical entailment or technical consistency.*

That means that all utopian visions have to be ruled out. For realism is a product of a decision, unique in world history, to put off utopian assaults upon reality, to defer any form of thought and action based on a passionately held conviction of the way things *ought* to be. Realism, in their view, is the cultural expression of a society which, because it is technologically innovative, can look forward to the overcoming *at some time* of the condition of scarcity and the division of men into classes that now characterize it, but which cannot really conceive that this utopian condition of genuine affluence might ever truly be attained. Because the experience of Western society has always been an experience of hierarchically distributed

*AUTHOR'S NOTE: Since writing this, I have been convinced by discussion with my colleagues at Wesleyan — and especially by Frank Kermode, Norman Rudich, and Victor Gourevitch — that my grouping of Auerbach with Popper and Gombrich obscures the differences in affective predisposition with which each of these three thinkers views the advent of the revolt against realism in the modern imagination. I am prepared to concede that Auerbach is much more inclined to view the apocalyptic aspects of this revolt with somewhat more sympathy than either Popper or Gombrich is inclined to do. And this because he has a somewhat more ample (specifically Hegelian) awareness of the creative possibilities of any revolution in consciousness, whether in the direction of formal consistency or in the direction of a "paratactical" resistance to such consistency. For the purposes of this paper, however, which is to characterize the cultural preconceptions of the centrist tradition in humanistic criticisms, the three thinkers can be conveniently grouped together. Auerbach would simply have to be conceived as a representative of the left wing of that tradition by virtue of the sympathy he is inclined to extend to attempted revolutions of the sort envisaged by the avant-garde of this century. The categories of his *analysis* of the situation appear to me to be substantially the same as those used by both Popper and Gombrich.

privileges and responsibilities, realism in thought necessarily consists in the discovery of internally differentiated and hierarchically ordered natural and social structures, even though it recognizes that the contents of these hierarchies have changed throughout time and space and might become more open, that is to say, internally more mobile, in specific situations of affluence from time to time.

The crucial question, however, is: Do art and thought need to be hierarchical in what they permit perception to find in the world and language to represent? If that were not the case, then we might be able to understand the current attack by artists on art, by writers on language, and so on; we might be able to show the essentially utopian content of the art they produce and link up the avant-garde in art with the radical wing of contemporary social movements.

What Gombrich, Auerbach, and Popper have seen in the new art and thought of this century is a repudiation, not only of a way of *viewing* reality, but also of the reality which that way of viewing was committed to find and map. The repudiation of realism appears as a repudiation of an external reality which is seen to be internally divisible *ad infinitum* and unifiable only in *theoria* never in *praxis*. The form of reality, in short, shares the attributes of the artistic and intellectual traditions that were developed in the West alone for its mapping and gradual conquest. Both the reality and the cultural traditions created by the attempt to map it are conceived to be *syntactical* in nature, by which I mean that both reality and the sole possible strategies for its encodation are regarded as homologously *hierarchical* in principle.

The word *syntactical* comes from two roots which when combined mean "to arrange together." Grammarians use the word *syntax* to refer to the rules of certain languages by which the elements of those languages are defined and their arrangement in certain acceptable combinations to constitute sentences is carried out. But the connotations of the notion of syntactical strategies are further ranging: syntactical linguistic conventions generate rules of combination by the tactic of subordination and stress. The important point is that a syntactical linguistic strategy permits the growth of vocabulary and the evolution of concepts of combination and therefore the mapping of new contents of experience, but it requires that, whatever the contents of language, those contents be organized in a relation of subordination and domination. It may well be that such linguistic strategies prevail in cultures which, like the Greek, are dynamically hierarchical, that is to say, hierarchically organized at any given time but, like their languages themselves, constantly changing the verbal contents which occupy the positions of subordination and domination. Auerbach uses the term *syntactical* to characterize the literary style of Homer and goes on to make the triumph of syntactical culture the mark of progress in the development of literary realism. This is certainly the kind of thing that Popper has in mind when he lauds the open society of the West over the closed societies of Asia and modern totalitarianism. That is to say, he envisages as the ideal those societies which are open to talent but in which only the individuals who have talent are presumed to deserve positions of privilege and responsibility, in contrast to those societies which simply confer privilege by right of birth or by adherence to some abstract or presumably timeless principle of selection.

But the term *syntactical* — whatever its use among grammarians — helps us to understand the revolutionary nature of much avant-garde art, pop culture, and current social rebellion, as well as the originality of the current avant-garde when compared with previous ones. For the current artistic rebellion, like the current social rebellion, is programmatically opposed to syntactical strategies for representing and organizing the experience of the world, on the one side, and for structuring society, on the other.

What the innovative artists and thinkers of this era have rebelled against is the very principle of a syntactically organized vision, the consciousness that requires the organization of reality into relationships of subordination and domination. The rebellion against perspective in art and against narrative in literature, like the rebellion against historical consciousness, reflects the feeling that hierarchical modes of relationship are no longer the fate either of perception, of representation, or of society.

As Auerbach himself tells us, the grammarians have a word that might be used to characterize the stylistic conventions being developed to figure such a world; they call them *paratactical*. Paratactical conventions try to resist any impulse to the hierarchical arrangement of images and perceptions and, as the roots of the word *parataxis* indicate, sanction their "arrangement together, side by side" — that is to say, indiscriminately, by simple listing in sequence, in what might be called a democracy of lateral coexistence, one next to another. As you can see, the term *paratactical* could be used to describe what aleatory music is about; it certainly applies to the Happening, to much of pop art, and to the techniques of *nouvelle vague* cinema and the anti-novel. It represents a class of stylistic conventions ideally suited to the representation of a world in which hierarchy, subordination and domination, tragic conflict, and psychic scarcity are conceived to have been transcended. The avant-garde is not interested in the substitution of a new syntactical convention for the older ones, and it is not trying to purge our vision of tired preconceptions so that we can reconstitute society and culture as yet another structure of subordination and domination.

The avant-garde of this century envisions the possibility of realistically conceiving a world in which hierachy, whether open or closed, has finally dissolved because the condition presupposed by these two models of society, the condition of material scarcity, is no longer a tragic inevitability. The avant-garde insists on a transformation of social and cultural practice that will not end in the substitution of a new elite for an old one, a new protocol of domination for the earlier ones, nor the institution of new privileged positions for old ones — whether of privileged positions in space (as in the old perspectival painting and sculpture), of privileged moments in time (as one finds in the older narrative art of fiction and in conventional historiography), of privileged places in society, of privileged areas in the consciousness (as in the conservative, that is to say, orthodox Freudian psychoanalytic theory), of privileged parts of the body (as the genitally organized sexual lore insists is "natural"), or of privileged positions in culture (on the basis of a presumed superior "taste") or in politics (on the basis of a presumed superior "wisdom").

The practitioners of the humanities know about paratactical styles, and they fear them, not the least because they deny the need for "critics." In fact, Auerbach associates them with archaic, or myth-dominated, cultures and with those periods of crisis in Western thought and art when the need for transcendental certitudes or the solaces of religion, or simply a boredom with formal disciplines, has asserted itself against the dominant realistic tradition — such periods as the fourth century A.D. in Rome, the seventeenth century in Western Europe, and, of course, our own age since about World War I. And they are probably correct in their belief that all previous paratactical deviations have finally ended as little more than ground-clearing operations, preparations for the crystallization of new syntactical conventions, as when Mannerism eroded Renaissance formalism only to give place to Neoclassicism. In short, paratactical conventions in thought and art have been recessive or subdominant strains in Western culture, at least since the Renaissance. And all previous mannerist movements are probably correctly viewed as manifestations of imperfectly repressed religious feelings or reflections of a mythic belief in fate or destiny that may still be present with us all. But — equally — it may well be that this conception of the historical function of the paratactical imagination is inadequate for an understanding of the current cultural rebellion against tradition, fiction, and perception and the combination of them that has sustained realism throughout its long history. And for this reason: the paratactical style is an intrinsically *communal* style, rather than a *societal* one; it is inherently democratic and egalitarian rather than aristocratic and elitist, and it is possible that the rebirth of parataxis in art and thought in this century does not represent the fall back into myth or the advent of a new totalitarianism so much as the demand for a change of consciousness that will finally make a unified humanity possible.

For although there is much that is merely exotic and perhaps even pathological in contemporary avant-garde art and utopian thought, what is characteristic of its best representatives — from Joyce and Yeats on down to Resnais, Robbe-Grillet, Cage, Merce Cunningham, Beckett, and the rest — is a seeming ability to live with the implications of a paratactical consciousness: a language of linear disjunctions rather than narrative sequences, of deperspectivized space, and of definalized culminations without any need for that mythic certitude that has always attended the flowering of such a consciousness in the past. And this may indicate that the current avant-garde is able to take as a fact what every previous one had to regard finally as only a hope — that is, that the condition of material scarcity is no longer an inevitability and that we are at last ready to enter into a utopia in which neither myth, religion, nor elites of taste and sensibility will be able to claim the right to define what the "true" aims of either art or life must be.

LOUIS MINK

5.
Art Without Artists

As far as aesthetics is concerned, the revolution is over. Like all successful revolutions, it was brought about by people who thought they were doing something else, and it occurred while no one was looking. One simply notices what one has known for some time, that the concept of beauty has disappeared from the discipline (if it can be called that) which was invented two hundred years ago by Baumgarten as the "science of beauty." The concept of beauty has long since chased the concept of the sublime into Limbo, and modern anthologists of aesthetics who feel that there should be a reference to beauty somewhere in their volume are forced to go back at least to Santayana for an appropriate title. An indication of a different sort is that the very term *avant-garde* has dwindled into a pastel period-concept, conjuring up faded photographs of the Beaux-Arts ball. Coined to refer to the tigers of wrath, it has been taken over by the horses of instruction, that is, by art historians. Even more indicative is the fact that modernism in art has moved, in little more than half a century, from the language of manifesto to the language of epitaph; the imperatives and exclamation marks which sprinkled the documents scratched out on the café tables of Paris, Zürich, and Berlin have been replaced by statements in the past tense and by question marks. Gathered for alumni seminars this summer, the still-questing graduates of Yale can choose as they will between "The Lost Image of Man (period)" and "The End of Art (question mark)."

No doubt each of us has his favorite epitaph. The one which has haunted me since I first read it years ago in that journal of mortuary science, *The New Yorker,* is the epitaph of the bourgeois novel written by that most bourgeois of all writers, John Cheever. "Some People, Places, and Things Which Will Not Appear in My Next Novel" is a collection of scenes and devices of which Cheever says, "Out they go; they throw so little true light on the way we live." The final section is about a writer, an old acquaintance of the narrator's, who after a career of incompetent creativity is dying in a *pensione* in Venice. The narrator brings him gifts of cheer, but too late, and sits in a broken chair by his bed.

"I'm working," he exclaimed. "I'm working. I can see it all. Listen to me!"
"Yes," I said.
"It begins like this," he said, and changed the level of his voice to correspond, I suppose, to the gravity of his narrative. "The Transalpini stops at Kirchbach at midnight," he said, looking in my direction to make sure that I had received the full impact of this poetic fact.
"Yes," I said.
"Here the passengers for Vienna continue on," he said sonorously, "while those for Padua must wait an hour. The station is kept open and heated for their convenience, and there is a bar where one may buy coffee and wine. One snowy night in March, three strangers at this bar fell into a conversation. The first was a tall bald-headed man, wearing a sable-lined coat that reached to his ankles. The second was a beautiful American woman going to Isvia to attend funeral services for her only son, who had been killed in a mountain-climbing accident. The third was a white-haired, heavy Italian woman in a black shawl, who was treated with great deference by the waiter. He bowed from the waist when he poured her a glass of cheap wine, and addressed her as 'Your Majesty.' Avalanche warnings had been posted earlier in the day. . . ." Then he put his head back on the pillow and died — indeed, these were his dying words, and the dying words, it seemed to me, of generations of storytellers, for how could this snowy and trumped-up pass, with its trio of travelers, hope to celebrate a world that lies spread out around us like a bewildering and stupendous dream?

In Cheever's final arching sentence, the word that does the work, I think, is the word *celebrate*. How better could one summon up the thought not only of the generations of storytellers but of the history of all the arts since the Renaissance, the celebrations of eye and heart which unite Michelangelo, David, and Cezanne; Telemann, Mozart, and Strauss; Racine, Wordsworth, and Brecht? The celebrations of art, one might say, are the functional substitutes which civilization has created to replace the feasts and rituals of communities which have no need for art or artists. But having reminded us of all this, Cheever then writes its epitaph. For the failed artifice, the trumpery of the imagined pass with its mysterious travelers, can stand for a whole repertoire of devices which have successfully solicited the imagination of generations of audiences; and by extension it stands for all the artifices of art which arouse, suspend, and ultimately satisfy our expectations of meaning — for the Golden Section and other concepts of ideal proportion in sculpture and architecture, for perspective inviting the eye in painting, for musical modulation through related keys returning at last to the tonic, for sonnet form, for the well-made plot. Now of course the obsolescence of devices and styles does not mean in any way the end of art. Braque did not bring painting to an end, nor Schönberg music, nor Pirandello and Brecht theater. But they did bring about what Harold Rosenberg has called, with especial reference to painting, instant art history, and instant art history has in turn transformed the cultivated perception of art, for which novelty ceases to be merely an attribute and becomes itself a value. That there is a tradition of the new is itself, ironically but inevitably, no longer a novel observation.

Yet if one surveys the literature of twentieth-century aesthetics, it might seem absurd to say that the revolution has already occurred. That claim is in part a gesture of modesty on my part — an avoidance, that is, of any suggestion that I am proclaiming or predicting a new art or a new world. To anyone familiar with philosophical aesthetics and with what John Passmore some years ago called "The Dreariness of Aesthetics" (in an article which for obvious reasons you will not find in anthologies of aesthetics), it must seem odd enough to speak of revolution at all. Consider such a recent volume as *Aesthetics in the Modern World*, edited by Harold Osborne. How modern "modern" is it does not say, but it was published in 1968 and consists of selected articles published in the last few volumes of the *Journal of the British Society of Aesthetics,* itself only ten years old. Scanning the Index of Names, however, one turns up the names of very few modern artists. It rather powerfully suggests that aestheticians spend long lives thinking about the works of art which came their way when they were young. The S's are a representative sample: they begin with Sartre (mentioned once, as a philosopher influenced by Husserl), but for the rest there are only Shakespeare, of course, Edith Sitwell, Gertrude Stein, Stendhal, Sterne, and Robert Louis Stevenson. It is no doubt by chance that these are all writers; elsewhere there are Gauguin, Giotto, and van Gogh, but except for Picasso no painter later than Whistler. Satie, Stravinsky, Schönberg, and Stockhausen are missing from the S's, but then so are Bach, Beethoven, Brahms, and Bruckner from the B's. Purcell is the only composer listed at all — no doubt a special negative bias of aesthetics in Britain, a country whose greatest musicians since Purcell are Handel and Delius. But the example serves well enough to typify recent philosophical aesthetics as a whole; and the implication was drawn long ago by Collingwood in the Introduction to his *Principles of Art:* "The aesthetician who sticks to classical artists is pretty sure to locate the essence of art not in what makes them artists but in what makes them classical, that is, acceptable to the academic mind."

Yet I should still say that the revolution has occurred; it is just that the implications of the shift from "What is beauty?" to "What is art?" have not yet been fully drawn and acknowledged. Aesthetics is of course a conceptual subject; it has to do with our understanding of art and its locus, not directly with individual works of art as such. And conceptual revolutions can be said to occur in any field, not with the elaboration of new theories, but in the first instance with the ability to ask new questions — new, that is, in the sense that only a fundamental conceptual shift makes them intelligible as questions at all. "What is the speed of light?" becomes an intelligible question only when it becomes conceptually possible to think of light as something having a velocity at all, and the question "Is the speed of light a constant?" becomes an intelligible question only when it becomes conceptually possible to think of motion in general as quantifiable.

Now the significance of the shift from "What is beauty?" to "What is art?" is that it makes the central concept of aesthetics dialectical for the first time. To put it another way, it hands over to artists the right to make any answer false. When the question was "What is beauty?" artists had very little to say about the answer. The cases to be examined were drawn from nature and from acknowledged masterpieces of art. There was therefore no problem of the borderline, peripheral, or ambiguous case. An unfinished Leonardo sketch might be enchanting or interesting, a saltcellar by Cellini sumptuous or elegant, but neither could raise *problems* for the theorists of the beautiful. When the conceptual focus shifts from beauty to works of art as such, however, conceptual reflection flip-flops from the centripetal to the centrifugal. Before, one ignores the periphery and focuses down on those masterworks at the center of the history of art to penetrate their secret. After, one works the ambiguous edges of the charmed circle, asking, "Is this child's unself-conscious dance a work of art? That fork? This automatic writing? My life?" In Joyce's *Portrait,* Stephen Dedalus accomplishes the flip-flop virtually between the beginning and end of a sentence. "I have a book at home," he says to Lynch, to whom he is expounding his aesthetic theory whether Lynch wants to hear it or not,

in which I have written down questions which are more amusing than yours were. . . . *Is a chair finely made tragic or comic? Is the portrait of Mona Lisa good if I desire to see it?* . . .*Can excrement or a child or a louse be a work of art? If not, why not?*"
— Why not, indeed? said Lynch, laughing.
— *If a man hacking in a fury at a block of wood,* Stephen continued, *make there an image of a cow, is that image a work of art? If not, why not?*

— That's a lovely one, said Lynch, laughing again. That has the true scholastic stink.

To be troubled by the cases which test the reference of our concepts is no doubt scholastic, but it is also in the schools that the changes come about which later are accounted revolutions — and successful revolutions at that, because otherwise they could not even be retrospectively described. The point here is that once the question about the accidental image of a cow is asked, it opens itself to the actions and choices of others, that is, to an unpredictable future. For it is at this point that artists can claim the right to falsify definitions by changing the experience which conceptual reflection must in the end acknowledge willy-nilly. In 1917 Duchamp turned a porcelain urinal upside down, signed it "R. Mutt," and submitted it under the title "Fountain" to the show of the Society of Independent Artists. The hanging committee rejected it, having its own answer to the question "If not, why not?" but of course nothing exhibited in that show has achieved the distinction in the history of art of Duchamp's rejected ready-made. Much the same could be said of other didactic oddities in modern art: Rauschenberg's carefully erased de Kooning drawing, for example, or John Cage's silent piece, exactly 4′33″ of inactivity and circumambient sounds, Jean Tinguely's self-destroying machine "Homage to New York," Ad Reinhardt's black paintings, Warhol's eight-hour film of the Empire State Building in which nothing happens except nightfall — or perhaps at the extreme, a Happening I know about but don't know about because its composer kept it secret even from those people who unwittingly moved through its scene and were its, so to speak, dramatis non-personae; and he has kept it secret from everyone else ever since.

Now it's not my intention to add to the very considerable body of explanations of the significance of these extreme works as individual works. Hilton Kramer summed up that side of the art world very neatly when he observed, "The more minimal the art, the more maximal the explanation." My point is not that such works transform consciousness, or reveal the crisis of contemporary life, or usher in the future of electronic postliterate man, or anything like that; it is simply that you don't mind my calling them works of art as long as I call them "extreme." There is no problem about calling them "extreme." It is obvious that centrifugal reflection has already brought us to the ambiguous periphery of the concept of art. The problem is why we are willing to recognize it as the periphery of *that* concept at all, how the very objects which over the last sixty years or so have been brought forth in raillery, rejection, and rebellion against some current definition of art have in a dialectical way wound up by being included in its concept.

Something like this has of course occurred in less dramatic and titillating ways. Sometime before the first world war, I should guess, whole collections of so-called primitive objects such as masks, pots, and shields were moved from the anthropological section of museums of natural history to museums of art; and somewhat more recently, at least post-Bauhaus, museums of fine art have mounted shows of industrial and domestic tools selected for "good design." But these evolutions of the concept of art have been gentle and incremental. They have had their own linguistic history to justify them, that is, the traditional terminology of the mechanical and industrial "arts" and of craftsmen as "artisans." Moreover, as objects they display intelligible form and are clearly the products of purpose and acquired skills. Aristotle himself classified the carpenter with the dramatist as both engaged in *poesis,* or making, as contrasted with theoretical activities such as science and practical activities such as politics. But the dialectical pressure exerted on the concept of art by the free action of artists is of another order, for it asks us not to reclassify objects with which we are already familiar under other aspects — such as tribal masks — but to assimilate objects which are new on the face of the earth.

In a very recent and short but subtle book on aesthetics, Richard Wollheim has listed what he calls some "very general principles which have historically been advanced concerning the essential characteristics of a work of art. Examples would be: that the object must be enduring, or at least that it must survive (not be consumed in) appreciation [this eliminates, for example, a dish of oysters Rockefeller]; that it must be apprehended by the 'theoretical' senses of sight and hearing [this again eliminates cuisine, as well as attempts to compose a symphony of smells or the feelies of *Brave New World*]; that it must exhibit internal differentiation, or be capable of being ordered [this eliminates, presumably, such things as a single sound or a single patch of color, however sensuously appealing]; and that it must not be inherently valuable [I'm not sure what import this criterion is intended to have, but perhaps it's intended to exclude such things as diamonds merely as such]." To these "essential characteristics" of a work of art most people would add at least three more: that its construction or performance require skill, preferably skill hard won and difficult to imitate; that it be the outcome of purposive intent; and that it belong to an identifiable genre, such as painting, sculpture, or the like. This sounds very abstract, but what the last three general characteristics sum up, of course, is the notion that nothing is a work of art unless it is produced by someone whom we could call an artist, however neophyte, engaged in an activity whose performance justifies (we think) that description. For the theory of beauty, art (like nature) is primary, and artists are simply those who produce or attempt to produce it. For the theory of art, artists or artistic activities are primary, and art is simply what these produce or call their products.

Now it is not important for my purpose that any such list of "essential characteristics" or criteria for applying the concept of "work of art" be complete or refined beyond dispute. For any definition of art is a gambit in the game between aesthetician and artist. The artist may accept it — as playwrights long accepted the "Unities" and, later, the idea of aesthetic distance incorporated in the device of the proscenium stage — or he may reject it and follow a different development, leaving the aesthetician with nothing but a stranded pawn and memories of what might have been. What Harold Rosenberg has called "art that thumbs its nose at art" can therefore be recognized across all the arts as definition-defeating art. In the increasingly spirited (and one-sided) contest between definition-producing aestheticians and definition-defeating artists, every one of the "essential characteristics of a work of art" listed above has been contravened by a whole class of examples. No doubt many of these are of no more fundamental interest than the case of Diogenes, who on being told that Plato had defined man as a featherless biped, plucked a chicken, saying, "Here is Plato's man." But some are, and I wish to call especial attention to that class of cases, illustrated in all the arts, in which techniques, often elaborate, have been developed for severing art from artist, that is, for preventing anything in the artist's imagination, feeling, purpose, belief, perception, or even technique from appearing in either form or content of the work itself. Such techniques are, paradoxically, ways of creating an infinitely extensible class of *objets trouvés,* or "found objects," and these constitute in effect a new or second nature, one created *ex nihilo* by human agency and yet as mysteriously Other and indifferent to our aspirations as first nature without divine Providence.

The idea of the found object may go back as far as Leonardo, with his advice to look observantly for the images in such things as damp-stained walls and the pattern of knots and knotholes in wooden planks, and no doubt it includes Hamlet, who saw a cloud as a camel, but then also very like a whale. It doesn't, of course, include sermons in stones, or the infinity in the palm of Blake's hand, or other attempts to read Nature as moral or symbolic.

It was the Surrealists, I believe, who introduced the notion of the *objet trouvé* into the language of art criticism, in an innocent and unproblematic way. The selection of a found object was based on the simple capacity to notice resemblance of form — of aesthetic quality, one might say — between natural objects, like pieces of gnarled driftwood or stones "carved" by wind and water, and sculptural forms already familiar to the contemporary eye. Duchamp's "ready-mades" were of course a different matter; their authentication as art was claimed, not on the basis of any resemblance of a bicycle wheel or a shovel to accredited forms, but for their lack of resemblance. In Duchamp's view — or at least what he said was his view — he chose his utilitarian objects for no reason at all. He imposed on himself the discipline of selecting only ready-mades which aroused no feeling whatever in him; moreover, although he had invented a technique which required so little time and effort that he could have produced an *oeuvre* of truly monumental proportions, he carefully limited his "production" to a relatively few objects. His claim was that merely by choosing these banal objects for single exhibition he had altered them. What he created was not a new object but a new thought toward an object.

Nevertheless, ready-mades are a cul-de-sac in the tradition of art without artists. It is even unfortunate that Duchamp and others should have turned into high-class show biz something which ideally everyone should have the pleasure of discovering for himself in the process of growing up, namely, that the world will reveal itself to us as pure spectacle whenever we will let it. Anyone who has ever ridden on a train remembers moments of pure absorption in the anapestic clack of the wheels or in the subtly varied swoop and dart of the telegraph lines along the track. I myself discovered what might be called the principle of the frame while riding in a bleak winter twilight on the Rapid Transit in Cleveland, Ohio, when it suddenly occurred to me that the window was like a picture frame and that by moving my head I could flick the drab industrial landscape into different compositions of gray-on-gray. This event is not recorded in any history of art and shouldn't be, because anyone should have the right to discover the experience for himself. But the world as pure spectacle is a world of qualities revealed to a consciousness which is a general human possibility, not especially to one which is an historical achievement and predicament. And it is the latter — the awareness of the *second* nature of found objects which are created rather than merely being selected — which bears on the revolution in aesthetics.

It is becoming commonplace now to speak of found poems, found sounds, and found images, although the word *found* is still as often as not left within quotation marks; the uncertainty expressed in this device is presumably uneasiness over whether something can rightly be called "found" which is also in some sense created. My point, of course, is that there is no contradiction. Early Dadaists created found poems by cutting words from newspapers, shuffling them in a bag, and drawing them out blindly one by one. Sequences seldom made much sense, of course, so usually they were intelligently shuffled into some sort of grammatical form. This spoiled the purity of the random method, to be sure, but at least it could be said that whatever the resulting poem says did not *originate* in anyone's imagination or intent. Computers can and do reduce even this reliance on selection and rearrangement, since they can be programmed to produce only well-formed or grammatical sentences, while the selection of syntactical forms as well as of each word — of *any* adjective in the available vocabulary to fill an adjective slot, for example — is made by reference to a table of random numbers. Here is a poem produced by such a program: its title is "Bassoons," but that was also selected at random.

> Is that the automaton that smells like tears of grass?
> All blows have glue, few toothpicks have wood,
> Direct a button but I may battle the ham,
> The crafty carnival's kite massacres the scalp.
>
> Yes, we would, you shall.
> Shall I not tighten a moose's parasite?

This is actually a very primitive computer poem. Its progam contained a vocabulary of 3500 words and 128 sentence structures, and there were no probability weightings. The chances that meter or rhyme will emerge, or that there will be connected imagery, can be very much increased by probability weightings, as slot machines can be adjusted to increase or decrease the frequency of pay-off combinations. Even in this poem the words *automaton, glue, toothpicks, button,* and *carnival* seem to me, although faintly, to cluster in something like a single impression of mechanical meanness, set off against the sentimental "tears of grass" and the zany, W. C. Fields exasperation of "I may battle the ham." But the point of dragging this poem in at all is not to parody literary criticism or to offend the memory of Charles Olson or to renew the endless debate about whether computers can be said to think.

The point is rather that just by existing — by being the case — the poem establishes beyond dispute several points we need in order to go on: (1) It *is* a poem. (2) It was not produced by a poet. (3) Human agency was undeniably involved in the process by which it was produced, but whoever designed the program for the RPC 4000 computer which produced it did not need ever to have read a poem or have written one or be capable of writing one with any qualities — whatever qualities you like — which this one lacks. (4) Infinitely many unique poems of any specifiable length and complexity can be produced by similar techniques. And if we sorted through this indefinitely accumulating print-out, no doubt we would find, among the chaotic and the banal, items which would seem to us enchanting or perceptive or intriguing or elevated or gnomic or hilarious or haunting or perhaps even apparently allegorical. (The most puzzling phenomenon of what might be called vanguard masterworks, I might add parenthetically, is their power to be apprehended as allegorical or symbolic even though they're not. They seem to be trying to tell us something, although they remain stubbornly on the far side of every attempt at interpretation. I have in mind, for example, not Beckett but Ionesco, or Pinter's early plays, or Resnais's *Last Year at Marienbad,* or Duchamp's famous *"Large Glass,"* cracks and all, or Rauschenberg's "Monogram," a "combine" of an angora goat with a tire round its middle and a little paint applied to both goat and tire. The description is comic, but the image is unforgettable, an icon in a time without iconography.)

The technique of producing found poems, or poems without poets, is a combination of indeterminacy and rigorously rule-governed procedure. The selection of a sentence frame or of a word from among the accessible stock of items is made strictly at random. *That* it is made from this stock and precisely at this point in the routine is totally determined in the program. The same exploration of the possibilities of chance and rule has been made, of course — and with the greatest ingenuity — in music. As even people who have never heard a performance of their compositions know by now, some composers, like Babbitt and Stockhausen, have gone the route of strict determination of composition, with every parameter except perhaps orchestration fixed by mathematically generated transformations. Others, most notably John Cage, have tried every possible way of letting each successive occurrence of sound and silence be determined by nothing but accident. To determine pitch, duration, loudness, source, simultaneity, and occurrence of each sound, Cage has used dice (the etymological meaning of the word *aleatory*), the *I Ching* (now computerized), the accidental imperfections of the particular piece of paper he was writing on, the unpredictable choices of performers from scores which do not even specify beginning or end of the performance, and the random fall of thrown objects, as of marked transparencies on star charts in his orchestral piece *Atlas Eclipticalis.* But perhaps not enough attention has been paid to the strict and elegant discipline with which these procedures, once chosen, have been carried out. Cage's career has been a continued affirmation, with respect to music, of "Anything goes," but a standing and uncompromising rejection of "Do what you please." And what he has accomplished, among other things, is to demonstrate that these are not equivalent. The *product* of the compositional process (whether one takes that to be the score or a performance of the score) has no antecedent restrictions in what may or may not belong to it; all sounds are born equal, and stay that way. The *process* of composition, however, is designed so that at no point does the composer permit himself to say, "What do I *want* to do here? What *effect* do I want? Is this really me — is it sincere — is it successful?" This seems like self-abnegation only because it is — the most abrupt sundering of the artist's personality and imagination from the perceptible qualities of the work of art since Michelangelo first asserted their connection.

Such works therefore are found objects, although quite unlike "found sounds" such as foghorns and the hiss of thermostats, which correspond to Duchamp's ready-mades. They are not objects regarded in a new way but *new objects,* although, unlike anything else in the history of art, they belong not to culture but to nature — the new or second nature which has dispensed with Providence. This description may give comfort to those who are outraged by what they perceive as the inhumanity of art-rejecting art. For what they object to is the idea that such works belong by right to the culture which man has created and which records his achievements and his possibilities. Found objects are art without celebration, the polar opposite of Lincoln Center as the temple of culture, where the liturgies of celebration are ritually performed. So it might be thought gratifying to relegate them to nature, even though a second nature, where they can remain at a comfortable distance along with such other inexplicable and irredeemably inhumane creatures as the cockroach, the lamprey, and the squid.

But the human project has always been to assimilate nature to culture, or in older language to justify the ways of God to man. And if I am right, the problem of aesthetics is to understand the consequences of its own revolution by assimilating the second nature of objects newly found to the history of the culture we have inherited, that is, to find even though only retrospectively the continuity in change. The change, as I have tried to indicate in several ways, is the sundering of art from artist — the complete and disciplined absence from the work of art *as we experience it* of any qualities or patterns which were intended by the artist or could be said to reflect anything in his imagination, feeling, or belief. The continuity, I believe, can be provided by a reformulation of what has come to be known as the expression theory of art. This suggestion may well seem among the least promising ways of adjusting aesthetics to the possibilities of art without artists, as even the briefest summary of the expression theory will make evident; for found objects, whether selected or created, are *prima facie* at the furthest remove from the kinds of art which the expression theory has found most congenial and illustrative.

The thesis of the expression theory is that what art is about is feeling or emotion, and that its particular way of being about emotion is, not to describe it, nor yet to arouse it in a spectator (although of course it *may* do that), but to *express* it. In the naive but popular form of the theory, which so far as I know has never actually been held by anyone who has tried to think it through, this is taken to mean that art is a complex way of evincing or revealing the artist's own emotional states. Its elemental forms would be a cry of pain, a grimace of anger, a little dance of pleasure, or a sigh of content. Such a view doesn't necessarily demean art and certainly doesn't diminish artists, for the assumption is that there is as much difference between the intensity, complexity, and uniqueness of the artist's emotions and more quotidian feelings as there is between *Swan Lake* and a child's spontaneous dance step. Nevertheless, the work of art remains, according to this romantic theory, a symptom, even though a particularly complex and sustained symptom, of the artist's emotional states. It is no doubt to this popular view that we owe the still widespread beliefs that suffering is good for artists, that major artists must have major emotions, and that, conversely, anyone who feels things intensely is thereby accredited for the life of art.

For more thoughtful versions of the expression theory, such as those argued by Cassirer, Collingwood, Susanne Langer, and more recently Richard Wollheim, a work of art is not a symptom of emotion, even emotion recollected in tranquillity, but a *symbol* of it. Langer calls a work of art a "presentational" symbol to distinguish it from discursive symbolisms such as language in its referential function, or conventional symbolism, such as the association of St. Mark with his lion. The characteristic of a presentational symbol is that it does not just refer to but presents or exhibits what it symbolizes, as a Mercator map *exhibits* the true compass directions among all of its points, although it only *refers* to, by a complicated system of mathematical translation, their relative distances. What a work of art exhibits or expresses, then, is not feeling as such but the forms of feeling — both dynamic forms, such as tension and release, and static forms, such as the ambivalent juxtaposition of feelings. Works of art are therefore the cognitive instruments through which we learn the *structure* of the life of feeling, something general rather than particular, even though important parts of the structure may well be limited to a particular epoch or culture. The *content* of the particular emotional states of others and even of ourselves we must still infer from the symptomatic ways in which they are not expressed but evinced or betrayed.

This theory has great merits. I believe that it is true, but since I can't possibly go into all of its obscurities and into the objections to it — even if I could get out again — I shall merely try to draw attention to the *weight* of some of its associated theses. First, the expression theory implies that we do not know the life of emotions, even our own, merely by having one. It is not by introspecting feelings but by expressing them or *finding* an expression of them that we come to know them. This accounts for the fact (although it is not therefore the only way of accounting for it) that often in the experience of art we think "That's it!" as if finding something remembered but lost, and also for the fact that we often want to call a work of art true or false although it *asserts* nothing.

Second, the theory implies that we do not know the life of emotions by describing it — which in turn implies that a psychology of the emotions is impossible. A good way of convincing oneself of this is to reflect on how meagre our vocabulary is for describing emotions. Consider the varieties of grief: offhand, I can think only of the descriptive nouns *sorrow, sadness, anguish, distress.* But even if we add adjectives of intensity and phrases such as "grief lightened by hope," our vocabulary remains a fragile and very wide-meshed net to dip into the sea of emotional nuances and tones in the hope of bringing anything to the surface. Although I haven't really tried to test this hypothesis, I am inclined to think that we have more words for differences of color than for differences of emotion. Moreover, emotional states and processes, we do know, are complex, yet we have no terms at all to *describe* the pattern or relations of feeling in a single state. Again, it seems true to say that in the life of emotion there are no oppositions, as Freud said that in the unconscious there is no negation, yet language requires us to regard love and hate, or anger and calm, as opposites and then try to correct this blunder with some further concept of oscillation or ambivalence. Yet again, we know that the experience of art is at least sometimes exquisitely clear, precise, and complex, so that one might say, "I felt — it felt — *I* felt just like the last scene in *Wild Strawberries*"; and that does the job economically and finally. Works of art, one might say, orient us to the life of emotions, actual and possible, as maps studied and remembered orient us to the external world beyond the horizon of vision.

Third, the theory sustains, although it doesn't entail, the view that there is a history of the forms of feeling and that it is through art alone that we can reconstruct the sensibilities of other times and cultures and, more importantly, identify and come to *know* novel and bewildering forms of feeling as they come into being in our own time. But it is important to know where to find the signs of the times. Dress and coiffure, for instance, are effective signals in the maintenance of behavioral systems, but as modes of expression they are unspeakably irrelevant; in themselves, in fact, they are prosthetic devices for expression.

Finally, the theory sustains, although again it does not entail, the view that emotion and reason are not mutually exclusive opposites but successive and interdependent stages in a single process. The forms of feeling exhibited in art look backward to the genesis of feeling and forward to the rational comprehension of a world which includes modes of explanation and possibilities of action as well as the energies of emotional life. A feeling is the childhood of an idea, or to put it the other way round, ideas — even ideas in logical and mathematical systems — have childhoods in feeling, which they may forget but never entirely escape. We have feelings, I should say, of separation and connection, of tension and resolution, of orientation and disorientation, which reason in its own history models more or less successfully and from which in any case it draws its energy.

The greatest danger one can imagine is the final rupture of thought and feeling. Schismatic feeling contains the terrifying possibilities of a giant and powerful child who can inflict on us at will his momentary hunger, anger, or even playfulness. The most terrifying of all of Goya's *Caprichos* is that of a traveler confronted on the road by just such a monstrous child, and what makes it frightening is the look of mindless glee on the child's face. On the other hand, schismatic thought leads straight to the crystal palace of technical reason, in which the only possible action is the execution of programmed imperatives, and experience is deduced rather than lived through.

Now of course I don't intend to claim as an argument for the expression theory of art such quick snapshots of the prospects of death by fire or death by ice. The fallacy of such a claim is so ancient that its name has never needed to be translated from the Latin. Nevertheless, there is merit in a view which enables us to answer in a coherent way the questions which our experience of art provokes; which makes it possible to understand that there are revolutions of emotional life as well as of political institutions and conceptual systems; and which sustains the possibility of holding in a single thought emotion and reason — as Yeats said that his fantasy "attempts to hold in a single thought reality and justice." Yet it would seem that the expression theory must founder on the resistance to it by the world of created found objects — of art without artists. For as the party of humanistic culture correctly perceives, whatever computer-generated poems or images, or indeterminate or totally determinate compositions, may do to our perception, however novel or interesting their qualities, whatever feelings they may *cause,* what they cannot do, in principle, is to *express* feeling or forms of feeling, for only artists can do that, and art is what they produce in the course of doing it.

But here I think that the expression theory can be revised. It does not even require a revolution in aesthetics, for that took place with the paradigm-shift from a conceptual system centered on the concept of beauty to a conceptual system centered on art objects. It is now a matter of picking up the pieces and going on. The concept of expression, insofar as it means a process of expressing the structures of feeling by impressing their complex form on enduring or recordable objects, did not belong to the theory of beauty and does not really belong to the theory of the art object, except as a special case. It came into currency in the stage of high Romanticism, which was the typically confused transitional period between the old aesthetics and the new — much as, for example, the now forgotten physical concept of impetus provided the relatively brief historical transition between the Aristotelian concept of force and the seventeenth-century concept of inertia. Combined with the idea of elite sensibility and the notion that belles lettres and the beaux arts could be clearly identified and separated from the vulgar and the utilitarian, the transitional concept of expression entailed that neither useful artifacts nor of course natural objects can be expressive. As recently as the publication of Susanne Langer's *Feeling and Form,* less than twenty years ago, there was some small protest over the fact that she began her main argument with a discussion of pots; a pot, it was charged, might have form, but not *expressive* form.

But we can now take the final step and say that objects as such, including natural objects, can have expressiveness as a quality, as they can have shape, density or luster. No doubt the recognition of expressiveness in objects is parasitical on our learning to recognize expressiveness in human actions and makings. But this is not an objection to the concept; it is rather an explanation of how we come to learn it, as of course all concepts must be learned. Through the open door of the concept of expressiveness, art without artists reenters the human world of culture and history, just as it was the obsessive presence of art without artists which forced us to hunt for the door in the first place.

The capacity of the expression theory of art to survive the many and astute criticisms which have been made of it can be attributed to its tenacious grasp on a common and profound human experience: works of art often, we find, look or sound just the way life feels. But of course some do not, others lose their power to do so, and sometimes the unexpressed burden of feeling finds nothing at all which corresponds to and expresses it. To substitute the concept of expressiveness (meaning expressive form wherever found) for the concept of expression (meaning the artful invention of complex form) leaves open the possibility that we may find, among the audible and visible juxtapositions of created found objects, those correspondences to the life of feeling which we can recognize more readily than we can invent. The incidence of such discoveries is unpredictable and may well be infrequent. Since few of us are likely to listen through miles of tape or sort through mountains of print-out in search of those portions which can be experienced as felt, it is possible that the world of art may support a new profession, the "selector," who as proxy audience culls and chooses what is to be reproduced and made further accessible. This would in effect merely separate from the creator of found objects a function which traditionally has been performed for themselves by intentional artists. The latter have always discarded (like a film director in the cutting room) what did not fulfill their intentions; a selector, sifting through the midden of second nature, would discard what lacks expressiveness. And he would, like the critics he would replace, receive and no doubt deserve the opprobrium of everyone.

No one can predict the future of art without artists, although it is safe to guess that it will not include Beethoven's Tenth. By now it is possible to discern some of the general *stylistic* qualities of created found objects in all media — such qualities as ephemerality and unrepeatability, the elimination of the boundaries of the object in space and the performance in time (as in Happenings), the abolition of genres, the disregard for every kind of illusion, and the tendency to include the process of generation in the product (as setting up the electronic equipment as part of the performance). But I have not intended to suggest that these can be regarded as fixing the style of our age, as baroque or neoclassical were styles which in their time supervened on all forms of expression. It is more likely that ours is the first age without a style, or rather with an unresolvable plurality of styles. Art without artists is, paradoxically, more likely to change the past than to prevision the future, in the same way that Eliot said that every new poem changes the history of poetry. For how we come to terms with the new, transforms to some extent our perception of the past; and the recognition of expressiveness in objects may very well lead us to reclassify and reexplore the histories of literature, music, and other arts, which have been constructed mainly to prove the inevitability and the immortality of masterpieces.

85 : *Art Without Artists*

A final point. The theory of the humanities since the Renaissance has shared with the theory of law a single structural idea, in the following way: Works of art, art criticism, and aesthetics have been most generally regarded as constituting a hierarchy of three levels corresponding to the hierarchy of public actions, positive law, and jurisprudence. In the latter hierarchy, principles of jurisprudence sanction both the decisions of courts and appeals against those judgments. The judicial process, in turn, finds the nature and degree of culpability of a given action according to the law. Now the humanities have for long been regarded as fundamentally similar. Works of art are like public actions: we even say that they are "published," that is, made public. The critical process, like the court, is both fact-finding and law-applying. It sets itself to describe a particular work for the sake of coming to a conclusion about its success or value; and in arriving at its final judgment, it appeals to canons or criteria of criticism. In turn, the proximate principles of criticism are supposed to be clarified, harmonized, codified, and grounded in first principles by aesthetics, corresponding to jurisprudence.

If aesthetics is the foundation of criticism, a revolution in aesthetics entails a revolution in criticism. Now aesthetics as the theory of beauty was explicitly normative, but aesthetics as the theory of the art object is not. If there are no first *normative* principles of aesthetics, then judicial criticism is at an end, and serious critics must exchange the judge's wig for the guide's cap, as indeed many already have. Critics can show us details and patterns and relations which we would not have seen or heard for ourselves, and it is through these and only through these that expressiveness can be recognized. But as the conceptual journey from the center to the periphery of the concept of art takes one into the unmapped territory of found objects, so after surveying it we can return to the center. Yet what we rediscover at that center is no longer immortal works, flawed masterpieces, feeble efforts, minor classics, failed attempts, or the Ten Best of 1952 — all solemn pronouncements of judicial criticism — but a world of objects, waiting silently for us to approach them.

6.
Revolution:
The Role of the Elders

It has not been the best of years at Wesleyan, in the American universities generally, in America at large. But it has not been the worst, either. When I was here before, I was most struck by a kind of civilized gaiety in the place, which was not in the least, I thought, inimical to intellectual enterprise. I'd been here ten weeks or so when Kennedy was killed. *Post,* not *propter hoc,* no doubt; but looking back one sees the progressive darkening of American intellectual life as having begun at that moment and continued until we find ourselves, in May 1970, in the midst of an enormous academic strike, held to be the only way available for the demonstration of a proper concern at an appalling constitutional crisis which, apparently, appalls few outside the universities and by many is regarded as a pure invention of the dissidents.

That is why this strange year is far from being the worst imaginable. Professors went along, over the years, with the 'establishment' assumption that 'pure' knowledge — the kind that is associated with the humanities — is and ought to be impotent and might therefore be freely expressed. Behind some of the irritation expressed by the powerful at manifestations of academic dissent there is the simple feeling that the professors and students are meddling in matters that are beyond their scope and have nothing to do with them. But this feeling is wrongly based, and it is on an understanding of the need to find practical applications for their potency that black and white, student and faculty, have come together. They cannot, as once they might, think it enough to discuss 'academically' — i.e., impotently — among themselves the untruths and injustices of public policy.

This is not to abandon disinterestedness as an academic virtue; or I at least think it isn't. But we have something like a revolution in the universities in this shocked new understanding of responsibilities, and it is hardly to be expected that all of the supporters of the revolution will be as careful to preserve what seems to them merely an amenity of the *ancien régime*. In this, and in other ways, we are compelled to consider revolutionary programs and demands much more radical than any that would be necessitated by the terms of my first two paragraphs; and the older one is, the more difficult it is to do so. Many of the demands of the 'counterculture' are beyond the imaginative sympathy of most people of my age; this is not an excuse for the kind of nonsense Robert Conquest recently wrote in *The New York Times*,* but it does complicate the issue, especially for such groups of largely middle-aged men who, throughout this year, have been discussing Revolution in the Humanities at the Center (off-campus) for Them. On the whole we were not gay, but we were usually patient and even distinterested at times. Also, we were able to get on with our work to a degree perhaps unusual in this academic year. In what follows I indulge myself in the luxury of trying to express my own mixed feelings as the footsteps of actual revolution caught up with our recorded versions of it, much like the strenuous work performed for us by Mr. Acconci at the height of the Cambodian shock.**

Most men of fifty or so are more intimate with another revolution, with the peculiar timebound apocalypse (for so we now see it) of the Thirties. There was almost pathetic testimony to this at a conference on The Future held at Rutgers University in 1965, where the discussion, dominated by well-known writers from New York, got stuck in the Thirties, as if the only true basis for prediction was in that period. I was never myself subjected to any experience comparable to the cauldron of New York left politics, but I could understand the fixation; my late teens were dominated by the Depression and the Spanish Civil War and the Moscow Trials and the Ribbentrop Pact. It is difficult, and probably useless, to go into this with the young. The Marxism of the time was cruder, the economic predictions on which we founded our certainties of disaster and renovation were wrong, and we all made, without thinking, certain reservations about our own roles in a transformed society which now seem naive or even dishonest. But there are, for all that, resemblances between then and now. It seemed quite certain that after the crisis there would be a wholly new state of affairs, not a modification of the

---

*Robert Conquest, "Everyone Hates US," *The New York Times Magazine*, May 10, 1970.

**Mr. Acconci gave his recorded footsteps a long start, but then caught up with them, displaying considerable physical energy in the process. Performance by Vito Hannibal Acconci, with tape and live voice, at Wesleyan Center for the Humanities, May 8, 1970.

old one. From where we were in the mid-Thirties it *seemed* there was simply nowhere to go except into a new kind of world — a certainty confirmed, for some of us, by the early poetry of Auden, strong and authoritative in its diagnosis of our hopeless ills, powerful though vague in its characterization of what was rushing at us "out of the future into actual history." And this revolution would be not merely political but a transformer of consciousness:

> Some possible dream, long coiled in the ammonite's slumber
> Is uncurling, prepared to lay on our talk and kindness
> Its military silence, its surgeon's idea of pain.

The master of this transformation was called Love, though we were not to understand by this concept anything involving regression. Eros was a force for discipline, affirmation, social responsibility. The compassion with which we would look at the necessarily shattered cities, the tracks of the refugees crawling westward, must be the compassion of the surgeon or the remote and helmeted airman. The polymorphousness of play was important, but for children, "casual as birds." So we lost our historical bets, or failed to anticipate time's peripeteias; but certainty there was, and confidence in love, and above all a rejection of the old guard — "holders of one position, wrong for years" — in favor of some counterculture.

What went wrong? *We* did, no doubt, with the excuse that a generational focus of attention is bound to be dissipated in any circumstances and especially amid the lies, the terrors, the general cheapening of thought, emotion, and intellect which few can escape during a world war. The greatest poetry of the war was Eliot's *Four Quartets*, as we are often told, and it is a poetry of patience and of private meditation; but *Little Gidding* came out in 1941, after the first blitz but before the nightmare had developed its full extravagance. In neutral America, Auden began a new education in aesthetics, ethics, and religion. I suppose the real wonder is that those years allowed anybody to think clearly or feel honestly at all. Anyway, they put an end to most possible dreams.

But we were wrong anyway. I don't mean simply wrong about Spain, about Stalin, about the proletarian revolution; we were wrong about history, including the histories of the arts in themselves and in their relation to conduct more generally considered. Insofar as we thought, with Lawrence (who was not much read in the Thirties) that an insufferable deadness had invaded our lives, that we needed, like Connie Chatterley, to be violently stirred into life, that intolerable social and emotional constraints grew daily upon us, we were right. But our predictions and solutions were too simple; we did not really imagine a need for cultural change which would radically affect what we wore or read or did with our wives or thought of our own personal place in the world. (The new counterculture, incidentally, is Lawrentian in its contempt for the notion of a responsibility toward one's own unique personality.) Consequently, when the war ended, we retreated into what William Empson, with a polemical blend of contempt and incredulity, calls Neo-Christianity, by which he means not only Christianity but all other forms of worshiping pain and denying the natural man. And only when that mood passed — it was shared, as a mood, by many who did not lapse doctrinally into Christianity — only when that passed and we began to assess the conduct and aspirations of the very young could we see, dimly enough, how it was that we were wrong, and why our arts and humanities had failed us. Above all, we had made a bad mistake about something we pride ourselves on cherishing, namely, history.

I will now try, with apologies for the necessary imprecision and dogmatism of the attempt, to explain the historical mistake we made.

In the arts and humanities the old world had already been rejected before 1914; the rejection was of the post-Renaissance world, and the villains were, according to taste, Descartes or Locke, and Newton, Huxley, and Darwin. The line may be traced through Nietzsche, Worringer, and, in the Anglo-American tradition, T. E. Hulme; but there are many other paths it followed, as students of Yeats know well. One of the consequences was a rancorous hatred of reason, or intellect, or 'positivism'; and already in the last years of the nineteenth century there was a venerable tradition of counterscience, astrological, magical, theosophical. The idea that we live "in disconnection, dead and spiritless," because we have lost a unity of being that flowered and decayed at the Renaissance is still commonplace, and many important movements in the arts up to the Twenties can hardly be understood without some reference to this "dissociation." At the same time, in the years before the First World War, there were revolutionary changes in philosophy, psychology, painting, the novel.

All this is what everybody has known for a long time, and I dwell briefly on it for one reason only: the implications of these changes in the arts and in related ways of understanding the world have not been fully understood. That is why I say the middle-aged are the victims of their own historical mistake. Perhaps we were taken in by what may be called the Hulme tradition, the authoritarian attitudes struck by some of the most influential writers; Hulme liked violence, had an abstract knuckleduster designed for him by Gaudier-Brzeska, and greatly affected Pound, Eliot, and Wyndham Lewis. He was very important for the antihumanist, crypto (at least) -fascist literary oligarchy of the Twenties. From this we derived a model of modernism which included a large and impressive requirement of order. It was not an order that one could easily perceive (Eliot asked, if one would understand modern poetry like his, for a "logic of imagination" and not a "logic of concepts"), and the whole notion of order, confusingly represented by some as a neoclassic revival, stemmed from the transcendent arrangements of *Symbolisme.* But literary order was demanded and related to more familiar forms of order, social and theological. We were encouraged, especially in the neo-Christian period, not to flinch at a society which reflected the order of a neoclassic poem, that is, a hierarchical and élitist society. Modernism, it seemed, was revolutionary in the arts only because it restored what was lost. And it could thrive only in a society which abhorred the dissidence of dissent, especially when that dissent proceeded from racial minorities. So we grew accustomed to apologizing, not only for the Mussolini-worship, but also for the antisemitism and hatred of the people, that we found in the great modernists.

It was partly because this was unattractive that we also welcomed, in the Thirties, a literature that seemed less arcane and less exclusive, a literature with at any rate some more immediate engagement with the horrible world about it, some concern for the secular fate of the poor and outcast. Auden, for example, loved and admired Eliot, but made no attempt to imitate his totalitarian forms or his totalitarian thinking; loose-mouthed, prolific, and apparently *engagé,* he explicitly refused to endorse the intense aspirations to wholeness that we associate with his elders. He reintroduced into poetry, it seemed to us, not only social seriousness but *play;* and his thinking originated in a different set of books. Marx, Freud, and less permanently venerated figures such as Layard, Groddeck, and Homer Lane. We were ready for a reaction against the ivory Symbolists; in the decade of decay and revolution we rejoiced in a new Marxist-Freudian literature, yet still adored the last oracular ranting of Yeats and the contemplations of Eliot, who abominated Marx and the "low dream" of the consulting room. We had all the fun of living in an overlap in history, having the last of the modernists and the first of the clever young men who reacted against them, at one and the same time.

What we had forgotten, of course, was a modernism much more radical than the one which required a neo-Christian generation to interpret it. We had forgotten a modernism which ridiculed 'order,' rejected the models which included it, and helped to invent the world we are going, for some time hence, to have to live in.

What we forgot was, to put it briefly, Dada. It began, as everybody knows, during the First World War, and in the violence of its programs and expressions of its programs it learned much from the war. It 'spat in the eye of the public,' despised *passéisme,* and condemned art for being recognizable as such by formal canons and types. It went a long way toward desacralizing the arts, which had been for some time looking more and more like religions; and for the first time (except, possibly, for some historical accidents) it created confusion between objects of art and jokes. It reacted to the horrible circumstances of 1916 in such a way as to give a violent kick at the entire notion of Art; and it didn't on the whole seem effective, partly because of its palpable excesses and apparent unseriousness. In the Twenties, Dadaists became Surrealists and were otherwise assimilated into a more intelligible tradition. But they invented the Happening, randomness as a policy, found art, and much else. And they changed, not only our relation to the norms of the art of the past, but our relation to norms of conduct. For in the long run these things are related, though it proved a surprisingly long run, partly, perhaps, because for a long time our attention was focused elsewhere.

This is, as I say, commonplace. But there was another thing we forgot — and still, I think, forget — though once it is pointed out, it also seems very obvious. I mean that in the first years of the century a really radical change occurred in the arts which was not flamboyant and destructive but in the end had at least as much effect as Dada, and the only derivation for it that I can think of is from technology. It may be argued that the most distinctive characteristic of twentieth-century thought is the switch of attention from the environment to the instrument. In the novel, for example, this takes place when writers such as Conrad (acting, of course, on hints from earlier writers) began to concern themselves, not with the formalities by which older novelists authenticated their stories, but with the form of the novel itself, so that all manner of things which had seemed of the essence of the novel — chronological narration, 'depth' in character, and so on — were seen as inert and decorative, and all the effort went, not into the direct rendering of the world, but into the refinement of the instrument. The end of this story is the position that the old virtues of *rondure,* etc., are lies and that the novel must make its way without the aid of the old, shared belief that its arbitrarinesses somehow represent a knowable world. In the same way, perspective and eventually all 'figurative' elements disappeared from painting, and the old diatonic structures of music were excised. It is unnecessary here to provide parallels with physics and technology. "An epoch," said Einstein, "is the history of its instruments." Airplanes no longer look like birds, or anything else other than airplanes.

We did not see this very well. We did not see that merely by directing our attention to essential formal qualities and by discarding all those which functioned only as a mimesis of the obsolescent, the novel and the poem (for *The Waste Land* belongs to this argument too) were providing us with a model of personal and social conduct in which there was no room for ritual imitation of older modes of behavior, but a terrifying amount of room for personal creative decisions. Add this to the more histrionic rejection of convention by Dada, and you have a situation in which a concern for the arts — always likely to induce some form of 'bohemianism' — is probably going to have repercussions in the field of conduct: rejection of restraints, rejection of the culture, rejection of the past. It did not happen at once; but, as Lionel Trilling has hinted, we made certain it would happen sometime by teaching many relevant works as modernist and world-changing. They were kept within the culture by various pressures, but sooner or later these would ease, and the chickens of modernism would come home to roost.

They have done so, as we all know, in the last decade or so. Detail is not called for; we are talking about — for short — the Rock generation. Mr. Fiedler's mutants, the generation we think of loosely as that of the long-haired, pot-smoking, past-hating young. They constitute a bohemia on a colossal scale, a very generalized bohemia opposed to a bourgeoisie consisting of nearly everything but themselves. And they are a new kind of bohemia because they have benefited from a breakthrough in the technique of bohemianism; the means by which one is *épatant* are themselves the focus of interest, usurping an older concern for social effect. The new interest is in the medium, not in the message; there is no 'significance' in long hair and random clothing, or anyway their main purpose is no longer to communicate disagreeableness to the elders. Just as the new arts of aleation no longer exist to proclaim alienation but to do their own thing, to devise their new and purer randomness, so the sexual and pharmacological preferences of a generation assert no longer a separation from the past and from the elders — it is taken for granted — so much as their own existence and variety. What Dada felt it must affirm with demonstrations — the death of art, the annihilation of personality — is now, in art and life, simply performed for its own sake. Even the Dada hint that out of these intellectual terrors and annihilations there would come a new and better age is not necessary to, though it is not wholly absent from, Neo-Dada. When the emphasis is, in my special use of the term, technological rather than mimetic, there is no longer any strong sense that what is happening is transitional, that the new arts and the new mores will themselves end, and that thenceforth a series of new times will begin.

In short, it is the modernism we neglected, and not the one we cultivated, that has, after lying dormant for half a century, erupted as the revolution of the counterculture.

The elders, it is well known, have a good deal of trouble understanding all this, in part because of the difficulty of saying anything about randomness in terms of an acceptable intellectual matrix. For example, nobody pays much attention to Oedipal explanations of the conduct of the young; they simply beg a large number of tedious questions. And if one applies the sort of criteria developed by the New Criticism to a lot of modern poetry, the effect is similar; the criteria are of no relevance except insofar as their irrelevance is part of the situation.

Let me therefore suggest a model that for all its desiccation and fundamental lack of interest may assist the present inquiry. Old ideas of order are, in the situation we are considering, discredited. In terms of information theory, they depend heavily upon redundancy. That is, there must, in a form which is likely to be called orderly or 'organic' or some other honorific epithet, be a degree of what hermeneuticists call *Vorverständnis*. You have to have some notion — it need not be exact — of what remains to be seen or heard of whatever it is you are reading, looking at, or hearing, before you can follow it or hope to get the message. The redundancy (that is, the quality of fulfilling expectation) will vary from moment to moment, and various peripeteias or graces will reduce it strikingly at times, but insofar as a work has 'form,' it cannot reach zero redundancy and will sometimes (at the end, for instance, of a conventional novel) possess it in a very high degree. The notion is basically simple: if I send you a message saying, "Thank you very much for the flowers," the letters *l o w e r s* have a high degree of redundancy. As Norbert Wiener puts it in a cybernetic epigram, a message is the negative of its entropy.[*]

[*]"Messages are themselves a form of pattern and organization. Indeed, it is possible to treat sets of messages as having an entropy like sets of states of the external world. Just as entropy is a measure of disorganization, the information carried by a set of messages is a measure of organization. In fact, it is possible to interpret the information carried by a message as essentially the negative of its entropy, and the negative logarithm of its probability." (*The Human Use of Human Beings* [New York: Doubleday, 1954], p. 21).

There is more to be said about conventional forms of art and behavior than that they have a degree of redundancy, but it is what nevertheless may be safely said. And now let us recall the two forces of revolution I have been talking about, Dada and technologism. Randomness, entropy, is essential to the program of Dada, and this is really revolutionary since it subverts conventional communication; a Dada 'message' is the positive of its entropy. And the second force, though it works differently and is easier for the elders to comprehend, arrives at similar effects. When a code of communication exists, it has to be founded on agreements to read the arbitrary units into which information is divided in accordance with conventions that the sender also accepts. Thus, in a novel, clues as to character, the order of reporting events, the credibility of the narrator, and so forth, are clues which the author knows his reader can interpret within narrow limits. The concord between them used to be so close that either party would have been surprised to be told that there *was* a conventional element involved. The history of how the conventional element came to be recognized and progressively rejected is a long one, but few would deny that it reached its climax in the early years of this century. The effect was not to discredit 'form' but to make it very much more arduous and markedly to reduce redundancy in all the arts. Eventually, as I have argued, conduct was affected; we are dealing, in the present revolutionary situation, with conduct that reflects the reduced measure of redundancy forced upon readers, listeners, and people looking at paintings two generations back. The earliest reactions were of outrage; but there is no longer any point in that, since where the conventions of redundancy do not exist, there is no probability and no measure of unexpectedness. Or, only the unexpected is predictable.

I have just been overstating the case, I admit; not all the conventions are dead, and some new ones have developed for us to learn. There may be — in fact, there almost certainly are — certain biological and cultural limitations on absolute randomness of conduct and on possible degrees of severance from the past. Still, we have now a diagrammatic representation of the situation in which the elders, or humanists as they are sometimes called, have to work. In itself it is not, I think, too dismaying. Ideas of order can be benign or malignant; so can randomness. When they conflict, as they did on certain campuses this spring, it is order that fires the guns. When the universities organize their protest, we see how unnatural and unstable their emergency forms of order must be, how entropy threatens their message; nevertheless, we prefer that to the bullets of redundant order.

But the immediate question is not of political sympathies; the question is how we elders, with our accumulated disabilities and errors, ought to behave in the new cultural situation. The difficulty, to put it simply, is that no matter how well we understand both Dadaism and technologism, the forces of counterredundancy, we are almost certainly committed to ideas of value that work only where there are formal qualities expressible as redundancies. We are critics (of one kind or another), teachers (of one kind or another), and our business is the transmission of values. I'm not, of course, calling these values absolute; I can see no way in which that claim could be substantiated. All that can be said is that humanists, using forms of persuasion which vary with each generation, transmit a notion of their inherited valuations to the young. There tends to be a canon, which is variable of course; and works that get into it are works particularly susceptible to the necessarily varying methods of talking and being persuasive about them. In the past there has also been some feedback of critical redundancies into works of art, which made the job easier. Of course there are rebel humanists who seem to deny that their task is the transmission of values; Northrop Frye is an obvious modern instance, but what he really says is that part of the work can be systematized on a value-free basis and that valuation and the transmission of values are unsystematic, which is by and large true. No humanist elder really likes the idea that he is the last person in history to suppose that what interests him has value; we all strive to the extent of our resources of sensibility and ingenuity to make it look as if it has and to persuade a new generation to join us in so believing. And this is as true of conduct as of art.

However, as redundancy diminishes and entropy increases, value criticism, which depends so much on the existence of formal relationships (and so on redundancy) loses relevance. Nor is there any evidence that the transmission of information about minimally redundant work has yet seemed to anybody a necessary, not to say a possible, task. Briefly, in relation to the new arts, the function of criticism seems principally to consist in providing a theoretical environment for the works discussed. Thus the only service a critic can perform for Mr. Cage's music is to explain how silence functions in a music situation or how, technologically, he goes about ensuring a maximum randomness. A great deal has been written about Duchamp's "Fountain," but nothing that cannot be described as the provision of theoretical context; the work clearly does not have the qualities that art historians devised their vocabulary to identify. The only other kind of criticism that seems to be possible is the sort of rhapsody or gossip that has long been anathematized in the older tradition. So there seems to be no obvious place for *our* kind of thing in their kind of thing. And this takes us back from the realm of speculation into the world of fact. What, given our mistakes and the way we have been conditioned, are we to do in our contacts, critical and pedagogical, with the revolutionary generation?

My answer to this question is partly, I suppose, the issue of my own temperamental noncombativeness. It seems to me a simple recognition of what has always been the case, that we have no imperial rights over the culture, only the right to argue by whatever means we choose that our thing is worth doing. This right, of course, we allow to everybody else, whatever *their* thing. We should certainly not take it upon ourselves to worry if people do not want to join us, preferring some world elsewhere.

In other words, we should not be so absurd as to teach and behave as if there were powerful forces not ourselves that more or less oblige aspiring human beings to be like us. This may seem obvious in 1970; I can only say that it has not been obvious for very long and was not obvious in the Wesleyan of 1963–64; there, as elsewhere, it was an unspoken assumption that students — if such a thing were possible — ought to be as cultivated as, and in the same ways as, faculty. We have to give it up. There are other worlds, and other fictions, than the ones we agree to cherish. Insofar as these eschew redundancy, the critical assumptions I, and most of my kind, tend to make will not enable us to say much about them. Whether today's students will in the end discover that their fictions are after all paradigmatic and radically redundant, and join us in some new alliance, I cannot say, though it seems not altogether unlikely. But for the time being we must cultivate our still ample garden and let others do the same. We ought cheerfully to resign our institutional powers; other social universes have their own reality-constructions, and an authoritarian institution would be obliged to 'nihilate' them, but the humanities are not such an institution and would destroy themselves by pretending to be.

Ways of making sense of the world are plural, incorrigibly so in our time. Living with the revolution means living with that. It does not mean abandoning our own ways of making sense. Perhaps, when the dust settles (if it ever does), some ways of establishing a virtual human space in the world will seem obviously better than others. But at present we can't make that judgment. We can only be patient, humane, tenacious, and, where its seems appropriate, absorptive.

This is not a sellout. There are some things about the counterculture which appear to be dangerous (insofar as it wants to nihilate *us*) and some that seem foolish. It can offer a refuge for ignorance and carelessness and megalomania and bullying. The worst thing it can do, probably, is to undermine the authentic cultural relationship between the teacher and the taught. This, of course, is essentially between more experienced, more mature, better informed people and less experienced, less mature, worse informed people. In the past there can be no doubt that the elders found it comfortable to institutionalize this relationship by means that now seem illicit: in short, by hypostasizing Authority. But this can and must be given up without the sacrifice of the truth, which is that if the teacher does not know more — if indeed he is not, in terms of what remains of the common culture, wiser — then he ought not to be there anyway. Well-known and eloquent teachers who say that their students are better equipped than they are to institute programs, that their students know more about the world than they do, and that they go to class as students of their students, ought at least to distribute their salaries among the class and pay tuition.

A university is a place where the generations are brought together for the purpose of transmitting from elder to younger (though again there is and ought to be 'feedback') information which is not transmitted genetically. It is not a place for experiments in group therapy or the submersion of individual in group aspirations. Sometimes I think that the extravagant abdications of some teachers at this moment will have the just effect that in a few years the students will be complaining that they are being systematically starved, and we shall have a reversion to Authority in the old bad sense. The authority we need is natural and simple, containing no element of privilege, simply proceeding from a fact of life that no intelligent, not to say civilized, relationship can ignore.

So teachers must teach. They can explain — they ought to explain — that they are using disciplinary matrices to which there are possible alternatives. They must, in the humanities at any rate, explain that survival depends on the effectiveness of the dialogue between teachers and taught who are alike ready to question *anything* and to refrain from authoritarian assertiveness. The fresh, necessarily naive skepticism of the young interacts with the cautious skepticism of men who know about change and have themselves changed — men who have made mistakes about history and everything else and want to make their mistakes creative.

And this takes us back to our revolution and to the reminiscences and speculations about revolution which were overhauled by the real thing. What surely is good about the changes of the last few years is that, if we are spared the worst follies, which might destroy the universities altogether (and these could

come from careless or desperate men on either extreme wing of the argument) —
if we are thus spared, we shall be able to claim that although teaching is
harder work now, we are doing it better than we did. We have changed and
must change again; we have learned something about our job, our
responsibilities, and the dangers which have always threatened us but which
used to be more easily ignored. We have learned that, after all, our innocent
and disinterested activities have a political dimension, and we have found out
our allies, the students. Among them, and among our colleagues too, there are
some who also threaten, who believe we should not be allowed to do our thing.
But we must go on doing it.

When the young were in one another's arms, Yeats' old man turned
reluctantly to monuments of unageing intellect. The young never wither, are
perpetually renewed by nature; our art is, as far as we can, to preserve
intellectual monuments unaged. We can't do this by junking the monuments.
Sometimes we can do it by showing how the new is transmissible on the same
terms as the old (how many of the 'best' exhibits at the big Metropolitan
show last winter seemed permanent, not because of their novelty, but because
they were, finally and surprisingly, subsumable under any old category such as
'painterly'!). Mostly we do it by patiently exploring new ways of making the
monuments new, taking them out of the temporal rat race, changing them
as needed.

And always we have to remember these things: We are not a church or an
empire; we are smaller than we thought, but with the rights that interest and
disinterest confer; we are humanly similar to the most dissident of our neighbors;
we have to go on living in change; and finally, our interest and disinterest are
of a kind that give us the right to speak, and properly to act, in concert with our
neighbors when what is common to our notions of humanity and justice is
outraged by men of power. After all our talk and kindness through the year, we
have, at its end, looked out of the window and seen that this may happen.

7.

Politics and the Literary Imagination

The famous speech on "degree" delivered by Ulysses in Shakespeare's *Troilus and Cressida* is not, of course, the voice of Shakespeare but that of one of his characters speaking in a particular dramatic situation; yet most readers and viewers of the play cannot help feeling that the author's conviction lies behind Ulysses' words. And there is abundant evidence from other plays and from the thought of the period that for Shakespeare "degree" was part of that order in which the health of the universe, of society and of individual man resided:

> The heavens themselves, the planets, and this center
> Observe degree, priority, and place,
> Insisture, course, proportion, season, form,
> Office, and custom, in all line of order.
> . . . .
> Take but degree away, untune that string,
> And hark what discord follows.

Shakespeare as artist, it might be argued, needed order even more than Shakespeare as Elizabethan or Jacobean. Literary art seems to bring form out of the chaos of unorganized experiences, to impose order on the bewildering fragments of diurnal reality. From one point of view, art has always been on the side of order. It is interesting to see how again and again in literary history the most individual and idiosyncratic minds have subscribed to some ideal of order and hierarchy, often relating it, as Shakespeare did, to something far beyond a social pattern — a cosmic dance, the course of the planets or the music of the spheres. Ben Jonson's strong and rugged mind brought itself to stoop before a vision of social order that had wide moral implications: "To Penshurst," one of the first English poems in praise of the Great House and its exemplary pattern of life, is both a compliment to noble friends and a vision of the good society:

And though thy walls be of the countrey stone,
They'are rear'd with no mans ruine, no mans grone,
There's none, that dwell about them, wish them downe;
But all come in, the farmer, and the clowne:
And no one empty-handed, to salute
Thy lord, and lady, though they have no sute.

Some bring a capon, some a rurall cake,
Some nuts, some apples; some that thinke they make
The better cheeses, bring'hem; or else send
By their ripe daughters, whom they would commend
This way to husbands; and whose baskets bear
An embleme of themselves, in plum, or peare.

In an earthier version of the concluding stanza of Yeats' "A Prayer for my Daughter," Yeats linked his idea of ordered, ceremonious Great House life to the neo-Platonic Dance of Life, but at the same time, like Jonson, he wanted a living, organic social order in which tradition was being continually both handed on and renewed. Yeats's first reaction to having been "deprived . . . of the simple-minded religion of [his] childhood" by nineteenth-century science was to seek for "almost an infallible church of poetic tradition, of a fardel of stories, and of personages, . . . passed on from generation to generation by poets and painters with some help from philosophers. . . . I wished for a world, where I could discover this tradition perpetually, and not in pictures and in poems only, but in tiles round the chimney-piece and in the hangings that kept out the draft."

The artist, then, needs order and tradition, and the more revolutionary the artist (or so it has been argued), the more he needs a tradition in the light of which his own originality can become meaningful. "No poet, no artist of any art, has his complete meaning alone. His significance, his appreciation is the appreciation of his relation to the dead poets and artists. You cannot value him alone; you must set him, for contrast and comparison, among the dead." These well-known words are those of T. S. Eliot, the most revolutionary poet of the English language in the present century. Is there a paradox here? In a lecture delivered in 1933, Eliot defended "the struggle of our time" as the struggle "to concentrate, not to dissipate; to renew our association with traditional wisdom;

to re-establish a vital connexion between the individual and the race; the struggle, in a word, against Liberalism." Could anything be more reactionary, more backward-looking than this? It was Eliot, too, who defined his position as "classicist in literature, royalist in politics, and anglo-catholic in religion." The term "royalist" as defining a political — or any other — position does not in fact have any meaning in the twentieth century. What was the great avant-garde poet doing using language like this?

The paradox goes much further than Eliot. The English critic T. E. Hulme, whose attacks on Romanticism and humanism between 1913 and 1915 pointed to a new classical ideal of impersonal discipline which sought to get back behind the Renaissance almost as the Pre-Raphaelites had sought to get back behind Raphael, was a militant avant-gardiste as a critic of the arts. He translated Georges Sorel's *Réflexions sur la violence;* he enormously influenced Eliot; he inspired the Imagist movement; he believed that authoritarianism and belief in original sin made for a better society and better art than any that could arise from democracy and a humanistic belief in man's unaided powers. Sorel is perhaps the clue here — Sorel, who asked "to be allowed, before descending into the grave, to see the humbling of the proud bourgeois democracies, today so cynically triumphant"; Sorel, who admired equally Lenin and Mussolini; Sorel, who in his strange career of political questing came to repudiate not only the principles of 1789 but those of the Enlightenment, of bourgeois democracy, of humanitarianism of any kind, to preach violence as "a very beautiful and heroic thing" and to move from belief in the heroic violence of the proleterian strike to join forces with the extreme nationalist, royalist Right. Throughout all the vagaries of Sorel's extraordinary career, one thing remained more or less constant: his contempt for the bourgeoisie.

Modernist art was always anti-bourgeois. Dadaism, Futurism, Surrealism, all those modernist movements of the earlier part of this century had a common aim (not necessarily the sole aim) of breaking up bourgeois conceptions about the nature of art, of language, of experience. Dada gloried in destructive irrationality in deliberate protest against bourgeois conceptions of order. Marinetti's Futurist program called for the destruction of museums equally with the destruction of the accepted forms of language and logic. The grotesque and flamboyantly dexterous nonsense poetry of Hans Arp was equally a challenge to accepted notions of language, order and meaning.

But where have we got to? If the artist in his capacity as artist needs tradition and order, and if this need may lead him to sympathy with the political Right, what are we to say of the modernist prophets of *dis*order who often moved to the Right (sometimes to the fascist Right) because bourgeois order seemed to them hypocritical and false? Sorel's career illustrates clearly how an anti-bourgeois position can move equally to the Right or to the Left: scorn of bourgeois democracy is voiced by Fascist and Communist in almost identical terms. Sorel's prayer to be allowed to see the humbling of the proud bourgeois democracies before he died might have been equally Lenin's or Hitler's. If the artist needs order, he might say that the order of the world of bourgeois democracy is not a true order and destroys the organic order of society (which is what Marx virtually said in the Communist Manifesto), and he then might seek either to revive a traditional social order in order to help his art (which is what Eliot did, at least theoretically) or to bring about a radically new order which requires for its coming into existence either the breaking down of all conventional expectations about language and experience or a new political system created by *putsch* or by revolution. The point is that Communist, Fascist, Anarchist and Ivory Towerist agreed on one basic article of faith: bourgeois democracy is a sham and an evil. And those who exposed this sham and this evil while thinking they served the Left were serving the extreme Right just as effectively — indeed, even more effectively, as the history of the Weimar Republic shows.

But the situation is more complicated even than this. For the man who looks backward to an earlier — and in his view more organic — social order with which to replace the unsatisfactory bourgeois order may, at the same time, agree with revolutionaries about the need to destroy all conventions about art and language and look, not backward to prebourgeois society, but forward to some not-yet-existing society, where the actual technique of his art is concerned. So we can get reactionaries in politics who are revolutionaries in art. And indeed, this is the position of many of the modernist writers of the twentieth century, including Eliot.

If the artist needs order, it might be argued that he is particularly sensitive to order and that a phony order or a hypocritical order or an inorganic order (and bourgeois order was criticized on all three grounds) would therefore not satisfy him. The great visions of ordered society of the kind we find in Renaissance literature, which are often linked with the Great Chain of Being or with neo-Platonic views of the nature of reality, cannot, if they arise in modern times, be related in any way to the social order as it is. Jonson's Penshurst really existed as he described it; Yeats' Great House was a symbol created out of his vision of what Lady Gregory's Coole Park might stand for. Bourgeois order tends to drive the artist away in a manner that medieval and Renaissance order did not.

But what is wrong with bourgeois order? Why has there been such unanimity on both the Right and the Left about the menace of the bourgeoisie? There is an element of masochism in these anti-bourgeois attacks, for the people who make them are in almost every case bourgeois themselves. The bourgeoisie in Europe have produced a great literature; indeed, since Chaucer and Shakespeare the most vital kinds of literary imagination, at least in English literature, have belonged to the bourgeois on the make. Whence, then, springs the notion that the bourgeoisie are Philistines, hostile to art; that there is inevitable warfare between the artist and the middle classes; that the artist is always in some sense alienated, exiled, free from the social and moral obligations that bind other people? We must go back behind the Aesthetic Movement and *l'art pour l'art*, back behind Matthew Arnold's fight against the Philistines in *Culture and Anarchy*, behind Ruskin's attack on industrial ugliness and his endeavor to associate the aesthetic, the moral and the social, behind the French idea of *la vie de Bohème*, behind Carlyle fulminating against the "cash nexus" as the only bond left between man and man.

The phenomenon begins in England and is associated in its beginning with the first impact of the Industrial Revolution on English sensibility. As early as 1800 Wordsworth deplored "the increasing accumulation of men in cities, where the uniformity of their occupations produces a craving for extraordinary incident" and a "degrading thirst after outrageous stimulation," thus linking conditions of urban living to a debasement of literary taste. But a more interesting clue is provided by a letter Walter Scott wrote to a friend early in 1820. Scott is trying to diagnose the cause of popular unrest:

> Formerly obliged to seek the sides of rapid streams for
> driving their machinery, manufacturers established themselves in
> sequestred spots and lodged their working people in villages
> around them. Hence arose a mutual dependence on each other
> between the employer & employd for in bad times the Master had
> to provide for these peoples sustenance else he could not have
> their service in good & the little establishment naturally
> looked up to him as their head. But this has ceased since
> manufacturers have been transferd to great towns where a Master
> calls together 100 workmen this week and pays them off the next

with far less interest in their future fate than in that of as
many worn-out shuttles.

Scott, who was a high Tory, is saying what Marx later said, that the
bourgeoisie has dehumanized human relations. The old vision of the organic
society is no longer possible. And this is attributed directly to the influence of
the Industrial Revolution. The bourgeois order is thus no real order. Twenty
years after Scott's death Carlyle made the point again, emphasizing that it was
not the *unhappiness* of the proletariat but the inorganic and meaningless routine
of their lives that is new and intolerable:

> Life was never a May-game for men: in all times the lot of the
> dumb millions born to toil was defaced with manifold sufferings,
> injustices, heavy burdens, avoidable and unavoidable: not play
> at all, but hard work that made the sinews sore and the heart
> sore. . . . And yet I will venture to believe that in no
> time, since the beginnings of Society, was the lot of those
> same dumb millions of toilers so entirely unbearable as it
> is even in the days now passing over us. It is not to die,
> or even to die of hunger, that makes a man wretched; many
> men have died; all men must die, — the last exit of all of
> us is in a Fire-Chariot of Pain. But it is to live miserable
> we know not why; to work sore and yet gain nothing; to be
> heart-worn, weary, yet isolated, unrelated, girt-in with a
> cold universal Laissez-faire: it is to die slowly all our
> life long, imprisoned in a deaf, dead, Infinite Injustice, as
> in the accursed iron belly of a Phalaris' Bull. . . . Do
> we wonder at French Revolutions, Chartisms, Revolts of Three
> Days? The times, if we will consider them, are really
> unexampled.

We get here the view that life has become *radically different:* "in no time,
since the beginnings of Society," was it what it is today. The Industrial Revolution
and its effects represent a unique evil, marking a watershed in history. The gap
between life before and after the Industrial Revolution is unbridgeable. Man
has been dehumanized, individuals have become "isolated, unrelated." It is the
difference between Jane Austen's world and the world of the later Dickens;
between the society presided over by a Darcy or a Knightley and the
nonsociety of the Veneerings' dinner parties in *Our Mutual Friend.* Even though
Carlyle concentrates here on the condition of the workers, it is really the

dehumanizing of society as a whole that he is talking about. If Carlyle went on to preach his ultra right-wing doctrine of the Hero, that simply goes to show that attack on what the middle classes have done to society can lead the attacker to seek solutions equally on the Right or on the Left. Ruskin, and even more William Morris, went to the Left for exactly the same reasons that sent Carlyle to the Right. "It is not that men are ill fed, but that they have no pleasure in the work by which they make their bread, and therefore look to wealth as the only means of pleasure," wrote Ruskin in *The Stones of Venice,* and it might have been Carlyle speaking. It was Morris who related these concerns most clearly to the concerns of the artist: "Surely anyone who professes to think that the question of art and cultivation must go before that of the knife and fork . . . does not understand what art means, or how that its roots must have a soil of a thriving and unanxious life."

Art requires order, but a genuine order, and if the world he knows seems to the artist to be based on an order which is not a real, organic order, and which does not take care of the human need to *relate* (the term is Carlyle's and is not taken from the sentimental social idealism of today's young), then the artist will attack it and seek either to revive something from the past or to create something radically new: either task will be conceived by him as at the service of the originality of his art. And his sense of the urgent need for originality will be increased if he feels, as Carlyle felt, as the later Dickens felt, as many young people today feel, that the problems of their time are *unique* — that "in no time, since the beginnings of Society," (in Carlyle's words) was life like this. This special sense of contemporary disaster did not first appear with the atom bomb; it arose early in the last century when people were confronted with what appeared to be insoluble socio-moral problems posed by the early Industrial Revolution.

II

Art, then, is bound up with a concept of order; the avant-garde artist rejects the order of the bourgeois world because it is hypocritical, unreal and stultifying (not necessarily all these things simultaneously) and turns to the visible order of the political Right, often a romanticized and politically inaccurate concept of such an order, rather more often than he turns to the political Left. But this is an oversimplified formula. For in a sense the artist needs disorder as much as he needs order; he needs liberty for his imagination; he needs an independence, even an arrogance, of mind and heart that allows him to trust his own vision implicity. And here, too, we have part of the explanation of why the modernist artist has turned to the Right more than to the Left. As Conor Cruise O'Brien put it in his essay on the politics of W. B. Yeats: "The politics of the left — any left, even a popular 'national movement' — impose, by their emphasis on collective effort and on sacrifice, a constraint on the artist, a constraint which may show itself in artificialities of style, vagueness or simple carelessness. Right-wing policies, with their emphasis on the freedom of the *élite,* impose less constraint, require less pretense, allow style to become more personal and direct." Of course, this applies only to right-wing policies as imagined by certain artists, not as they may turn out to be in actual practice. The true innovator in any of the arts got equally short shrift from Hitler and from Stalin: at the end of the day Nazi and Stalinist conceptions of art are seen to be identical, involving a pretense of representational literalness while in fact imposing on the pretended mimetic ideal the insistent demands of crude didacticism and even (in literature) of generalized fable.

Politically, then, modernist art is Janus-faced, combining a revolutionary urge to smash the existing system with an ideal vision of order which is often politically reactionary. Sometimes, of course, revolution in art is associated with left-wing revolution in politics, but no successful revolution, on the Left or on the Right, can tolerate for long the free and disturbing imagination of the artist. However much the modern artist is welcomed in the initial stages of a revolution, as he was in the early days of Soviet Russia, it is not long before he is pushed out and more docile servants of the régime exalted as the true exemplars of the good artist. The interesting point about what emerges is that the official art of a postrevolutionary society is grossly Philistine, possessing to an exaggerated degree the very faults that truly original artists fulminated against in the prerevolutionary bourgeois society. The artistic tastes of Hitler, as of Khrushchev, were startlingly like those of an uncultivated Victorian petit bourgeois.

But there are even more paradoxes involved in this question of art and order. However much the artist requires a sense of order with respect to artistic *form,* his imaginative vitality will tend to work against this and, at least in the case of the literary artist, exhibit moments of local energy within a work which make for anarchy at least as much as they make for order. The greatest artists always have this local energy. Levin Schücking called it "episodic intentification" in Shakespeare and explained it historically, but it is in fact something more than this, something intimately bound up with the way the literary imagination works. George Orwell, in his essay on Dickens, called attention to the way in which Dickens tends to create vivid details in excess of the formal demands of the novel.

Most great writers do this in some way or other, although our modern critical habit of "proving" the perfect formal relationship between all the parts of a literary work has obscured this truth. When Eliot suddenly brings in De Bailhache, Fresca, and Mrs. Cammel toward the end of "Gerontion," the critic and explicator may be tempted to search for a specific reason why precisely these persons should be named at this point and to establish their identity, but the fact is they derive from the imaginative exuberance — a sort of aesthetic gaitey — that in the last analysis is what keeps a poet or a novelist or a dramatist going. This exuberance goes beyond form and even leans toward chaos. The artist, it is often said, imposes order on the chaos of diurnal experience, and of course in a sense and up to a point this is true; but this opposition between the disorder of life and the order of art can never be wholly sustained. That is what Yeats's poem "Byzantium" is about: you oppose the impersonal order of timeless art to the time-bound, biologically conditioned, tumultuously changing human condition, only to find in the end that you cannot leave that tumultuously changing human condition out of your art, for that is its ultimate source and inspiration. When Yeats returned, at the end of his life, to what he called "the foul rag-and-bone shop of the heart," he was testifying to the pull of chaos over order.

III

When imaginative writers are in rebellion against the society of their time, it is often because the forms and norms of that society work against the local vitality, the element of chaos, that every literary artist needs in some degree. Shakespeare did not rebel against the society of his time because it allowed free play to his imaginative vitality. Even the political watchfulness which resulted in the temporary imprisonment of those who had acted in a performance of *Richard II,* and the sort of censorship associated with it, presented no real constraint to Shakespeare. He lived in an age of rapid change, turbulent feeling, national exuberance, linguistic excitement and emotional liberation; the national ideal of the Tudor monarchy, however distasteful it may be to a modern democrat, provided a symbol and a ceremony that was the "objective correlative" of much in the national state of mind; while the Elizabethan theater, with its extraordinary cross-class appeal, enabled dramatists to appeal simultaneously on a great number of levels, addressing rich and poor, noblemen and 'prentices, heroes and whores, in a language which could be at the time ceremonious and bawdy, elegantly ordered and wildly and disturbingly eloquent.

This was a real society, and they were a real audience for art. But the dinner parties of the Veneerings in Dickens' *Our Mutual Friend* represented a nonsociety, in which people, having suddenly got rich by buying and selling shares, appeared from nowhere to indulge in hypocritical gestures of friendship before disappearing again when their speculations went wrong and even their financial hollowness was found out. The Veneerings and Podsnap are at once convincing characters in their own right and brilliant symbols of what a man of sensibility and imagination looked for and could not find in the society of *nouveaux riches* Victorians. Of course, they are to be seen in the complex context of the novel as a whole, but Dickens' capacity for what I have called local energy enables them also to be appreciated in isolated scenes. Similarly, Dickens does not argue against the Manchester school of economics; he creates Mr. Gradgrind in *Hard Times* and shows us the human price paid by acting on what is assumed to be Manchester theories.

It is not tyrants in the simple political sense that most threaten the artist, for there has been great art under absolute rulers; it is depersonalization, dehumanization. Novelists, dramatists and poets can cope with villains; evil may be a problem, but the probing of it in an *Othello* or a *King Lear* is a victory, not a defeat. The real threat of defeat for the artist comes when something in the code of society suppresses the realities of human personality. Ben Jonson in *Volpone* projects a tremendous picture of two men who have surrendered their humanity for money; but their behavior is shown to be superbly grotesque, fascinatingly monstrous and perverse, and the language of the play shows at each point that this is so, that there is a norm that is being continually flouted. What caused the later Dickens and the so-called Victorian prophets such agony of spirit was that the norm had given way, without any change in society's use of the language of traditional morality, before the depersonalizing process of keeping up respectability, of "what will the neighbours say?", of keeping up with the Joneses, of replacing altogether the man by the mask. And here literature has saved us. Not only did the Victorian prophets protest; more importantly and more fundamentally, the great Victorian novelists kept the awkward vitality of the human animal before the eyes of their readers: they kept the bourgeois imagination lively in spite of itself. And so our young bourgeois critics of society are in a position to rebel today.

This brings me to my main point. Great literature militates against abstractions, against any reduction of human experience to formulae, and works always with the concrete and the lively. In that sense all great literature is anti-political, turning away from statements about how society should be governed, turning away from slogans and polarizations between "goodies" and "baddies," in order to project and illuminate the ambiguities and ambivalences of human character. In that sense all political literature is bad literature. When D. H. Lawrence illustrates the difficulties and complexities of human relationships in a careful patterning of symbolically suggestive and at the same time realistically persuasive scenes in *The Rainbow* and *Women In Love*, we admire the artist and accept the illumination. When he pauses to theorize or denounce, we become irritated and resentful. And in those last verses, when, ill and desperate, he expresses his sense of his own superiority as artist and man of sensibility to the dehumanized masses of modern industrial society, his voice becomes shrill and offensive. One could quote passages from Lawrence's later poetry which are disturbing because they show in their attitude to people that very dehumanization against which his best novels and stories so effectively protested. The direct political utterance is not good for imaginative literature. All political utterance polarizes, and all polarization obscures the fecundity and variety of the human scene. This is not to say that politics and political utterances are not necessary; but they cannot tell the truth about man. Propaganda, even in a good cause, corrupts language and perverts the truth. For the truth — at least the truth about people, about men and women — is a mass of contradictions of a kind that politics cannot tolerate. While Marxist students in America proclaim the necessity of joining forces with the workers against the "ruling classes" and "their" war in Vietnam, genuine manual workers beat up left-wing students and proclaim their love of the "establishment" and their support of the Vietnam war. What goes on in their minds? What is their vision of the world? Does it matter? If they are on the wrong side, they are on the wrong side — and the enemy. One can ask the same question about policemen and National Guardsmen.

Democratic politics are far from being an exception to the rule that political utterance can never tell the whole truth, for the demands of party politics force just the kind of polarization that impoverishes the imagination and prevents it from achieving some vision of the complexity of the whole truth. Is it possible to carry over into politics some of the insights into the human situation which are achieved by literature? Would a generation nourished on literary classics be in a position to understand more profoundly the ambiguities of human character which account for attitudes and actions which lie behind people's political views?

In a totally polarized situation, such as that which immediately precedes civil war or revolution, this would clearly be quite out of the question. (In most national civil wars the committed on either side are relatively few. Most people simply find themselves fighting on one side or the other, bewildered, confused, fatalistic or often plain reluctant.) But in a position which has not yet reached that stage and where *persuasion* of those who differ from you or who are neutral is still a serious political objective, there might be an argument for the application of the literary imagination to politics. The rhetoric of democratic politics is, of course, in itself irredeemable, especially in a two-party system that poses a crude black-and-white situation. For that matter, the rhetoric of revolutionary politics is even more irredeemable, for in the movement from argument to slogan to action, active revolutionaries have long left the first stage far behind, and language for them is a very blunt instrument indeed. But if the objective is to enable people to *see* what the world is really like (or even to see what their own lives are really like) as a preliminary to getting them to help to change it, and if this is an honestly held objective and not a rhetorical gambit, then I think that the literary imagination is relevant.

There are two dangers in political polarization, and they are related. The first is the lack of human understanding that such polarization brings: people are bludgeoned into being either "us" or "them," and the realities of the human situation are denied. The second is that, to someone who has accepted this simple division, the conviction of his own rightness is overpowering, and as a result he becomes priggish and self-righteous. The more idealistic and committed he is, the greater is this danger. For the cynical machine-politician, no conviction of his own rightness is necessary; he is concerned only with his own interest. It is the bourgeois intellectual who, virtually alone in the total class picture, is capable of furthering policies which work against his own material interests. (I write this just before the British general election of June 1970, and I intend to vote for the party under which I personally will be less well off materially.) For this very reason the bourgeois intellectual is most prone to self-righteousness.

Now self-righteousness sets up a formidable barrier not only to communication but also to understanding. So you get the paradox that the bourgeois intellectual, for all his better education and higher intelligence, is often less able to communicate and understand on the simple human level than less articulate and less well educated people, who may be incapable of seeing any further than their own noses but who by the same token do not adapt their vision to a theory. One of the workers for a British opinion poll recently rang a doorbell of a lower-middle-class home and asked a rather dumb housewife one of the standard questions: Party politics aside, did she believe Harold Wilson or Edward Heath more capable of running affairs? To which she replied: "Well, a lot of people don't trust a middle-aged bachelor and say that Heath ought to have married, but *I* say that if he isn't married, he has all the more time to give to government affairs." This is political nonsense, one might well exclaim, and is not an answer to the question. But it was a real, human answer, however limited or indeed however stupid. If she had said instead, "Heath is a prime example of that social mobility which enables a man to move up until he becomes a prisoner of the ruling class and must therefore be regarded as the spokesman of that class's self-interest and fears, while Wilson, in spite of being nominally to the left of Heath, has compromised with American imperialism and is therefore a classic example of the impotence of the reformist Left" — if she had said that, would she have said anything more real, more precise? It is enough to say that the housewife's answer could not have been predicted — it was a genuine, if ridiculously limited, answer to the question — while the second answer could have been ritually intoned by thousands of doctrinaire left-wingers. What can be ritually intoned by thousands is not necessarily untrue, but if it is true, its truth lives in the realm of cliché and ceases to be operative on the human level. My own response to litanies is the same frisson of horror with which I regard the carrying around and public display of enormous blown-up photographs of political leaders, whether they be Hitler, Stalin, Mao or for that matter a saint of the Church.

IV

These thoughts were prompted by talking with students of Wesleyan University at the time of the student "strike" as a protest against Nixon's moving American troops into Cambodia (an action which, I agree, deserved the strongest possible protest). Some students spent their liberated time in ringing doorbells in the town in an attempt to persuade ordinary citizens of the evils of Nixon's government and the necessity of protest. But few of them apparently separated out the issue either of the Vietnam war or of the position of the American Negro, the two issues in which liberal feeling is most strongly engaged. They raised the more general question of the total rottenness, the fascist nature, of American society. But when they put this point to a small shopkeeper who had emigrated many years before from poverty, squalor and hopelessness in a little town in Sicily and who owned his own business, had just paid off the mortgage on his house, had educated his children, and lived in middle-class cleanliness and comfort in an attractive American town, they were astonished by his reaction. They had never realized what the background of such a man was, had never asked themselves how he would think and feel about the present situation in America, and *they could think of nothing to say* to the simple, human, pragmatic arguments put forward in reply to their invitation to revolt. Instead of the students educating the simple citizen, it was the simple citizen who was educating the students — educating them in some of the basic realities of middle-class thought and feeling. To say to that shopkeeper, "Up against the wall, ruling class!" would be the most irrelevant rhetoric. He did not regard himself as a member of the ruling class; he was content to be ruled the way he was. Life was better than he had ever known it. Similarly, if doorbell-ringing students encountered a man who had come to America as a refugee from Hitler and all of whose relatives had been killed in Auschwitz or Dachau and invited him to condemn American society as fascist (or even, as was occasionally done, as "worse than Germany under the Nazis"), they met someone who knew that what he was told was simply untrue and who could give them chapter and verse to prove it. Ah well, you might say, it was not true for him, but it was and is true for some people in America, for inhabitants of Negro ghettoes, for example. Yet even if we concede this — and there is surely a difference between a policy pursued in an underhand way in defiance of the declared policy of the government and a policy officially initiated and made compulsory by the government, as Nazi racial policy was — there remains the problem of coming to terms with the attitude of that shopkeeper and that refugee.

Lenin once said that there is no such instrument as a "sincerometer" which could test people's sincerity: they could only be judged by their actions, which would enable them to be classified as for or against the revolution, as goodies or baddies. This is clearly a position at which the revolutionary is bound to arrive. If you have reached the point where "the" revolution is *ipso facto* a good thing, you lose sight of the human complexities of the situation out of which you wish the revolution to arise. You ignore awkward truths — it might even be said that you ignore the truth, because it is bound to be awkward — and concentrate on a struggle of light against dark. As most human beings are gray or parti-colored, awareness of the realities about human beings is the first casualty of such a revolution polarization. Many revolutionaries concede this and consider the sacrifice worth while. But the end of this line of thought is to accept revolution for the sake of revolution, not for the sake of people. What may have begun in humane concern ends in dehumanization. That, in fact, is the story of most revolutions.

Can the novelist and the poet help us here? Can a deep engagement with the literary imagination of great writers encourage the "cultivated heart" and bring a new human dimension into political discourse? All politics is Procrustean, chopping off bits of the recalcitrant human reality to fit the policy being propounded. Oppressed Negroes are suffering innocents; policemen are evil; white Southerners are malignant racists; capitalist bourgeois society directly or indirectly supports the oppression, the evil, the racism, and so it is supremely evil. But all this is terribly abstract. What is it *really* like to be a young Negro growing up in a Chicago ghetto? What is it *really* like to be a young National Guardsman panicking in the face of jeering and stone-throwing students? Can we get inward with the experience of others in such a way as fully to understand what makes them tick, why they are desperate, or frightened, or cruel? I myself hold the view that evil is very often (though far from always) less the product of a deliberate conspiracy on the part of the malignant than a by-product of all sorts of confusions, fears, doubts and inconsistencies* which in spite of everything are not wholly impervious to humane and rational discourse. But we cannot begin that discourse without imaginative understanding. That understanding, indeed, should be historical as well as literary, for a knowledge of how people came to be the way they are in a given society is as important as the imaginative ability to empathize with their fears and confusions, if we are to have any chance of communicating with them and changing their minds.

This raises the question of the logic of student "strikes." I know that these strikes are often directed not against the universities but against the government or against the forces which control society; and the idea appears to be that in the time freed by not attending lectures and seminars and not writing examinations, students can help spread the radical faith and get more and more people involved in effective protest. (There are of course those who wish simply to destroy the universities, together with other institutions of bourgeois society, but I am not now concerned with them.) The notion that we can and should shelve humanistic culture, the nurse of the imagination, while we man the barricades seems to me to

*Of course one can attribute these inconsistencies to the structure of society, as Marxism does, and argue that once you have destroyed that structure, they will disappear. But I can see no evidence of this in history or anywhere else. I don't think that Marx was wrong in general in his analysis of capitalism. But though his diagnosis was right, I grow increasingly dubious about both his prognosis and his prescription.

be naive. I do not believe that we should give up our belief in the humanities so easily. All great literature is, to use that modish word, relevant, and those who do not find it so are not reading it properly. It is unfortunately true that literary scholarship in universities is often calculated to obscure rather than reveal this aspect of literature, and there is a lot of discontent with the way humanities are sometimes taught which I fully share. To this extent a strike that really was against the university, if it were directed against the pedantic and inhumane treatment of such a subject as literature, would be more logical than the present kind of strike. But in making this point I am not endorsing the simpleminded demand for an immediate, easy, superficial "relevance" that is voiced by some students these days. Discovery of the supreme relevance of great literature requires the willing cooperation of the reader's imagination. There is no use slopping about in a genial semiliteracy, hailing as "relevant" anything that uses the jargon of the radical Left of today and dismissing as "irrelevant" anything that requires some effort to penetrate. The most relevant works of literature demand the greatest effort for their full appreciation. That radical students — or some of them — should join the right-wing know-nothings in a view of the history of culture that implies a contempt for anything except the strictly modish and contemporary, I find deeply disturbing.

Man lives in history and in nature. He has modified — and increasingly polluted — the green world of nature to build his cities and produce his technology, and through all the changes that this constant modification of his natural environment has produced, his own patterns of social organization have been modified in consequence. *Everything* is ultimately relevant, everything that man has done and suffered. Civilization can no more live significantly without a memory than can a human being without continuity of personality. We are what time and history have made us, and if we want to control our own future, we must know how we got to where we are today. Society today is not uniquely bad (it has generally been worse), nor is today's "generation gap" unprecedented. The sense of that gap is itself a part of history; it is produced by history and explicable in historical terms. "A long time ago this world began," and man's dreams of Utopia are almost as old as his life on this planet. Life at its best is mixed and fragile. Its ultimate absurdity is that growth and maturity lead inevitably to decay and death, that young love grows old, that wisdom, if it persists long enough, turns into dotage. We *ought* to aim at Utopia, at the elimination of all injustice; we *ought* to bend all our efforts to improving the lot of man on earth. But we cannot bypass the true facts of the human condition: those who have tried to do so in the past have produced appalling disaster. And it is the great novelists, dramatists and poets who have most to tell us about the true facts of the human condition. Here is relevance as it can be found nowhere else. If we return to politics with our imagination nourished by literature and our understanding sharpened by historical study, I think we may well find that we shall ring those doorbells more effectively.

HAROLD ROSENBERG

8.
Politics of Illusion

In his account of the coup d'etat of Louis Bonaparte, Marx introduced aesthetic categories. "All great world-historical facts and personages," he began, quoting Hegel, "occur, as it were, twice"; then he added, "the first time as tragedy, the second as farce."* Louis, Marx set out to demonstrate, was a caricature of Napoleon Bonaparte, and his seizure of power in December 1851 a parody of Napoleon's coup half a century earlier. To underline his theme of historic repetition, Marx called his book *The Eighteenth Brumaire of Louis Bonaparte,* a satiric reference to the date on which, according to the new calendar of the Great French Revolution, Napoleon I concentrated political power in his hands.

The aesthetics, or dramatistics (to use Kenneth Burke's term), of Marx have not been widely discussed, except in relation to theories that consider works of art and literature to be "reflections" of social developments. In dealing with history, Marxists restrict themselves to material, social and ideological factors. In *The Eighteenth Brumaire,* however, the concepts of drama and poetic illusion are applied by Marx not to literature but to revolutionary situations. Moreover, the label *tragedy* or *farce* is applied as an absolute judgment of the events.

To deal with modern revolutions Marx supplements his theory of the conflict of social classes with an analysis of the mechanism of deception and self-deception in politics. Unreality appears as serving a specific historical function — indeed, two contrary functions. In times of revolutionary crisis, Marx found, class conflict, the normal condition of civilized societies, is either veiled or actually arrested. Heroes come to the fore, and theater forces itself upon history. The great French Revolution took on the appearance of a classical revival. "Camille-Desmoulins,

*Karl Marx, *The Eighteenth Brumaire of Louis Bonaparte,* ed. C. P. Duff (New York: International Publishers, 1964).

Danton, Robespierre, Saint-Just, Napoleon," said Marx, "the heroes, as well as the parties and the masses of the old French Revolution, performed the task of their time in Roman costume and with Roman phrases." This casting backward in the imagination in order to advance in reality was conceived by Marx as a law of the collective psyche in critical situations — a law that led him to consider revolutions as tragic. "The tradition of all the dead generations," he announced in a celebrated sentence, "weighs like a nightmare on the brain of the living. And just when they seem engaged in revolutionizing themselves and things, in creating something entirely new, precisely in such epochs of revolutionary crisis they anxiously conjure up the spirits of the past to their service and borrow from them names, battle slogans and costumes, in order to present the new scene of world history in this time-honored disguise and this borrowed language."

In Marx's theory of social creation, reversion to the past is automatic, a reflex of the crisis that has made creation necessary. (Some may wish to compare this creative escape from the present with Freud's theory of sublimation.) The tragedy consists in the grip of the past upon the psyche, in the fact that, to use Marx's phrase in *Capital, "le mort saisit le vif."* In twentieth-century aesthetics it is assumed that the dead can be driven out by the avant-garde will, as when Apollinaire in *The Cubist Painters* instructs the reader that "you cannot forever carry around the corpse of your dead father." Picasso, Miró, Modigliani, however, and Pound and Eliot — by their foragings in ancient Greece, medieval Europe, seventeenth-century Italy and Holland, ageless Africa — have accepted in practice Marx's principle of "conjuring up the spirits of the past to their service" and borrowing earlier images in order "to present the new scene in time-honored disguise."

The twentieth-century artists act on the basis of a consciousness of history, while the actors of the late eigtheenth century were automatically thrown back among the dead by the enthusiasm of revolutionary creation. It may be that the element of farce in Picasso, Miró, Eliot is related to the self-consciousness of their historical revivals. The great revolutions, as Marx sees them, were naive. The new was born, as it were, surreptitiously, while its creators, in a trance of glory, were emulating the heroes of past epochs. History in those great periods had lost its sense of time. It had been captivated by form and become incapable, so to speak, of thinking historically, that is to say, of itself.

For society, as for Stephen Dedalus in revolt against tradition, "history is a nightmare from which I am trying to awake." Marx could have agreed with Joyce's conception in *Finnegans Wake* that man is a dreamer "with that fellow fearing of his own misshapes." Marx's problem, however, was more complex than Joyce's, since he was speaking of the condition of the psyche in relation to political action. A dream confined to the mind of the dreamer is a constantly changing spectacle, but a dream performed as a public event is drama, either tragic, as in Sophocles' *Ajax*, or farcical, as in *The Merry Wives of Windsor*. Delusion in politics is not merely a disorder of language and imagery but a recasting of circumstances in defiance of those solid, continuous and comprehensible conditions known as reality. Acting in history is *acting*, both as performance and as doing.

Hence Marx is not content to compare the present and the past, Napoleon and Caesar. History is not mere appearance. To the politics of illusion Marx applies his materialistic dialectic of class struggle, in order to distinguish between tragedy and farce on the basis of the social character of events. For him the issue of seriousness or absurdity, social creation or social impotence, depends not on the stature of the individual protagonists but on the state of development of the social classes which they represent and on the capacity of those classes to meet the needs of the time. Behind the playacting of the heroes operates the destiny of the class, so that without being aware of it the Robespierres and Napoleons are guided by the subplot of class struggle — which is in turn geared into impersonal economic and social processes, equivalent to the all-regulating divinities of Greek theater. Propelled by a vigorous class, the "nightmare" of the heroes will thus serve a creative end; in the French Revolution it supplied (to quote *The Eighteenth Brumaire*) "the self-deceptions that they needed in order to conceal from themselves the limitations of the content of their struggles and to keep their passions at the height of the great historical tragedy." In its poetic frenzy the revolution of 1789 destroyed feudalism and set up the foundations of middle-class society, while Napoleon's military campaigns created a favorable environment for the new bourgeois order throughout much of Europe.

Once these ends had been achieved, the French middle class woke up from their grand dream-gestures on the battlefield and in the forum to what Marx calls "the sober reality" of industrial production, economic competition and profits. With this denouement the costume play was at an end. "The new social formation once established," writes Marx, "the antediluvian Colossuses disappeared and with them the resurrected Romans." In the daylight of Monday through Friday the new business society could no longer comprehend, Marx explains, "that ghosts from the days of Rome had watched over its cradle." One might add that in the strictly political daylight, Marxists, applying the principles of *Capital* and techniques of Socialist recruitment, could no longer comprehend that dramatic mimesis and tragic and farcical illusion constitute essential ingredients of Marx's conception of history.

The Eighteenth Brumaire presents "the great historical tragedy" of 1789 as a prologue to the coup of Louis Bonaparte in 1851 in order to draw the contrast between a genuine revolution and a counterfeit one. In both, the politics of illusion prevailed. With Marx, the issue was not reason and fact, as the trademark of genuine revolution, versus deception and fantasy, as marks of a fake. The issue was illusion versus illusion. Both the coup of Napoleon and the coup of Louis endeavored to resolve social crises through seeing the present in the disguise of the past — in Marx's phrase, through "conjurings up of the dead." Through the tragic theatricalism of the first revolution a tremendous social transformation was consummated, while the absurd heroics of Louis' repetition of the old gestures brought forth nothing new. "The awakening of the dead," which according to Marx had once served to stimulate the struggle for innovation, now provided a comical parody of the great days of the past. With Napoleon myth "magnified historical tasks in the imagination"; with Louis it was a means for escaping from reality.

The difference between historical playacting that tragically accomplishes social creation and playacting that is a farcical pantomime concealing social impotence is determined, as mentioned, by the subplot of class struggle. In the French Revolution the energies of the emerging middle class changed performing into doing and introduced a new social order. In the Revolution of 1848 all classes were stalemated — the middle class was *already* in decline — and the class struggle could reach no outcome. Once the June insurrection of the workingmen had been suppressed, society became politically lifeless — its conflicts lacked direction and, according to Marx, "wearied with constant repetition of the same tensions and relaxations" (the description of a society in a state of neurosis). "If any section of history," Marx comments, "has been painted grey on grey, this is it." The proletariat, in his words, has "passed into the background of the revolutionary stage. Henceforth, it seeks to achieve its salvation behind society's back."

With the workers out of the way, the middle class fights itself. One layer after another is disarmed through force, threats, parliamentary intrigue or political ineptitude, until, Marx reports, "all classes with which the proletariat had contended in June themselves lie prostrate beside it." Once the class struggle has been liquidated, history loses its content. It becomes mere stage performance, featuring personifications of past glory, marshals chattering in gibberish, outbursts of meaningless violence — in a word, farce. In Napoleon III, Marx contends, underlining the power of the class to determine the quality of the hero, the French "have not only a caricature of the old Napoleon, they have the old Napoleon himself, caricatured as he would inevitably appear in the middle of the 19th century." The passage of time has transformed the hero into a clown. In the absence of the revolutionary bourgeoisie, the Napoleonic politics of illusion has become an illusion of politics. Marx goes so far as to speak of "history without events."

Evidently, the class struggle can be dissolved. Then history, as Marx conceives it, stops — though this does not prevent people from being slaughtered in non-events. At any rate, the dialectical materialistic method of interpretation ceases to apply, since there is nothing for it to interpret. Or rather, the method applies *in reverse*. Instead of explaining political actions in terms of class struggle, it explains their futility by the failure of the social classes to function politically. Since history now has no direction, the conclusion of the analysis is qualitative: this is an age of farce. *The Eighteenth Brumaire* is the most important work of Karl Marx for the twentieth century because it deals with the characteristic political situation of the twentieth century: social crisis in which the socioeconomic classes — farmers, wageworkers, middle class — lack cohesion, fail to act politically and leave history to be given its shape (or "misshape") by nonclass elements. Under these circumstances, events are determined, not by economic and social needs and developments, but by the theatrics of revolutionary revivals, including costumes, salutes, cult jargon (e. g., new calendars such as that of Mussolini's Year One) and the cult of the leader.

To meet this type of situation Marx discards economic analysis, except to account for the disintegration of classes, and concentrates on qualitative labeling and ironical exposure designed to shatter popular illusions. Very little attention is paid in *The Eighteenth Brumaire* to the current economy of France, which under the Second Empire was to enter into a new wave of expanded production, trade and profiteering. Economics has become historically irrelevant to the degree that the social classes of France have been rendered politically inactive. Marx analyzes the economic condition of the classes only to explain why nothing is to be expected of them. Two years after the defeat of the proletarian uprising in 1848, he finds the workers "forgetting the revolutionary interest of their class for a momentary ease and comfort" — a familiar accusation heard on the Left in America and Europe for the past hundred years — and he concludes that "the historical process would have to go forward *over* their heads," italicizing *over*. *That history can take place over the heads of classes is for Marxism a highly unorthodox idea.* As for the middle class, "the ordinary bourgeois," says Marx, "is always inclined to sacrifice the general interest of his class for this or that private motive" — an inclination which the bourgeois seems to share with members of all classes, including the proletariat. Marx could have used his findings in *The Eighteenth Brumaire* to disprove his theory that the class struggle can be relied on as the motor of history.

In any case, it is the suspension of the class struggle in 1848–1851 that dooms representative government in its combat with the pretender. At one point, Marx wistfully suggests that to save freedom, the parliamentary parties, whose primary demand had become law and order, "ought to have allowed the class struggle more elbow room." To safeguard its property, however, the middle class, Marx found, was prepared to abandon its social values. Historically, this class is in conflict with its own ideals of liberty and progress and is prepared in times of stress to condemn them, even in their mildest forms, as socialistic.

The accompaniment of the political disintegration of the classes is the rise to power of the clown-hero Louis by means of a politics of sleight of hand — imposture, bribery, behind-the-scenes deals and conspiracies, even bedroom intrigues. Through the election of December 10, 1848, Louis had become president of the Republic, but a fictitious president, since from the start he intended to do away with the Republic he headed in order to assume the imperial throne of his glorified uncle. His ambition was realized for him primarily through the self-defeat of his opponents, that is to say, of all the solid elements of French society — in the manner comparable to a husband bringing about the success of his wife's lover through his own behavior in traditional French comedy.

"The Constitution of 1848," says Marx, "was overthrown not by a head but fell at the touch of a mere hat; this hat, to be sure, was a three-cornered Napoleonic Hat." The degree to which a society has become undermined is difficult to spot; and Louis, cautious to the point of cowardice compared to his uncle's dash, kept vacillating for months about the timing of his coup while all of Paris talked about the secret. The Pretender's presence swelled as normal politics shrank, with the propertied classes constantly thrown off balance by the Red Specter used as a weapon against one party after another. The conservative Party of Order tightened the vise around the National Assembly until Louis was in a position to tighten the vise around the Party of Order. The final choice was embodied in the principle, "Rather an end with terror than terror without end." In the demand for a regime of order above classes, the Pretender, who owed allegiance to no class, had the advantage over class parties. Bonaparte offered himself as leader of all the people as against any or all sections of the people. His program is translated by Marx into a philanthropic swindle: "He would like to steal the whole of France in order to be able to make a present of her to France." The rise of Louis is the comedy of respectable values turned inside out: "Only disorder can save order." "Only war can save peace." And so on.

Louis can claim to rise above the friction of classes and bring order and stability because he himself belongs to no class. In Marx's terms he is the "princely *lumpenproletarian*," the Emperor of la Bohème. In him the negation of classes finds its physical embodiment; he is the chief and representative of the disorderly, antisocial elements in France. His private army, the Society of December 10, is the complement of the moral and political decay of French society; it is, in fact, the direct product of that decay. Marx's analysis of the *lumpenproletarian*, or bohemian, composition of the Society of December 10 is one of his most valuable contributions to modern political dynamics. Bohemians are a phenomenon of middle-class societies and can therefore be understood only by reference to the particular layers — aristrocratic, capitalist, worker, peasant — from which they have separated themselves. The political impotence of the social classes in times of crisis opens the door to adventures on the part of the socially declassed. Among the declassed the myths of all classes, from utopian socialism to anarchy and cultural elitism, mingle and converge. Intellectual unreality is the vertical line that unites all levels of bohemia in a common impulse toward extreme behavior. For Marx the economic philosophy of bohemianism is based on the hope of living at the expense of society.

On his tours through France, Marx relates, Louis was accompanied by associates of the Society of December 10. In their army of myth, founded by Louis on the pretext of a benevolent society, "the *lumpenproletariat* of Paris," says Marx, had been organized into secret sections, each section being led by Bonapartist agents, with a Bonapartist general at the head of the whole.

Alongside decayed roués with doubtful means of subsistence and doubtful origin, alongside ruined and adventurous offshoots of the bourgeoisie, were vagabonds, discharged soldiers, discharged jail-birds, escaped galley-slaves, swindlers, mountebanks, lazzaroni, pickpockets, tricksters, gamblers, maquereaux, brothel-keepers, porters, *literati,* organ grinders, rag-pickers, knife grinders, tinkers, beggars, in short the whole indefinite, disintegrated mass thrown hither and thither which the French term *la Bohéme.* From this kindred element Bonaparte formed the basis of the Society of December 10. This Bonaparte who constitutes himself chief of the *lumpenproletariat,* who here alone rediscovers in mass form the interests which he personally pursues, who recognizes in this scum, offal, *refuse of all classes,* the only class weapon on which he can base himself unconditionally, he is the real Bonaparte. An old crafty "roué," he conceives the historical life of the nations and their principal and state actions as comedy in the most vulgar sense, as a masquerade where the grand costumes, words and postures merely serve to mask the pettiest knavishness.

Continuing in the same vein, Marx concludes that, given the present absurdity of French middle-class conflicts, "the adventurer who took the comedy as plain comedy was bound to conquer."

Marx's description of the lumpenproletariat and their leader is the crux of his Shakespearian vision of how politics as farce can overwhelm society in periods of crisis.

The Society of December 10 was for Bonaparte the party force peculiar to him. On his journeys the detachments of this Society packing the railways had to improvise a public for him, display the public enthusiasm, howl *vive l'Empereur,* insult and thrash the republicans, of course, under the protection of the police. On his return journeys to Paris they had to form the advance guard, forestall counter-demonstrations or disperse them.

The Society, says Marx, unwittingly crediting Louis as a prophet of twentieth-century action parties, was Louis' own work, his very own idea.

Whatever else he appropriates is put into his hands by force of circumstance; whatever else he does, the circumstances do for him or he is content to copy from the deeds of others. But Bonaparte with the official phrase of order, religion, family, property before him, behind him the secret society of disorder, prostitution and theft, that is Bonaparte himself as original author, and the history of the Society of December 10 is his own history.

Here Louis is no longer the farcical imitator, but the serious originator of farcical anti-class dictatorships.

Other voices confirm aspects of Marx's testimony. Says Albert Guérard in his short biography of Louis Bonaparte: "The Bohemian emperor, a revolutionary at heart, had 'saved society,' 'stemmed the Red tide,' restored order, bolstered property. The Czar and the Catholic hierarchy had heartily approved the Coup d'État."

Bonaparte was compelled officially to disband the Society because of its acts of violence and plots for assassinations. In reality, however, Marx contends, "the Society of December 10 was to remain the private army of Bonaparte until he succeeded in transforming the public army into a Society of December 10."

I shall pass briefly over other anti-class forces marshalled against society by the above-class Pretender. Complementing the Paris Bohemians were the small peasants, for Marx a rural *lumpenproletariat* bypassed by capitalism, who, though they share common economic and cultural characteristics "do not form a class." Politically they "belong to the underworld of history" (another unorthodoxy for Marxists to meditate on).

> To the four million (including children, etc.) officially recognized paupers, vagabonds, criminals and prostitutes in France, must be added five millions who hover on the margin of existence and either have their haunts in the countryside itself or, with their rags and their children, continually desert the countryside for the towns and the towns for the countryside.

In addition, there were the bureaucracy, swelled out by Louis as an "artificial caste" existing "alongside the actual classes of society," and the army, no longer as in the days of Napoleon "the flower of the peasant youth" but "the swampflower of the peasant *lumpenproletariat*." These static and unproductive human aggregations constitute the social reality behind the Napoleonic idea of grandeur. To Marx the height of the comedy is the enthusiastic acceptance of the power of this mob by the respectable elements of France: "Only the chief of the Society of December 10 can now save bourgeois society; only theft can save property; only perjury, religion; only bastardy, the family; only disorder, order."

Unfortunately, it was not consistent with Marx's class theory of history to take the *lumpenproletariat* seriously — to say nothing of the philistinism that hovers over his description of society's victims, outcasts and enemies. He understood the farce of the bohemian emperor and that in real life farce can be deadly. But he could think of Louis' coup only as a temporary deviation from real history; he could not conceive the farcical dictatorship of the nonclass King Ubu as a recurrent condition with which man might have to deal. *The Eighteenth Brumaire* proposes no prescription for coping with this type of political crisis, nor any theory as to the likely effects of the adventurer's victory. "All great world-historical facts and personages occur, as it were, twice, the first time as tragedy, the second as farce." The farce follows the tragedy and puts an end to its illusions once and for all. But why twice? Why not three times? Four? Five? An indefinite series?

For Marx, bourgeois heroics could only manifest themselves *twice* because the proletariat stood in the wings — and the next act was theirs. The illusory politics of Louis would be followed by "the sober reality" of working-class revolution, as the illusory politics of Napoleon was followed by the sober reality of the new middle-class order. The all-powerful state set up by Louis, Marx says, contained the "germ" of the working-class revolution. Marx's hopes went even further. The farce of Louis' coup would be the last seizure of society by the nightmare of history, whether tragic or heroic. The socialist uprising would have a new style, the style of realistic apprehension of historical tasks. The proletariat would release history from mimicry of the past and from theater. "The social revolution of the nineteenth century," Marx interjected into *The Eighteenth Brumaire*, "cannot draw its poetry from the past, but only from the future. It cannot begin with itself before it has stripped off all superstition in regard to the past. Earlier revolutions required world-historical recollections in order to drug themselves concerning their own content. In order to arrive at its own content, the revolution of the nineteenth century must let the dead bury their dead. There the phrase went beyond the content; here the content goes beyond the phrase." Here Marx speaks of the socialist revolution as "the revolution of the nineteenth century." He sees the uprising of the workers as imminent, as history's *next act.*

The Bohemian Emperor thus seems to Marx to be realizing the same objective as that of Marx himself in writing *The Eighteenth Brumaire,* that is, the task of dissolving the Napoleonic myth. Louis and Marx might be said to be collaborating in what Marx termed "this tremendous mental revolution," the overthrow of the cult of the leader. In Marx's view, Louis' farcical duplication of Napoleon in action would be even more decisive than his own exposure of the farce in words. History would be purged by history. Thus the concluding sentence of *The Eighteenth Brumaire* is oracular: "If the imperial mantle finally falls on the shoulders of Louis Bonaparte, the iron statue of Napoleon will crash from the top of the Vendôme column."

And the Bohemians? the *lumpenproletariat* of both the big cities and the countryside? Presumably, they would vanish automatically with the victory of the working class. In the communist, classless society there would be no classes for individuals to defect from. All would be productive citizens.

Instead of passing the torch, however, from class to class, history has preferred to explode into frenzies of motion without direction. Instead of the prosaic self-scrutiny, the "criticism of weapons," of the proletariat, bands undefined by class are formed, united by rituals, leaders and costumes (shirts, hoods, hairdos) — the armies of the politics of illusion. As the study of a false revolution, a a repetition in which nothing new is created, *The Eighteenth Brumaire* is more pertinent to the history of this century than Marx's efforts to demonstrate how the class struggle would be resolved in proletarian victory. For the very reason that *The Eighteenth Brumaire* is the study of a spurious event, it goes to the heart of our epoch of false appearances and aimless adventures. It is the political complement of our culture of nonplot theater, art made by chance, avant-gardism without a program or message.

Seen in the perspective of *The Eighteenth Brumaire,* contemporary class societies seem to have entered, not so much a crisis, as a crisis-series from which they cannot recover unless a new historical protagonist appears. There is no evidence, however, that such a protagonist is in the course of emerging. Hence the general pattern of 1848–51 — political self-defeat by the social classes, "heroic" calls to order — will probably keep repeating itself. Under these circumstances, self-deception and the deception of others become the normal procedures of political life; falsification is even regarded as morally laudable in that it contributes to stability. In feverish crusades for discipline and calm, absurd persons, absurd events, absurd slogans cease to arouse surprise or resentment. Political candidates publicly make themselves up as pseudo-personages in order to convince the public of their integrity. The techniques of advertising and mass entertainment are used to recast events to blend with popular fiction, or events are simply concocted out of the whole cloth to provide occasions for actions or formulations of policy. History is regarded as consisting, not of events that have happened, but of the books that have been written about them. With professional actors aspiring to the highest office, professional historians are brought into government administrations in order to guarantee that the desired account of their deeds will be transmitted to posterity.

The Eighteenth Brumaire warns, however, that there is a social dimension to farce in modern politics: it represents the spreading paralysis of the productive classes of society and the abandonment of their traditional values. A recent editorial in *The New Yorker* describes this condition as currently prevalent in the United States. (That *The New Yorker* is a "comic" magazine may have contributed to its deep insight in this instance.) It speaks of "a rapidly developing national crisis" in which "the politicians and the men in the press from whom we might expect a defense of liberty are strangely silent and seem to be in disarray. Instead of mustering and rallying their forces, they appear to sit puzzled and becalmed — almost oblivious of what is going on. The concerned citizen is apt to follow the crumbling of our democracy in the back pages of his newspaper." The editorial goes on to quote the Mayor of New York as complaining that people "are being tempted into a simplistic faith in repression as an answer to deep-seated, complex dilemmas" and deploring "the strange silence of so many in public life."

Evidently, American society is responding to its present crisis with a class inertia matching that of the classes of France from 1848 to 1851. Hopes for a leader are synchronized with promises of "law and order." All that is missing for the preparation of a coup is the personification of a myth and the emergence of the *lumpenproletariat* as a force to rule the streets. So far these have failed to appear, perhaps because America has too many myths and wealth enough to provide prosperity among the unproductive. Yet the fact that the middle class can no longer be relied upon for leadership marks a decisive break in American political and cultural history.

III. The Politics of the Humanities

RICHARD POIRIER

9.

Rock of Ages

As the generation gap becomes an increasingly compulsive subject, the
suspicion grows that it is perhaps less a barrier to apprehending the present and
the future than a comfort station on the way. Quite possibly, the gap is becoming
a place to hide, where all other issues get miniaturized to its proportions and
then dissipated without examination. This is particularly true for those indulgent
liberals who find a home there and who treat the rage of the young as a kind of
period style, when it is instead a compelling "performance" of the social and
political atrocities of the period. More agitated by the personal manners of dissent
(after all, the young *are* their neighbors, their allies, their children) than by the
evident causes of dissent, they fail to learn anything about the peculiarity
of their own manners, their own intellectual and political performances.

In the flood of writings which have poured the terror and confusion of the
times into the generation gap, three works can be brought together as illustrations
of the use and abuse of age as a metaphor for other issues. In one of these,
a special number of *Rolling Stone* magazine, the young can be seen attacking
themselves for having made their invented country — the rock festivals — into
a tawdry imitation of America. In the second, the young are, as it were, met
halfway: *In The Country of the Young,* by John Aldridge, a member of the paternal
generation, attacks America but sees the young not merely as its victims but
as its further spoilers. In a third, *Culture and Commitment: A Study of the
Generation Gap,* a most distinguished grandmother, Margaret Mead, wants to
defend nearly everyone. Feeling that the country and the young are in a state of
transition to a new world culture, she sounds not only (and irresistibly) like
affectionate grandma but also, in her awe of the children of electronics, like
Frankenstein surveying his creation.

It might be concluded that the older the observer and the more general the view, the more favorable will be the treatment of the young. Small comfort, for me at least. It turns out that favorable views are supported by modes of response and analysis very like those which support negative ones and are just as inadequate. In this as in most other matters, arguments are initiated by essentially aesthetic responses which can only do an injustice to the young and the old equally. The emphasis on generational differences is best seen as the expression of a much more pervasive terror in the face of new emergent forms of energy which are not generational at all, which are a mystery to people of all ages, and for which our "educated" responses are worse than useless; they contribute to still further anxiety and confusion. These three works, while not agreeing on targets or ranges of inquiry and disagreeing in their assessments, are important together in revealing a shared failure — an inability to make room for the pressures waiting, wanting to get expressed, in the experience with which they are trying to cope.

Nearly the entire twenty-seven-page, January 21, 1970, issue of *Rolling Stone,* the most authoritative, influential, and brilliantly assembled of the rock magazines, was given to a multi-authored account of the horrors of the rock festival held the month before at the Altamont Raceway in California for some 300,000 young people. The article is entitled "Let It Bleed," obviously to suggest some real connections between the author of a song of that title, Mick Jagger of the Rolling Stones (who are said to have dominated the festival), and the murderous violence that occurred there — three accidental deaths; hundreds of minor injuries; lots of bad trips on even good acid, due to the bad "vibes" presumably felt by most of the crowd; and the murder of Meredith Hunter, a black eighteen-year-old who was allegedly running toward the stage brandishing a gun. He was allegedly knifed and stomped to death by a gang of Hell's Angels, one of whom is now charged with the crime, thanks to a filming of it by cameramen who might be said to have stuck too closely to their assignment. For $500 in beer — and despite their reputation for violence and for social, mental, and political retardation — the Angels had been hired to guard the stage by the road manager for the Rolling Stones and by the festival organizer, who happens to manage a group called Grateful Dead.

Even the names involved in the event make it difficult for anyone who wants to argue against the journalistic, if not legal, indictment of the festival. Nonetheless, one must ask whether the accidental deaths (two by hit-and-run, one by drowning) or the acts of violence or the bad trips should be ascribed to the festival, or whether they would have been if a murder had not occurred there. Wasn't it shock at the fact of a murder that encouraged the bringing together of events that don't necessarily belong together? This is a question that has been asked by no one who has written or spoken about Altamont. One murder is one too many, but should a murder be used as a focus by which the accidental violence occurring in the same vicinity is made to seem evidence of some larger social, cultural, or political decadence? I would suppose that the good citizens of Dallas or Memphis or Los Angeles, for example, might well give some thought to this question whenever they feel urged, because of a murder at a rock festival, to condemn the rock scene or the Rolling Stones, who are among the radical heroes of it, or the young.

I am raising a real and at the same time rhetorically disarming issue. Not that it would disarm *Rolling Stone* or its writers, any more than it induced caution in Albert Goldman, a teacher of Greek and Roman classics at Columbia and a writer about rock music for *Life* and other publications. In *The New York Times Magazine,* using "Let It Bleed" for support, he unleashed some exultant ironies against the illusion that "the counter-culture is founded on some genuine ethical ideal or that it makes in any significant way a break with the prevailing capitalistic system." Obviously one must start with illusions before they can be shattered, and perhaps I simply never shared those of Mr. Goldman or of the writers in *Rolling Stone* when it comes to the economics of rock. Nor do I share the even more pervasive illusion that the communications one receives while listening to rock music ought to be, any more than are communications from reading a great novelist or a great poet, coherent with the economic ambitions of the artist and his managers or with the private lives of any of them.

Not restrained by scruples of this kind, *Rolling Stone* put together in "Let It Bleed" a cultural and social indictment of nearly irresistible persuasiveness. When, at the end, a note identifies eleven "writers of this special issue on the Altamont disaster," the reader becomes aware of how powerfully he has been worked upon by the very absence of a strongly organizing or stylizing ego. In its suggestions of choral testimony, in its cumulative repetitions, in the air of reality imparted by the clumsiness of its transitions — as if, really, "it" were just too large, too appalling, to encompass — in the sudden shifts from bookkeeping detail to theatrical and mythical metaphors, the piece seems to emanate from the group impersonality of the experience itself. Or rather, it seems to emanate from a tensed configuration of personalities brought together by chance and then brought closer together by shock. Disagreeing on emphases, even on where to place the blame, they all agree that some major disaster has occurred, some psychic numbing. And yet, for all its seeming artlessness, the piece is contrived to end, or nearly so — there follows a kind of all-passion-spent little coda — with some quotations from the columnist Ralph J. Gleason to which it has in fact been rather carefully building:

Somebody stabbed that man five times in the back. Overkill, like Pinkville. Like a Chicago cop's reaction to long hair. Is this the new community? Is this what Woodstock promised? Gathered together *as* a tribe, what happened? Brutality, murder, despoliation, you name it. . . . Whoever goes to the movie [he is referring to a film made for and about the Stones for which Altamont was to supply footage] paid for the Altamont religious community. All right, let me ask the question. Are Mick Jagger, Sam Cutler, Emmet Grogan, and Rock Scully any less guilty of that Black man's death than Sheriff Madigan is of the death of James Rector?

The organization of the entire piece provides a license, but is much too shrewd to provide explicit endorsement, for this kind of puffing. In its structure it moves from the identification of certain persons and circumstances to characterizations of these as somehow typical of larger forces. In its language there is a corresponding change: an escalation from a language of accusation for particular misdemeanors to an apocalyptic verbiage. The assemblage of particulars, gradually insinuated into various relationships of cause and effect, is transformed into a summary indictment for the betrayal of cultural or social ideals. Familiar enough in the less distinguished radical criticisms of the American "system," the method has not until recently been used in so concentrated a way by members of a so-called counterculture on themselves.

Rolling Stone's "Let It Bleed" and the reactions it records and produces are important as evidence of factionalism where none was expected: on the youth side of the generation gap. But to take that as its only significance would be for me to contradict the argument I've been trying to make — namely, that the gap between the generations is more apparent than real, that it is a metaphor in which nearly everyone has taken shelter, and that the real gap is between, on the one side, new dispositions of human power, both demographic and psychic, new forms of energy and, on the other, the inadequacy of our customary ways of seeing, listening, and interpreting. "Let It Bleed" is a document of major importance, not because of any indictment of the Rolling Stones as failed radical heroes of the rock scene nor of the Altamont festival "as a sort of culmination" (in the words of one writer) "of the worst trends in the rock and roll," but rather because it is a wholly unembarrassed illustration of the outmoded aesthetics which governed the participants, spectators, and reporters. An example of what Richard Gilman would call "the confusion of realms," it reveals, more extraordinarily than anything else I've read, how contemporary performances are taken as a species of theater, how people bring to them persistently literary expectations, and how, when these expectations are thwarted, the resultant trauma issues into uncontrolled verbal enlargements or distortions of the experience. Their language begins to be hyperbolic when reality intrudes into that art form through which they have chosen to look at the world around them — in the case of Altamont, a rock festival — the art form which they want to take for reality itself.

It seems that nobody at Altamont knew for sure at any given moment where he was, or, more to the point, in what kind of performance he was involved. Which is not merely a dressy way of saying that everyone had a different version of what happened. That's nearly always the case when different people, sharing roughly the same opportunity to hear or see something, are asked afterward what "really" occurred. What's important in illustration of my argument, however, is not so much what people reported after the festival as what they anticipated before they got there. It is here that the article in *Rolling Stone* is so remarkably useful as a cultural document. It consistently asks about what might be called the contemporary genres within which the people who went to Altamont had already placed their anticipated experience, much as one gives a prior categorization to the parties one is to attend, to an evening at the theater, to a wedding, to a funeral.

What was Altamont, in the minds of those who went there, before anything happened? That dangerously low stage, easily straddled; that muddy tract without the minimum hygienic and medical facilities for so huge an audience; those sounds that didn't reach far enough into the crowd, most of which didn't even know that murder and violence were an accompaniment to the music — what expectations preceded such realities? With what generic anticipations did the various people come to the work, the performance, the event? Mick Jagger promised "a Christmas and Hannukah rite to American youth," which isn't at all the genre in which he himself planned to perform. At least in some large part of his consciousness, he was instead performing in a movie. Not satisfied with Godard's film about the Stones, *Sympathy for the Devil,* Jagger had arranged for a filming of the Rolling Stones tour, some of the principal footage of which was to be a festival in San Francisco. This plan was in large part responsible for the difficulties in locating a site and for the final decision to have the concert at the

Altamont Raceway. And it was very possibly the filming that made Jagger less responsive to the violence when it occurred than critics think he should have been, though he had reason for caution in fearing a stampede. "They knew," we learn from "Let It Bleed," "what kind of movie they were after before they started. They wanted it groovy." Thus, while observing the old rule that the show must go on, Jagger was also aware that the film could be edited to make Altamont look "groovy": even murder can be edited out.

Jagger wanted something like Woodstock all over again. Woodstock is what might be called the principle genre in which most people were anticipating their experience. They went to Altamont to relive the Woodstock experience, or rather to live what most of them had read about Woodstock in the papers, in *Life,* and in an earlier and equally stunning issue of *Rolling Stone* now available as a separate pamphlet. Some also thought they were going to the original Monterey rock festival of 1967. These included poor murdered Meredith Hunter, and one of the saddest moments in "Let It Bleed" is the simple testimony of his sister, who reported that he'd gone to the festival at Monterey, had a good time, and went to Altamont thinking "it would be just the same." He went to see the Stones, she said, "just like everyone else."

Even as experienced a hand as Sam Cutler, the road manager for the Rolling Stones, had his version of the Woodstock or Monterey expectation, and it led to perhaps the most fateful decision in the preparations for Altamont. He was thinking of an earlier Hyde Park festival, where he'd used a branch of Hell's Angels for guards and where "everything was nice and pleasant." According to Ron Schneider of Stones Productions, Ltd., Cutler thought he had the same kind of situation in San Francisco. The idea of "San Francisco" also was in the head of Mick Taylor, fresh to the tours as the newest Rolling Stone. He had heard of what he calls "the incredible violence of America," but because of San Francisco he had expected a nice sort of peaceful concert: "I didn't expect anything like that in San Francisco because they are so used to nice things there. That's where free concerts started, and I thought a society like San Francisco would have done much better."

And so the expectations proliferated, including rather exotic cinematic ones. Some spectators report having felt from the beginning that they were in a film, not the one being made at Altamont, but ones they'd already seen. During the preparations "everyone was remarking how much it was like a Fellini movie," and a passenger on the helicopter which ferried the Stones over the crowd looked at the convergence of cars and thought of "the traffic jam in *Weekend.*"

Altamont, like some work of art, was supposed to follow certain conventions, meet certain expectations, satisfy the need for mythologies created at other similar gatherings. While "Let It Bleed" invites this interpretation, none of its writers inquires into the connection between these mythical, metaphorical, or cinematic "dreams" of Altamont and the extraordinary vituperation, the explosive metaphors used afterward to describe it: Pinkville, Chicago cops. From being an alternative to the America which some of the young describe in similarly violent synecdoches, Altamont became America. In that sense the Altamont festival, as accounted for in "Let It Bleed," was a betrayal of a history whose central event, elevated to the status of a myth, was the Woodstock festival.

It scarcely needs to be pointed out that this treatment of rock festivals reveals in the young an essentially conservative cast of mind. Another kind of conservatism, using other precedents, would have resulted in a wholly different and altogether more temperate kind of response. What if, in planning to join over 300,000 people on a field at Altamont, one's anticipations were governed, not by the metaphor of Woodstock, but by the metaphor of mass meetings at which everyone expects intoxication, usually some forms of violence, and sometimes even death? Soccer and football games would be examples; so would some religious revival meetings and political rallies. The difference, of course, is rock music. Rock is supposed to excite feelings unlike those released at other mass meetings. It is supposed to bring people, especially those helped on by drugs, into feelings of communal love and spirit voyaging.

This attitude toward rock exemplifies, in turn, an old-fashioned and preposterous faith on the part of some young people in the power of artistic performance to control social forces. When the performance fails to do so, there follows the further illusion that the art form has somehow betrayed a social and historical mission. It is possible, that is, to be as wrong-headed about rock as is George Steiner about high culture. If the approaches to Altamont were along the high roads of art, the later repudiation was based on the shock of recognition not only of the low roads of art but of the limits of art, in this case of rock. Both the anticipatory mythologizing and the retrospective demonizing are the result of a fundamentally academic ideal of the relations between art, on the one hand, and history, economics, politics, and social conduct, on the other. Ellen Willis, in *The New York Review of Books*, can thus find in the films *Easy Rider* and *Alice's Restaurant* "a pervasive feeling that everything is disintegrating, including the counterculture itself," while Albert Goldman, in the aforementioned piece, manages to set up a chronology in which the deterioration of "counterculture" is synchronized with "the industrialization of the art" of rock. Such slick passage from art works of whatever quality to historical generalizations was discredited in literary criticism (bad as it is) some decades ago, and its resurgence in criticisms of rock and film is among the more disappointing proofs of the failure to meet the demands and opportunities of the new with not even the best of the old.

The notion that the emergence of cultural health or cultural decadence can be inferred from the career of a particular art form misses the truly important fact about works of art, in which I'd include, though in a quite different way than does "Let It Bleed," not only rock music but rock performances and festivals. Rock cannot avoid expressing, in some way or other, the health *and* the decadence working their way through the circuits of the whole culture. It is astonishing, perhaps, that the young were capable of Woodstock, and surely it says something good about the parental generations that they were. It is not at all astonishing that they were capable also of Altamont; and that, too, says something not only about the young but about the older generations. Violence, exploitation, and shabby and inhuman management are to be anticipated in any effort of expression that takes place within the present culture. The components of Altamont weren't created by the young alone — neither were those at Woodstock — or by the old alone. They belong to all of us. Which is why it is deplorable that current attacks on the young, by the young as well as by the not so young, depend on a prior idealization, a separation of them from history. To treat them as if they alone, of all the elements of society, are so exonerated as to represent some saving remnant, is ultimately murderous. How else account for the note of aggrieved betrayal in Goldman's observation that

> it is beginning to look as if J. Edgar Hoover, Spiro T. Agnew, Mayor Daley, Judge Hoffman and Ronald Reagan, the deans of our great universities and the police and sanitation departments of our cities no longer have any cause to fear an uprising from the red Maoist masses of American youth. The generation that three years ago seemed destined to uproot traditional moral values and revolutionize our culture has now begun to drift aimlessly along the lines of least resistance. We need no longer fear that the Washington Monument will be blown up or the White House levitated.

Though the ironies here pretty much cancel one another out, Mr. Goldman might have wondered, as he ticked off the names at the beginning, that any generation could escape demoralization. Listening to his tone, full of a mockery that is at once bullying and, in its archness and callow wit, protected from retaliation, it is impossible to know what cultural values in Mr. Goldman are worth defending against the betrayals of the young. What culture is embodied in *that* prose? We're all in this imbroglio together, and the terrible price of our having invented and believed in the generation gap is that it has proved a license for the old to war on the young, rather than on our corporate life; and the young, now convinced of their special status on one side of the gap, have begun a war on themselves for having failed in a role foisted upon them by a society which will not recognize in youthful dissent an expression of its own goodness and in the repression of that dissent an expression of its agony of self-hatred.

An abundance of such self-hatred, along with a hopelessly literary reading of the young and of the problems of contemporary life and contemporary American culture, vitiates even the better parts (and there are few enough) of John Aldridge's *In the Country of the Young.* Aldridge doesn't seem to know that the finger he is shaking at his juniors is all the time pointed with a kind of frenzy at his own head. The poignancy of Aldrige's situation is nearly obscured, however, by foibles, these probably being, since I can't find any other illustrations, the parts of the book which A. Alvarez described as "witty." Aldridge doesn't like the hair of the male hippies ("worn like a pubic growth covering indiscriminately head, face, groin, and armpits, so that the entire person becomes a sex organ"), or their dress ("walking around in the exhumed costumery of another age is no more interesting or daring than capitulating to the system and becoming a General Motors slave. In fact, the truly radical gesture today would be to do just that"), or their speech ("the slack and derivative speech of the young seems to be the perfect idiom of their fecklessness"), or their intellectual manners ("untidy, perhaps because the capacity or the paranoia required for intellectual precision is not there"). By such invective Aldridge tries to provoke an adversary, even in himself; but more often than not, the target isn't the young so much as American society and the quality of American life since the Civil War.

One would expect that Aldridge's distaste for America might generate in him a degree of sympathy for counterculture and for youthful dissent. Aldridge, however, stands above that battle, damning both houses from the perspective, so far as one is discoverable, of an eighteenth-century gentility leaning on misremembered amenities and pretentions to high culture. At other times he seems to imagine himself a kind of H. L. Mencken fighting against the whole damn show, a Mencken who is said to have taken "the side of intelligence against stupidity, sophistication against provincialism." Mostly, however, the posture in the style is an emulation of Norman Mailer, who, though not mentioned in this book, is the subject of Aldridge's next. Aldridge, like Mailer — and wholly unlike the young, as either sees them — would be *productively* alienated," intensely "personal in rebellion."

So many literary replicas and platitudes govern the thinking in this book that it reads more like an account of a mind dispossessing itself of spells than the exploration of a subject. Aldridge's America is barely distinguishable, in the charges he makes against the poverty of its social and cultural life, from the America criticized for its cultural barrenness by James Fenimore Cooper, Hawthorne, and especially James, whom he quotes at length on the subject. T. S. Eliot, who also found American culture less than he could bear, supplies Aldridge with the metaphors for two of his most embarrassing characterizations of the young — that they are "suffering from a massive dissociation of sensibility," and that they lack "an objective correlative for their sense of grievance." But then, why not? Mailer, when running for mayor, said that New York lacked an "objective correlative." Apparently the political market value for the more dubious of Eliot's formulations is going up in the eyes of everyone who hasn't bothered to look closely into them. The Mailer who is the big influence in the book is the Mailer who gets out there and brawls that he may discover how to fight, and then fights that he may find out from his opposition, often his alter ego, where he truly stands. But Aldridge, I'm afraid, merely thrashes around without ever locating himself. Nor does he learn much from the Mailer who enters into combative association with the young, both in *Armies of the Night* and in *Miami and the Siege of Chicago*.

Indeed, the tip-off about the real subject of this book is that while it shows little indebtedness to Mailer's treatment of the young, it owes a great deal to his critique of the "liberal imagination" and to Lionel Trilling's valuable definition of it. However different in their styles, Trilling and Mailer are (as Aldridge is not) personally gauged, chastened, and disciplined by acutely temperamental involvements with the historical forces they write about. There is an absence in this book of any such personal element, despite gustatory evocations of it and willful attempts at sounding personally contentious. Perhaps as a result, his shifts, now to one, now to another literary perspective, far from revealing what he claims to be looking at, tend instead to determine what he sees.

Just as the "country" of his title, technology not withstanding, is no different from James Fenimore Cooper's, so the "young" of his title, sartorial differences waived, turn out to be liberals resurrected from the forties and fifties to be thrashed in the sixties and seventies. His charges against the young — that they care about quantitative and material problems but not at all about questions of quality, that their appetite for reform is limited to the merely administrative and legislative, that their psychological identification with the masses and their primary concern for collective salvation has blinded them to standards of cultural and even environmental life — are familiar charges made any number of times against the liberal mentality, especially the academic liberal mentality. (See the beautifully subtle arguments of Trilling's *The Liberal Imagination* or Mailer's chapter in *Armies of the Night* entitled "The Liberal Party.") But as directed against the young, they are so obviously off the mark, so clearly denoting the reverse of the kind of radical mentality the young are exhibiting, as to suggest that Aldridge, without quite knowing it, is talking about some other subject. As for so many others, "the young" are for Aldridge an inappropriate and bedeviled metaphor for ills he can't or won't face up to.

And what are they? Reading this curiously muddled book, one feels a kind of reluctant affection for a man who can't sort out his own futility from the futility, as he sees it, of his own generation in America. The pathos is perhaps most evident in his yearnings for the amenities he imagines as the necessary concomitants of culture and in his subscription to preposterous myths about America that could now be held only by a dotty Englishman: "Almost anywhere enroute between New York and San Francisco food and shelter are plentifully available at the lunchroom and the Y.M.C.A. level but if one wants something better one is out of luck." But his myths about Europe are his own: "It was just such an aristocracy, reinforced by monarchial rule and enormous wealth, that created the cultural institutions of Europe and that civilized and humanized a total way of life in Europe, making it impossible, at least in certain countries, to distinguish between the landscape produced by high culture and the environment in general." That humanization of the "total way of life" was not obvious, one suspects, to the children who even in England were being worked to death in coal mines well into the twentieth century.

A possible explanation for such remarks from a man of intelligence is that Aldridge is trying vainly, and unfortunately in public, to localize his anguish about his place in history. He believes with Mailer, for whom it is less a belief than a compulsion, in being personally engaged; and he believes that the trouble with the young, which separates them from him and from other older worthies, is to be found in their abstractness and in the ritualistic vocabulary that goes with abstractness, their dependence on terms such as *power structure, system, establishment, bureaucracy,* and *technology.* In fact, the gap isn't between him

141 : *Rock of Ages*

and the young but between all of them and the changed nature of the problems they confront.

Perhaps the real issues now can be talked about *only* by inventing realities that answer to the terms he's objecting to. It's absurd to talk about becoming "personally engaged" with an issue like pollution — and to say that the young don't care about environment is in this instance notably obtuse — or "personally engaged" with the military budget, the effects of media, or the Indo-China adventure. How else is one to explain the American involvement in Southeast Asia except by inventing terminologies and mysterious connections, especially when even those who support the war admit that they don't know how they got into it? So trapped is he within his own mythological basket-weavings — the alleged political abstractness of the young expresses, Aldridge thinks, a peculiarly American abstractness from physical environment — that he ignores the evident fact, that the political vocabulary he's criticizing isn't American in derivation. It is instead specifically European, coming from Hegel, Marx, and Marcuse. These men can scarcely be said to have suffered, any more than have the young of other nations who yet dress, think, and act much as do the American young, from the deficiencies of a specifically American cultural and physical milieu.

Aldridge's localizations with respect to America and the young can therefore exist only in a world of discredited literary myths, and his critique manages to make the young into precisely the kind of liberal whom they recognize only as their enemy. But in the stunning blatency of these very faults, there are some signs of attractively eager and thwarted life. Something must happen to me now or it never will — this is what the book's masochistic badness communicates, almost as if the author wants to be beaten for his argument. The young are the unfortunate victims of these confusions and mislocations however — of self-criticisms that emerge as criticisms of them, because of his need to mythologize social and personal discontents. The treatment of the young in this book is thus symtomatic of the way they've been used for a decade and are now being used by themselves: as a substitute for other problems we haven't yet learned to talk about.

Aldridge's book illustrates that not infrequent effort of older generations to find a scapegoat for the unacknowledged depth of their own alienation from contemporary American life. By turning his anger as much on the young as on the country, he wishes to suggest that his own alienation is still alive and kicking, and he does so by an illusory engagement with the stuff of experience. Evoking the "infinite and disturbing variety" of experience and the "infinite and disturbing variety" of men, he is nonetheless unable to disguise the fact that he, more than the young, is subject to the accusation he makes against them: that they are guilty of "coldly generalizing abstractions about experience." Aldridge is not "coldly generalizing," only vociferously so; and when he is not generalizing, his treatment of the particularities of American life is abstracted from them by his persistent literary and cultural fustianism.

In contrast, Margaret Mead is not bothered by particulars at all. Indeed, she happily announces, in her *Culture and Commitment: A Study of the Generation Gap,* that "concentration on particulars can only hinder the search for an explanatory principle." Her reason for thinking so — and let me say at once that, while her thinking may be clumsy, the basis for it seems to be right — rests on the insistence that "the primary evidence that our present situation is unique, without parallel in the past, is that the generation gap is worldwide."

No mere "country of the young" for Miss Mead; we are instead all part of "a world community," all "approaching a worldwide culture." Who is to say that this is not so? If it is, however, then all the more reason for precisely that "concentration on particulars" which she finds so generally objectionable and which she herself too successfully avoids. The problem isn't simply that in her talk about the young she hardly mentions those real, stubborn, specific issues which make them rebellious, revolutionary, or passive in their helpless disgust. Still more debilitating is her confidence, which is of a kind I've been challenging, that cultural changes as unprecedented in scope as those now going on necessarily also herald a change in consciousness, a change in customary responses and perceptions of contemporary life. Instead, it seems to me the central problem of our time that the cultural changes to which we have all been witness do not necessarily promote any corresponding developments of consciousness and haven't in any discernible way produced them. This is as true of the young, who were born into a changed world, as of older people who have felt the transitions from an earlier one.

However charming, her hopefulness prevents Miss Mead from asking, in a manner that would promise anything like a satisfactory answer, the question of how any of us is to *know* the constituencies of the world culture to which she says we now belong. Does the mere fact that they own transistor radios or tape recorders permit one to say, as Miss Mead does of the people of Tambunam in New Guinea, that "they shared our world and could contribute to it in a new way"? I don't know whose world is "our world" or what would be so good about sharing it, even assuming that one could share a world so easily. Electronics over the past twenty-five years has undoubtedly done more than merely expand means of communication; it has changed the nature of communication and therefore the nature of social intercourse, of history and politics. While being happy to announce this news, Miss Mead unfortunately invests it with certain platitudes that bedevil not only hers but almost all talk about the media in its relation to the generations and to contemporary culture: "Worldwide rapid air travel and globe-encircling television satellites have turned us into one community in which events taking place on one side of the earth become immediately and simultaneously available to people everywhere else. No artist or political censor has time to intervene and edit as a leader is shot or a flag planted on the moon."

Making an image or a communication "simultaneously available" even to two people, much less to "people everywhere," is notoriously no guarantee that they will be thereby brought closer together in spirit or understanding. In the instances Miss Mead is talking about, furthermore, the availability depends on media developed and largely dominated within certain cultures rather than in others. The people who run these media select what is to be made "available," select what it is that we are all to "know." Crucial to Miss Mead's argument is an assumption that we can "know" the present better than we can ever know the past, that the capacity even now to comprehend the past differs from the capacity to comprehend the present because the past has been edited and altered in the very act of preserving it in books or in other records. Thanks to electronics, so she thinks, the present cannot be so easily distorted: "no artist or political censor has time to intervene." Sometimes they do; other times they don't. The essential point, however, is that if modes of preservation alter the past, then to the same degree, though in a different way, modes of presentation, through whatever media, alter the present.

It is important to insist, however, that media alone cannot be held responsible for this situation. The apprehension of the present is screened, not only because of the way any given event is made available to us, but also because of the multitudinous and circuitous ways by which we are able to make *ourselves* available to it. Again, who were the "selves" at Altamont, who is the "self" in Aldridge's book? Art intervenes at every step, even if no artist or political censor does, and what is needed isn't more availability or more tape recorders or televisions in remote villages. What is needed is a revolution of self-inquiry into our general modes of receptivity, investigation, and appreciation. This revolution will be forestalled by the persistence of the illusion that it is now easy, or even possible, to know what we need to know about the present, much less the future.

Miss Mead's argument necessarily leads her to the loosest kind of thinking about the relationship of young and old to the developments that have changed the world since World War II. It only sounds reasonable to say that "these are the two generations — pioneers in a new era and their children — who have as yet to find a way of communicating about the world in which they both live, though their perceptions are so different." Are they *really* so different? Not on the basis of such a document as "Let It Bleed" which shares the moralistic, predetermined aesthetic responses so disastrous to the perceptions in Mr. Aldridge's book. Even if there is some difference, is it such that "there are no adults anywhere in the world from whom the young can learn what the next step would be"? While we can assume that no one's experience of an event is ever identical with anyone else's and that this is more terrifyingly apparent when people come from different cultures, different generations, or both, it doesn't at all follow as a matter of consequence to cultural analysis that "there are no elders who know what those who have been reared within the last twenty years know about the world into which they were born."

We do not, again, all have the same experience; and that means, I suppose, that we therefore all "know" different things. But this is not at all to say that any one of us, of whatever generation, is uniquely in touch with the world as it now is. After such knowledge as Miss Mead gives the young, what forgiveness? We all need to explore our common ignorance before we can even begin to forgive one another and start together on the hard job of learning how we see and how many other ways there are to see the things we now fear.

Mostly we fear the freedom offered, as well as demanded, by emergent elements of power within the population, which means within ourselves. We fear, too, the revelation that the realities which stabilize social and political institutions turn out so often, on inquiry, to be some species of theater already a parody of itself, or nearly so, before Jerry Rubin and his Yippies turn it into what they call "demonstration theater." The Yippies are no more absurd or theatrical than is the conformity they disrupt. A characteristic of death is conformity; a characteristic of life is the disruption of conformity, the revelation of differences, of a tensed variety that makes every element aware of every other and especially of itself, of its unique and authentic shape. Our society will prosper insofar as it promotes rather than merely allows differences among its parts. Only by the encouragement of eccentricity will it be able to locate, scrutinize, and continually shift its center. When Miss Mead applauds the uniqueness of the generations,

145 : *Rock of Ages*

rather than insisting on gaps between them, and when she reminds us of the varieties rather than of any promised uniformity of culture, she writes on behalf of life and hope in the future.

Social evolution now depends on the older generation's willingness to try out new styles, new tones, new movements of mind learned from the younger generation it is also teaching, and on a corresponding capacity of technologically sophisticated societies to learn from the technologically primitive ones to whom it can bring the benefit of tools and machines. Everyone must study himself in those who otherwise seem alien. *All* of what we are is what we are.

IV. Projections

LESLIE A. FIEDLER

10.
The Children's Hour:
or,
The Return of the Vanishing Longfellow:
Some Reflections of the Future of Poetry

We live, I am convinced, at a moment when a contradiction which our culture
has endured for more than a century now, by keeping it just below the level of full
awareness, threatens to erupt into our consciousness, which is to say, threatens to
become no longer tolerable. I am thinking of the conflict between two quite
different, sometimes downright contradictory notions of what poetry is or ought to
be which have operated in our muddled heads and divided hearts for the last
hundred years or so — notions sometimes implicitly responded to, sometimes
explicitly stated, though (up until our own time) most often by different spokesmen
to different audiences, existing in mutual ignorance or contempt of each other.

To define either or both of these notions of poetry too precisely at the beginning
of such an argument as I propose to make would be inevitably to mislead any
audience which could be imagined as attending to it; and therefore I shall forgo
the illusion of security sustained by such an initial definition, in favor of a step-by-
step exploration of the two types of verse: an exploration which will, however
deviously and belatedly, *end* in a kind of definition. To start, I should like only to
suggest that one of these two operative notions underlies and determines the tone,
texture and structure, as well as the basic appeal of popular verse wherever it
flourishes at this moment: in the classroom verse everyone remembers and
sometimes recites, with more nostalgia than reverence; in the sentimental songs
everyone sings or at least listens to willy-nilly, riding in cars, waiting for food in

restaurants or for planes, trains and buses; in the pornographic parodies of those songs transmitted orally from generation to generation; in the graffiti inscribed in public toilets; in Mother Goose rimes, children's game chants, greeting-card verse, etc. etc.

The other assumed definition functions, usually quite explicitly, in everything which we mean when we refer to serious verse, high poetry, highbrow poetry, i.e., most poetry included in hardcover anthologies or in slim volumes intended for sale to other poets and certain special libraries, which means also most poetry taught in classes or recommended for "outside reading" to enrolled students. It makes no difference in this regard what are the political or cultural commitments of that poetry: whether it identify itself in stance and theme with the Right or Left, academic traditionalism or the various anti-traditionalist conventions of Black Mountain or East Village or whatever. Left elitist or Right elitist, established elitist or underground elitist, committed or disengaged, it remains still radically different from what most readers and listeners most of the time think of as essential verse. As a matter of fact, behind it all there is a programmatic insistence on seeming different in precisely this way.

Certain superficial characteristics of the second sort of verse as it is practiced in the reigning modes will suggest themselves immediately to anyone likely to be reading these words. It does not rime, for instance, fanatically, insistently does not rime; it avoids all traditional, or, indeed, all clearly identifiable, all easily scannable metres ("Break the Iamb!" is its slogan — formulated long before the birth of many if its practitioners, but possessing for them still the cachet of something new and revolutionary). Most often its patterns are indicated, sometimes even dictated, by typography, the relationship of blank space and print on the pages of a book or a magazine; for it is a truly post-Gutenberg poetry, a kind of verse not merely reproduced but in some sense produced by movable type.

It tends at an extreme to become, in fact, *iconic,* "palpable and mute," as its earlier exponents like to put it, evoking the metaphors of Japanese calligraphy or of a "well-wrought urn" out of the Classical past. "Concrete" is the term which recurs more and more often in recent times, however, as our age grows shamelessly technological and gives away the secret. But the "concrete" icon is at a maximum distance from the fluidity of song — at the furthest remove from any intimate association with and loving subservience to the exigencies of a tune, which exists before and outside of meaning, whether that tune be actually heard or only implied. This flight from song, however, no matter how fundamental, is only *one* aspect of Modernist poetry, which is to say, the particular variety of highbrow verse we have especially honored over the past century; just as is the flight from myth-making (myth-analysis or parody is another matter) in Modernist prose narrative.

But to identify other aspects, and thus go further and deeper, we must, I think, have before us some examples, especially of the Pop tradition, which is less easily evoked by general allusions, existing as it does in the memory of the ear rather than that of the eye. Or to put it another and perhaps more accurate way, Pop poetry (and the reader should be warned that I am using the term to describe, not campy or condescending or tongue-in-cheek emulations of more disreputable genres, but those genres themselves) is known not so much by having it in our heads as by having learned it, in that lovely and significant Pop phrase, "by heart." The reader must, then, imagine me, as he reads the next pages, saying or singing, as is more appropriate, the following verses, not necessarily well but affectionately. What I am trying to do is to make for anyone interested enough to stay with me a little anthology of Pop poems, or rather of stanzas from Pop poems, selected not quite at random, though I might well have picked them out of the air.

My mini-anthology was in fact compiled by me in collaboration with three other lovers of such poetry (three less ambivalent lovers, let me state frankly) ranging in age from fifteen to twenty, two of them my own daughters, the other a girl friend of theirs. The point of choosing coeditors who are female as well as young I trust will become clear before I am through; but that does not finally matter as much as putting on record my method of selection and the possibilities of bias inseparable from it. Let it further be clear that I am offering as samples parts of poems admired to the point of having got them "by heart," not by utterly naive listeners who only know and respond to the kind to which they all belong, but by fairly sophisticated members of a young audience which also listens to and applauds, say, Robert Creeley and Allen Ginsberg, Gary Snyder and Diane Wakoski. I shall, in any case, not leave these popular poems in the sole context of each other; but will also reproduce — as a kind of control — an excerpt from a poem in the other tradition written quite recently by a twenty-six-year-old, which is to say, a "serious poet" about the same age or a shade younger than some of the Pop poets I am representing, like Bob Dylan or John Lennon.

The Modernist poem I have really picked at random, by flipping through the pages, and letting my fingers rest at the place they stopped riffling (a kind of post-Modernist *sortes Virgilianae*), of the most recently published poetry anthology on my shelves, a little paperback called *Quickly Aging Here: Some Poets of the 1970's.* This anthology was edited by another quite young man, whose photograph on the back cover presents his disarming credentials: properly long hair, denim shirt open at the collar, etc.; yet it was sent to me (I cannot resist underlining the paradox) by a presumably close-cropped, buttoned-up publisher, dreaming of classroom adoptions.

For me at least, the conjunction of the two kinds of poetry suggests a pair of questions which I shall introduce by way of a preface to my little anthology and to which I shall return later. First, for how long can the audience which responds sentimentally, viscerally, passionately to the first sort of poetry (I mean the members of the youth subculture, what is often called the adversary or counterculture) continue also to respond with equal fervor to the second, either on the page or as performed at poetry readings? And second, even if it is possible for an audience actually produced by a cultural revolution which calls into question all of the underlying values of the first kind of poetry to accept both, separating them out by occasion (no longer making the distinction of "high" and "low" so congenial to their immediate ancestors, but associating the one with records or tapes and Rock festivals, the other with books)—how long can young poets continue to supply elitist poems for books and little magazines? Will they find it sufficient forever merely to adapt the styles of Eliot / Pound / Williams / Olson to newly fashionable attitudes: the praise of drugs and tribal life, the condemnation of the war in Vietnam or the pollution of the natural environment?

After all, as important an influence on their sensibility as any political ideology, as Marxism or modern ecological thinking, more important perhaps, is the beat of the music which they have grown up hearing almost constantly at full volume, *making* almost constantly with each other in states of exaltation as inseparable from what that music is saying as from certain drugs. But the words they have been hearing and singing to that music, much more akin to the verse of certain despised poets of the mid-nineteenth century than to those of the early twentieth-century avant-garde, resemble the following:

It's been a hard day's night,
And I've been working like a dog.
It's been a hard day's night,
I should be sleeping like a log,
But when I get home to you,
I find the thing that you do—
Will make me feel all right.

When I'm home, everything seems to be all right.
When I'm home feeling you holding me tight, tight;
Yeah. . . .

I suppose there is, in fact, scarcely a song in the world better known than this one by John Lennon and Paul McCartney, published not only on records, endlessly rebroadcast, but featured also in the first and most popular of the Beatles' movies. But it is closely followed in popularity by a score of songs created and sung by Bob Dylan, a special favorite of the adversary culture, though by no means their exclusive property (two of the finalist groups in the National Irish Ballad Competition held in Sligo in 1969, for instance, sang his songs along with ballads in Gaelic); and of his erotic — as opposed to his political or religious — lyrics none lives more securely in the memories of the young than

> Lay, Lady, lay,
> lay across my big brass bed;
> Lay, Lady, lay,
> lay across my big brass bed.
>
> Whatever colors you have in your mind,
> I'll show them to you
> and you'll see them shine.
> Lay, Lady, lay
> lay across my big brass bed;
> Stay, Lady, stay,
> stay with your man a while.
> Until the break of day,
> let me see you make him smile.
>
> His clothes are dirty but his,
> his hands are clean;
> And you're the best thing
> that he's ever seen.
> Stay, Lady, stay,
> stay with your man a while. . . .

Both the Beatles and Dylan, however, belong primarily to the white man's world, which is to say, to Europe and its enclaves, and to the ex-European nine-tenths of the United States. The only songwriter who speaks for Black America, as Lennon (influenced himself by black musicians) or Dylan (whose work is modeled after white Country and Western prototypes) for White America, is, I suppose, Smokey Robinson. In a way, Robinson's lyrics are more "literary" than those of the early Beatles or the Dylan of "Lay, Lady, Lay," i.e., they try to imitate certain outmoded "high art"

153 : *The Children's Hour*

models, whereas the latter emulate "folk" conventions. For example, Robinson's use of the colloquial "dodged" as a rime for "mirage" in the song "The Love I Saw in You Was Just a Mirage" is a warrant of a kind of authenticity which more sophisticated or educated songwriters do not quite attain.

[The copyright proprietors of the lyrics I originally quoted here have insisted on fees of permission too exorbitant to bear thinking about, much less paying. The reader is therefore requested to turn on his record-player at this point and listen to the Miracles sing "The Love I Saw in You Was Just a Mirage."]

There is, however, nothing inevitably damaging in a certain note of pretentiousness or literary aspiration introduced into Pop, so long as it is not too up-to-date, too "Modernist." Joni Mitchell's "Both Sides Now" is a case in point:

> Bows and flows of angel hair,
> And ice cream castles in the air,
> And feathered canyons everywhere,
> I've looked at clouds that way.
>
> But now they only block the sun,
> They rain and snow on everyone,
> So many things I would have done,
> But clouds got in my way.
>
> Moons and Junes and ferris wheels,
> The dizzy dancing way you feel,
> As every fairy tale comes real,
> I've looked at love that way.
>
> But now it's just another show —
> You leave 'em laughin' when you go,
> And if you care don't let them know,
> Don't give yourself away.

And so, too, is "Little Boy in Corduroy"* by Donovan:

> A little boy in corduroy
> A little girl in lace,
> A little coy, jump for joy,
> Color in a space.

*"Little Boy in Corduroy": lyrics written by Donovan Leitch; copyright © 1967 by Donovan (Music), Limited; sole selling agent, Peer International Corporation; used by permission.

Little boy in corduroy,
After me say,
Save a wish for a rainy day.
How many wishes can you wish in a day?
Wish I had a wish to wish a wish away. . . .

Most literary by far of all recent writers of Pop songs is Leonard Cohen, who
had written verse for publication in cold print, as well as fiction, before he ever
attempted to reach a larger audience through records; and who is, clearly, not a
singer at all in any professional sense of the word. Indeed, when he himself
performs his own songs, they seem to be aspiring toward rather than actually
achieving musical form — seem quite different in fact from the same songs sung
by Judy Collins, for whom the lyrics of Joni Mitchell are far more apt. And in this
sense, Cohen is a test case, a touchstone for distinguishing between Pop and high
poetry on the very borders of the two, as is evident in "Sisters of Mercy": *

Well, I've been where you're hanging
I think I can see how you're pinned.
When you're not feeling holy,
Your loneliness says that you've sinned.

Well they lay down beside me
I made my confession to them
They touched both my eyes
And I touched the dew on their hem.
If your life is a leaf
That the seasons tear off and condemn
They will bind you with love
That is graceful and green as a stem.

When I left they were sleeping
I hope you run into them soon.
Don't turn on the lights,
You can read their address by the moon . . .

155 : *The Children's Hour*

It would be foolish to deny the real differences which separate Cohen's cadences and fiction from, say, Smokey Robinson's; but it would be even more misleading to overlook the resemblances between their lyrics, all that joins them together and separates them both — along with Lennon and Dylan and Joni Mitchell — from any and all practioners of avant-garde or underground verse. My sample, in fact, might well have been extended (though it is fairly wide as is, including a couple of Americans, a pair of Englishmen, a woman, a black;) it will, I am sure, be extended in the heads of any of my readers who know popular songs. Given another occasion and other collaborators, say, my own sons, I myself might well have added lines from a Country and Western singer — Johnny Cash, by preference, for the sake of his double link, back to the Carter family and forward to Dylan — and some harder, more revolutionary exploiters of Rock, I suppose the Rolling Stones. Such additional examples, however, would merely have made clearer the point, already well enough established, that over their whole wide and varied gamut, Pop lyrics where they are most like each other are most sharply distinguishable from what is common to most "Modernist," i.e., iconic or "concrete" poems.

They are so, first of all, in their insistence on subordinating normal speech rhythms or natural breath groups to metrical form; and, secondly, in their almost compulsive playing with sound patterns: end rhymes, internal rhymes, echo, assonance and consonance — to the point where sound seems to dictate sense, or even to compel nonsense; where not the medium, perhaps, but surely the patterning of sound (think especially of Donovan and Joni Mitchell) *is* the message. All of which is another way of saying that these poems are aniconic, anti-iconic; there is almost nothing in them for the eye, even when they are printed out on record jackets; for they exist, and we with them, in the pre-Gutenberg world or in a post-Gutenberg one.

There is, of course, an obvious rejoinder to such an argument. "But of course," I can imagine some unconvinced reader responding at this point, *"naturally,* all of this is so, since songs are songs, which is to say, words to music; and the particular ones you have adduced are immune even to the necessity, imposed on songwriters until only yesterday, to reproduce their lyrics in printed songsheets to insure their wide transmission. These songs were recorded on tapes or discs, or perhaps even existed for the first time — being composed by blending and editing in the sound studio — on tapes or discs. But all of this has nothing to do with poetry not composed to be sung or recorded electronically, only to be printed and read, whether aloud or to oneself. Such poetry has every right to be (if the notion of rights can be properly raised at all in the free realm of art) quite like any of the poems reprinted in *Quickly Aging Here,* which are resolutely visual, being as much influenced by the linotype machine as Pop poetry by multitrack tape recorders." And at this point, I imagine my opponent quoting against me — or rather displaying before me on the printed page — precisely the poem I came upon riffling through the pages of that earnest anthology, a poem called, aptly enough, "Icons":

Change
compels me more
than responsibility
for change.

●

one separates two

●

middle
shared

●

EYES
unity of spirit
behind
quality of form

●

Holding
the two ends
you hold it
by the middle . . .

●

air	air	air
earth	water	earth
earth	earth	earth

157 : *The Children's Hour*

•

Centrifugal
water slides down
the convex surface.

•

Down the concave surface
water slides
towards the center.

•

away
from the center
it multiplies

•

All
that is given up
remains.

I suppose it is evident to everyone, with the possible exception of the author
and the editor who reprinted it, that this poem is a conspicuously bad example
of its kind; but that is beside the point I am trying to make, which is that it is bad
in a *way* none of my earlier selections could possibly be, since the goals it
proposes, the prototypes on which it is modeled, embody a different notion of
what poetry is and does than any which the writers of Pop lyrics have in mind.
Theirs comes, I suppose, from the long tradition of songwriting itself, and more
particularly from the poetics of bourgeois Romanticism as developed in the
mid-nineteenth century, when, for instance, Stephen Collins Foster (who always
wrote for music) and Henry Wadsworth Longfellow (who composed poems
to be read) subscribed to common poetic values. The author of "Icons," however,
declares his allegiance to quite another tradition, not only implicitly, but quite
explicitly as well in a manifesto appended to the anthology in which he appears.
"I'm twenty-six and married," he informs us, and then goes on to cite his models:
"My favorite poets are Machado, Vallejo, Paz, Eliot, Williams, Roethke, Michaux.
Concretism has clearly influenced me. . . ."

"And why not?" the tolerant critic is inclined to say, "Why should some not be influenced by Eliot and Williams and Michaux while others are moved by Woody Guthrie or Ray Charles or whomever? Let a hundred flowers bloom in two separate gardens." Indeed, it is tempting to fall back on the old principle that whatever is is right, and declare that not only does our culture produce and relish two different kinds of verse, but it *should:* one kind intended to be backed up by electronic or acoustic instruments and danced to, or at least attended to on large, public Dionysiac occasions; and the other intended to be read on the page, discussed in classrooms, even attended to when read aloud, with or without musical background, on somewhat different, large Dionysiac occasions.

Having evoked images of the Rock Concert and the Poetry Reading side by side, however, we are forced to ask if, in fact, our two kinds of poetry are still all that different functionally. Did not the Beats by moving poetry out of libraries and schools into cafés and associating its reading with Pop music (even if the Pop they preferred was Jazz rather than Rock, i.e., an *ex*-popular form of song on its way to becoming highbrow and elitist, even obsolescent)— did they not begin as early as the fifties to break down the functional separation of the two kinds, thus threatening formalist distinctions as well? Certainly I, in a cultural world utterly changed by the Beat Revolution, have been present at evenings, events, happenings, where the two kinds of verse, sung and spoken, blended into each other, fell together in ecstacy.

Moreover, just as it is true that much recent underground poetry is not only performed on such ecstatic occasions but even written with them in mind, so also it is true that young men in universities, who have grown up on Rock and Poetry Readings, begin to compile school anthologies and Freshman readers in which the lyrics of Bob Dylan and Grace Slick are extracted from their musical contexts, from the total events which seem their natural setting, and are reprinted side-by-side with verse by Creeley or Bly or James Dickey or Bill Knott — not just as monuments to their living selves, or approximate reminders (like a bad snapshot of a beloved child), but as quite satisfactory complete works. Furthermore, once such lyrics are detached from their music and denominated "poems" in a traditional sense, they are treated as "poems," which is to say, commented on in classical critical fashion by academics trained to analyze the poetry of John Donne or Ezra Pound.

Some years ago I remember having been asked to contribute to a volume of such critical essays on the poetry of Bob Dylan; and though I have never seen it (presumably it aborted somewhere along the way), I did come across sometime back a similar sort of "new critical" approach to the lyrics of the Beatles, which was written by Richard Poirier, an editor of the *Partisan Review*, and appeared in that magazine, which is to say, at the very heart of the establishment. That some appropriate critical approaches should be, will be whether they should or not, worked out for this sort of poetry I have no doubt; but I remain profoundly uneasy about attempts like Poirier's to adapt to their analysis and evaluation methods appropriate only to the other kind of verse. For they are not of the same kind; and any attempt to dignify them by pretending they are (even when carried on by men who love such lyrics and are motivated by love) can only lead to grief, certainly will not redeem either in the eyes or ears of those committed only to one kind.

Finally, in any event, it is not only with the lyrics of Pop songs that we critics and readers brought up on the "New Poetry" must come to terms; for the other kind of poetry, verse written as if the *Symboliste* revolt had never occurred, T. S. Eliot never been born, continues to appear among us and to be prized by the young audience in forms which are only fictionally, metaphorically song. I am thinking of certain verses called honorifically "songs" in the context of a novel, but in actuality intended to be read and only *imagined* as sung, specifically of the verse included in J. R. R. Tolkien's vast and immensely popular trilogy, *The Lord of the Rings*. Some of these songs have in fact been set to music since their initial appearance in print and can be heard on records as performed by Michael Swann; but set to actual music, they seem disappointing, anticlimaxes to our fantasies of them sung to unheard tunes.

They are authentic pseudosongs, whose imaginary setting and accompaniment is intended chiefly to defend them against the anti-song sanctions of the Modernists, put off by imaginary lutes and tabors quite as successfully as by real drums and electric guitars; and I reproduce samples from two of them to indicate even more clearly the kind of poetry (this time without contemporary allusions or fashionable attitudes) preferred by the young men and women of our counterculture when they are truest to themselves, i.e., least influenced by vestiges of the "Modernist" past:

> The Road goes ever on and on
>   Down from the door where it began.
> Now far ahead the Road has gone,
>   And I must follow, if I can,
> Pursuing it with eager feet,
>   Until it joins some larger way

Where many paths and errands meet.
　And whither then? I cannot say.

and

Long was the way that fate them bore,
　O'er stony mountains cold and grey,
Through hall of iron and darkling door,
　And woods of nightshade morrowless,
The Sundering Seas between them lay,
　And yet at last they met once more,
And long ago they passed away
　In the forest singing sorrowless.

What should be manifestly clear at this point is that the verses which Tolkien attributes to his Hobbits and Elves have in common with the lyrics of Pop songs not only the magic of rhyme and metre but also a kind of shamelessness which permits them to present unguarded feelings in the traditional shorthand of familiar phrases, clichés, if you will. They are equally available to child and adult, naif and sophisticate, because they reject, along with Pound's injunction to "Break the Iamb," his second commandment, "MAKE IT NEW!" They are, in short, sentimental and banal, rather than ironical and recherché.

To realize the importance of sentimentality and the cliché — over against anti-rhyme and anti-meter — in determining to which kind various poems belong, one need only remember the revival of Formalist verse, a return to rich rhyme and complex metrical form, just after World War II, which did not escape the limits of Modernism, only shifted allegiance from its more populist modes to more genteel and elegant ones.

In this kind of verse at its best, in the witty and urbane poems of Richard Wilbur, for example, the sensitive reader can perceive a longing to escape from the parochialism of the avant-garde to the larger world; but the movement is short-circuited somehow, turning into a flight which leads only from the Latin Quarter and Greenwich Village to Westchester County and the Ivy League colleges — at its boldest, to Broadway, as once more in the case of Wilbur collaborating with Lillian Hellman on *Candide*. Finally, despite its musicality and grace, his verse remains committed to allusion and irony, buttressed against sentimentality by learning and what used to be called "serious wit." Indeed, the whole school to which he belongs was still obsessed with avoiding banality at all cost, submitting, as most of our gifted poets have submitted for a long time, to what the French critic Jean Paulhan has called "the Terror."

Jean Paulhan has in recent years attained a small fame in this country as the possible author, or perhaps only sponsor, of the pornographic novel, *The Story of O*, claimed since his death by a former mistress, though earlier attributed to him. But the work which is relevant to my present concerns is not imaginative fiction at all, much less porn, but a longish critical essay called *Les Fleurs de Tarbe*. It is a work which I first discovered more than twenty years ago and to which I have returned over and over again ever since, with the baffled feeling that someplace, someday, somehow (right here, it turns out, right now, and in just this way) it would provide me a key to open a door against which I have long been banging my head in vain. Its title, *The Flowers of Tarbe*, refers to a garden in a small French city, or rather to a sign posted on the gates of that garden, reading: IT IS FORBIDDEN TO ENTER THE GARDEN BEARING FLOWERS, which injunction Paulhan took as a piece of restrictive idiocy precisely analogous to the Modernist critics' injunction against bringing into the new poem lovely commonplaces, long-honored phrases, language blessed by association with other poems, everything which the American folk poet Will Carleton (to whom I shall return later) still called in the Introduction to his *Farm Ballads*, published in 1873, "the flowers of poesy."

That puritanical, authoritarian, police-state ban, that deliberate impoverishment of possibility, Paulhan chose to name, evoking the darkest aspects of the French Revolution, "the Terror"; and the metaphor seems to me apt, for there is an especial kind of self-righteousness joined to a particular brand of chutzpah in the interdiction of the cliché — of the sort which only movements convinced they are truly revolutionary can afford. But all revolutions become, alas, institutionalized, confronting the future they never quite imagine as counterrevolutions, even when they do not betray their own past. And it is high time, at any rate, for us to be through with a Terror set up to defend the achievements of a cultural revolution now a century old and ready to fight to the death the next one, God forbid that we too should end by setting up a counter-Terror: require the cliché as opposed to the eternal pursuit of originality, demand sentimentality in place of irony, forbid free verse in the name of song.

I am, in fact, in this time of too many demands, resolved to demand nothing, merely to try for a chance to notice something instead; since cultural revolutions — unlike political ones — only come into consciousness after they have already happened, or more properly have begun to happen. Indeed, until they have been *noticed* they cannot be said to have finally happened at all. There are many reasons, I presume, for this initial invisibility of cultural revolutions; but surely in our post-Gutenberg age, a chief reason is that our cultural revolutions are likely to begin in the popular arts, which we can never manage to believe (being children of a time which thought of them as manipulated by the establishment) are as truly subversive as they prove to be over and over again.

We have, however, come past the early stage of unawareness in the present cultural revolution, as the very fact of this essay attests, and have reached the point where not a single lonely prophet but a considerable group of men — artists, entertainers, social and literary critics — are trying to close the gap between high art and Pop in the areas I have been discussing. This closing of the gap occurs from both sides of our split culture at once: certain makers of Pop songs extending their range of tone and diction in the direction of the ironical-elegant mode of the avant-garde, at the same moment that some of the practitioners of that mode are trying to open up their poems to the kind of Pop banality and sentimentality banned under the Terror. Bob Dylan provides many examples of the former tendency, particularly in the songs he was writing (convinced temporarily by the literary critics who had been assuring him that he was in the traditional sense a "true poet") just before the appearance of his *John Wesley Harding* album and his deliberate return to Country and Western. And examples of the latter impulse are demonstrated in the work of a whole host of post-Modernists, ranging all the way from LeRoi Jones to Edward Albee.

Somewhere on Jones's long, troubled road — what he himself calls his "Black Magical" road — from the poetry of Black Mountain (which is, of course, not black at all in any ethnic sense) to the polemical anti-verse of black art (which he would dearly love to believe is not poetry at all in any white man's sense), he passed through a period in which he made some verses modeled on the songs most of his people actually love: songs without overt political protest, though more subversive, as I have been arguing, of "European" aesthetics than most of Jones's earlier and later work. An example, of which I quote only two out of four stanzas, is called "T. T. Jackson Sings," a title which declares the popular musical intent that motivated him:

> I fucked your mother
> On the top of a house
> when I got through
> she thought she was
> Mickey Mouse

. . . .

I fucked your mother
and she hollered 0000
she thought I was
fu man chu

As close as this comes, however, to the authentic sources of anti-elitist art, it is
still hedged about with typical modernist devices — especially the bravura tone of
the pornography, which becomes thus an ironical shield against the surrender to
triteness and sentiment which characterizes Smokey Robinson and, indeed, all truly
popular black singers from the Supremes to James Robinson.

White writers tend to be even more evasive and apologetic when making similar
attempts to draw on their own anti-art traditions, except when, as in the case of
Leonard Cohen, they are actually producing lyrics to be sung and recorded. On
the printed page, they coyly flirt with, rather than passionately embrace, Pop
forms. Robert Creeley is a case in point, carrying on in certain of his earlier poems
precisely such an unconsummated flirtation, then later moving in quite other
directions. "Ballad of the Despairing Husband," for instance, opens with an only
slightly condescending evocation of a song everyone knows:

My wife and I lived all alone,
contention was our only bone,
I fought with her, she fought with me
and things went on right merrily

. . . .

Oh wife, oh wife—I tell you true,
I never loved no one but you.
I never will, it cannot be
another woman is for me.

But even before the end of the poem, the trite metrical pattern and the pat rhymes
begin to blur and distort as Modernist impulses assert themselves:

Oh, loveliest of ladies, than whom none is more fair, more
    gracious, beautiful.
Oh loveliest of ladies, whether you are just or unjust,
    merciful, indifferent or cruel. . . .

And certainly in his more recent poetry, Creeley has quite abandoned even that game of approach-and-retreat in regard to Pop as he has accepted the mantle of heir-in-chief to Charles Olson.

Perhaps really to escape from the elitist trap one would have to be a foreigner, to whom English is a second language and whose head, therefore, is likely to be fuller of the cadences and end rhymes of popular songs than the devices of post-Eliotic verse. Bertolt Brecht suggests that possibility, as does Cesare Pavese. But Brecht's best English (or more precisely American) poem was written to a Kurt Weill tune:

> Oh show us the way to the next whiskey bar,
> Oh don't ask why, oh, don't ask why . . .
> For if we don't find the next whiskey bar
> I tell you we must die!
> Oh, moon of Alabama . . .

And though Pavese's "Last Blues" was composed to be printed on the page and read in privacy and silence, and was born precisely at the point where his spiritual love for the kind of American literature represented by Melville and Whitman joined his more carnal passion for American Pop art, represented by a certain beloved and unattainable Hollywood starlet, it seems somehow dated, trapped in the time of just-after-World-War-II:

> T'was only a flirt
> you sure did know —
> some one was hurt
> long time ago.
>
> . . . .
>
> Some one has died
> long time ago —
> some one who tried
> but didn't know.

Yet their examples are suggestive, since even to native Americans brought up in the traditions of high art, the language of Pop is a foreign tongue, which must be learned quite like, say, pidgin. And, indeed, some recent writers aware of this problem make it the subject of works which must be thought of as mediating between the two cultures and their separate languages. Edward Albee's latest play, *Box-Mao-Box,* is, in this sense, precisely about the situation which produces it. His chief charcters, enclosed on the stage in a transparent box, speak the language appropriate to their condition — suburban WASP all of them, heirs to the traditions of high culture in the West, ecclesiastical and aesthetic. But that language turns out to be a polite, elegant, allusive, mutually incomprehensible jargon, another version of the box they are in, the trap that encloses them.

Outside of that box, however, speaking other tongues (as incomprehensible to those inside as their own to each other) are the representatives of past and future, Grandma and Chairman Mao, apparently as alien to each other as both are to the spokesmen of the decadent present. And yet in the production, perhaps in the script itself, there are from time to time tantalizing suggestions that they somehow understand each other, manage to communicate around, over and under the boxed-in chatterers at the center of the stage. What Mao speaks in his mask of Oriental foreignness are not his poems (atrociously old-fashioned inside his own tradition) but his political opinions out of the famous Red Book. What Grandma speaks, in her mask of provincial simplicity and advanced age, are precisely old-fashioned poems, quotations from the works of Will Carleton, favorite "people's poet" during the last three or four decades of the nineteenth century — specifically, the verses of "Over the Hill to the Poor House," repeated, and repeated, until they seem more a mantra of the commonplace, intended to stir belief, than an evocation of outmoded clichés, intended to set us tittering:

> Over the hill to the poor-house I'm trudgin' my weary way —
> I, a woman of seventy, and only a trifle gray —
> I, who am smart an' chipper, for all the years I've told,
> As many another woman that's only half as old.

> . . . .

> What is the use of heapin' on me a pauper's shame?
> Am I lazy or crazy? am I blind or lame?
> True, I am not so supple, not yet so awful stout;
> But charity ain't no favor, if one can live without.

> . . . .

> Over the hill to the poor-house — my childr'n dear, good-by!
> Many a night I've watched you when only God was nigh;

And God'll judge between us; but I al'ays pray
That you shall never suffer the half I do today.

Somewhat similar in its approach (and more interesting in a way because it
sets the popular verse in a Modernist poetic rather than dramatic frame) is a poem
which appeared in the *Paris Review* for Summer 1969, the work of a very young
poet called Charlie Vermont. Quite obviously a personal reminiscence, as its title,
"My Father's Retirement Dinner," insists, the poem leads up to the point where
the author is moved to intervene in what seems to him the long, after-dinner farce
of valedictory speeches, but cannot.

I wanted to make a speech with my long hair so they could all feel good
I wanted to make the farce real. . . .

But he can find no language for that invention and is doubly pleased when his old
man manages to find one for him:

and my father says it
He turns to me and I'm with him and all the farce is there and he says

When I was a young lad I used to
have a great interest in
books (and he turns to me, though
my son doesn't believe it . . .)
. . . and one day
in one of these stores I picked up a
plaque with a poem on it
which since then has served as my motto . . .
We can't all play a winning game.
Someone is sure to lose.
Yet we can play that our name
No one may dare accuse,
That when the master referee
Scores against our name
It won't be whether we've won or lost
But how we've played the game.
and I'm small and looking up at the plaque and
I'm on my feet roaring
because that was between me and him and because
that was right for him

167 : *The Children's Hour*

in the context of respectability and because I
            had taken it for myself

on another level. . . .

  In both Albee's case and Charlie Vermont's, the poetry in which banality and
sentiment call the tune is qualified and apologized for by the very act of quotation,
of being put in the mouth of someone quite clearly different from the poet,
someone who speaks old-fashioned metre rather than up-to-date stage prose or
fashionable "projective verse." And the candor of the younger man's poem makes
quite explicit the condescension entrusted to the campy tone of the more practised
playwright's work: "that was right for him . . . I / had taken it for myself / on
another level." Yet we have come a long way in both instances from T.S. Eliot's
typical way of dealing with the Pop material enclosed in his poem ("0 0 0 0 that
Shakespearian Rag — / It's so elegant / So intelligent . . ."); for though
condescension remains in both living writers, it is an inclusive rather than an
exclusive condescension. In both, the imperative is clearly to close the gap between
Modernist high art and Pop: not to open the distance between the poet-dandy and
the alien masses, but to join together the alienated long-haired son and his
short-haired father, the fashionable playwright and his dead grandma — which is
to say, to make all of us once more (or perhaps for the first time) members of a
single community of taste and feeling with all our lost fathers and grandmothers.
Moreover, such strategies for closing the gap between present and past imply
necessarily closing a similar one between present and future — the future that is
already in us if not on us — sealing into that single community of the living and
the dead also the not-yet-born.
  The point is worth lingering over for a moment, for it can lead us from the initial
questions: Where are we and how did we get there? to the final one: What is to be
done? And it has become clear to us, as it always does at revolutionary moments,
cultural as well as political, that in order to possess the future we must first
repossess the past; in order to invent the future, first reinvent the past — if need
be, a *new* past, a history we never lived. In terms of creating a new poetry, this
means finding in that past, counterfeiting out of it if necessity compels, a model,
a set of ideal ancestors. It is intriguing to speculate, while prophecy is still possible
in this regard, who these half-imaginary ancestors will be: who will play for the
poetic revolution in the last three decades of the twentieth century the role played
by John Donne (Eliot's John Donne) during the first three decades and by Walt

Whitman (Allen Ginsberg's Walt Whitman) during the two that followed. And my answer, an answer by which I assume no attentive reader will be surprised at this point of my argument (though I take it few will be delighted), is Henry Wadsworth Longfellow, plus, perhaps, Stephen Collins Foster; Longfellow and Foster will be our Donne and Whitman.

It should be clear enough, in any event, that Will Carleton or the anonymous author of the Charlie Vermont poem will not do, for they are too entirely on the other side, not figures of mediation at all but representatives of the ultimate pole of Pop. No, we need rather figures who closed the gap before most readers in America quite knew it had opened; figures who stood at the center of an age when popular song and printed verse still drew on a single implicit notion of what poetry was, when the serious contemporary anthologist (E. C. Stedman, for example) could put the most popular of the songwriters and the most widely read of the printed poets side by side in the same collection — with no sense of doing something radical or superchic, or even a little daring. It is, then, to the mid-nineteenth century that we must return, back through the intervening years during which the divorce between popular song and serious verse grew ever more extreme, reaching a climax at the moment when T. S. Eliot was writing *Prufrock* for his tiny audience and Irving Berlin was teaching everyone else to sing "Alexander's Ragtime Band."

It is with this simultaneous invention of white jazz (called ragtime in that initial stage) and *Symboliste* poetry in English (called "the New Poetry" in that age of innocence) that the crisis is reached, a crisis not yet resolved, though some have attempted to. The Beats, as we have already noticed, made a try as early as the fifties; but, despite all their talk about Charlie Parker, none of them was really singing like a bird (Allen Ginsberg is just learning to do so now with his settings of William Blake), merely shouting like Walt Whitman. And Walt, whatever his real merits and his populist myth of himself, never was and never can be a really popular poet — with the sole exception of the single poem in which he abandoned his eccentric voice to make rhymes and honor sentiment, "O Captain! My Captain!" which, disconcertingly, alone among all his verse, has been learned "by heart" by the mass audience, child and adult.

It is not, therefore, to the mid-nineteenth century of Walt Whitman that we must return, or even to that of Herman Melville (think, for instance, of *Clarel* as a model for verse-making); not to F.O. Matthiessen's "American Renaissance" at all, but to the *other* mid-nineteenth century defined by Longfellow and James Russell Lowell and Oliver Wendell Holmes, by Harriet Beecher Stowe and Julia Ward

Howe and Stephen Foster — not to the alienated symbolist works prized exclusively (I hope we shall continue to prize them forever, though not to the exclusion of the counter-Renaissance, the bourgeois "white" Romantics) in the recent past by critics, including me, who assumed a hierarchy of literary works in prose and in verse, which provided at its broad, not-quite-respectable base a vast demi-literature available to everyone, but at its narrow summit offered only a few winnowed works to be appreciated by select handful of readers, who turned out to be, in fact, not merely adults as opposed to children, sophisticated as opposed to naive, ironical as opposed to sentimental, but also male as opposed to female, white as opposed to black.

It was Longfellow and Foster (the latter of whom, neither accidentally nor incidentally, tried to redeem the language of verse by remodeling its inherited diction after the example provided by Negro slaves) who, not absolutely to be sure, but approximately at least, joined together an audience of men and women, children and adults, privileged and underprivileged. Of Harriet Beecher Stowe, Emerson was moved to say from the other side of the barricades, as it were, that she was read in the parlor, the kitchen and the nursery; and Longfellow pleased an audience analogously heterogeneous — as attested by the story that when he went to England for an audience with Queen Victoria, he was asked first to go down into the servants' quarters to receive the plaudits of the larger and more demonstrative group of readers awaiting him there.

It is a parabolic story which teases the fancy of the contemporary artist, ordinarily pleased with his audience "fit though few"; for he knows that so broad an appeal means also — switching to individual psychological, rather than mass sociological terms — that the work of writers like Longfellow, not merely did not separate class from class, but also did not alienate the adult reader from the child he once was, by asking him to respond exclusively to works of art quite different in kind from those that had moved and molded him when he was first learning to read. This impresses us especially at this moment when (as I have argued elsewhere, thinking chiefly of prose rather than verse) a creative, dissenting minority among the young, from whose midst the storytellers and minstrels who give a special savor to our time almost entirely come, have been rejecting or radically undercutting traditional concepts of "growing up" — questioning not merely Freudian doctrine, which preaches that maturity entails moving on from the polymorphous-perverse sexuality of infancy to full genitality, but also the Arnoldian theory that adulthood entails a surrender of fairy tales and comic books, science fiction and pornography and Westerns, in favor of the kind of literature that makes one feel old and established merely by virtue of appreciating it: the novels of Henry James, for instance, or the poetry of T. S. Eliot.

We are living, in short, in the Children's Hour come round once more, and who can more appropriately be resurrected to serve as its laureate than the author who presided over a similar era more than a century ago? The very name which comes to my mind when I try to describe the moment at which we stand is the title of what was once Longfellow's best-loved short poem, the lines of which have never ceased to ring in my head:

> Between the dark and the daylight,
>   When the night is beginning to lower,
> Comes a pause in the day's occupations,
>   That is known as the Children's Hour.
>
> I hear in the chamber above me
>   The patter of little feet,
> The sound of a door that is opened,
>   And voices soft and sweet.
>
> . . . .
>
> Do you think, O blue-eyed banditti,
>   Because you have scaled the wall,
> Such an old moustache as I am
>   Is not a match for you all!
>
> I have you fast in my fortress,
>   And will not let you depart,
> But put you down into the dungeon
>   In the round-tower of my heart.
>
> And there will I keep you forever,
>   Yes, forever and a day,
> Till the walls shall crumble to ruin,
>   And moulder in dust away.

It is, however, a poem which has not survived (critics and editors seem convinced) the Modernist revolution in taste, which for a while banned Longfellow completely from the loftier levels of art and, even when its spokesmen relented enough to let him back in with the status of minor poet, insisted he be loved for quite other poems than the ones which had compelled tears and sighs of admiration at the time of his greatest popularity. I do not find "The Children's Hour" for instance, in the new collection of Longfellow's verse compiled by the neo-Genteel poet Howard Nemerov in 1959, or in the anthologies of American literature compiled by Professor Charvat, on the one hand, or Professors Bradley, Beatty and Long, on the other, in the early sixties. For them, at least, that poem was relegated to the nursery once and for all. Yet if we would really revive Longfellow in a time when living politics has become a Children's Crusade and fewer and fewer of the young are content to surrender the privileges of childhood at any point short of the grave, it is Longfellow the children's poet (rather than Longfellow the fully adult translator of Dante or the maker of sonnets about him) we must be willing to evoke.

Not where he is most like the *Symbolistes,* but where he is furthest from them, Longfellow is capable of redeeming us, teaching us why we have continued to love Blake's *"Songs of Innocence"* and the songs of Burns in a time not really congenial to such work, and permitting us, without reservation or shame, to love also Will Carleton and James Greenleaf Whittier, Eugene Field and Robert Service, along with the poems of A. E. Housman, Oscar Wilde's "The Ballad of Reading Gaol" and "Woodman, Spare That Tree!" by G. P. Morris, laureate-before-the-fact of all modern ecologists. For too long we have honored only the difficult and far-fetched metaphor, catachresis or the conceit, that yoking of dissimilars which stirs us to admire the virtuosity of the author and the subtlety of our own minds. Under the aegis of Longfellow, we will remember to pay homage, too, perhaps first of all, to the easy metaphor, the obvious connection, those marriages not of Beauty and the Beast, but of neighbors and friends, which create immediately (it takes no repetition to make a real cliché) figures we feel we have always known, might well have invented ourselves and therefore have no scruples about borrowing.

The blending of similars moves us to admire all that is easiest in art and to appreciate the generosity in ourselves which prompts us to give our love where it is not earned or merited by effort or achievement. To prize John Donne is an act of wilful pride; to appreciate Longfellow is an act of shameless surrender. The one gives us the sense of having distinguished ourselves among men, the other an awareness of how little such distinctions finally mean. And it was to express the latter that song was first invented, as we dare never forget.

When I first began to formulate these notions a year or two ago, they seemed to me pure prophecy, more vision than fact, maybe more wish than either; but in the intervening months I have discovered that Longfellow has begun to haunt more minds than my own, to manifest himself, indeed, on both sides of the gap I have been insisting must be closed with the aid of his example. At the recent funeral of Jack Kerouac, for instance, a group of his old friends, comakers with him of the Beat Revolution, which meant the beginning of the end of American Modernism, gathered together when the services were done. They were feeling somehow out of it all — not only out of the family gathering, which naturally excluded them, but out of the big world itself, since scarcely any representatives of that world, hardly any young writers, for instance, had appeared to mourn the death or celebrate the accomplishment of Kerouac. And alone together, they decided (Robert Creeley and Gregory Corso and Allen Ginsberg among others) to read poems to one another which turned out to be not their own, not even those of their masters, Whitman or Williams or Pound or Olson, but rather of James Russell Lowell and Henry Wadsworth Longfellow.

And at just about the same moment, hundreds of thousands of television viewers (not quite large enough in number, for the program has been discontinued since) watching the current episode of "Here Comes Bronson," saw superimposed over the image of the demi-long-haired hero of that series, on his motorbike as ever riding down that lonely road, the words: THIS IS THE FOREST PRIMEVAL, the opening line, in fact, of Longfellow's sentimental sub-epic, *Evangeline*. And a little later those viewers heard, in the interstices of Bronson's stuttering speech, at his moment of supreme wonder before the natural beauties of Big Sur and over the twisted frame of his busted bike — heard the voice of Michael Parke (the actor who plays him and also records Pop songs) speaking more of those opening lines, lines one was sure until very recently could never be listened to again by an audience, young or old, without embarrassed tittering or rude remarks:

> This is the forest primeval. The murmuring pines and the hemlocks,
> Bearded with moss, and in garments green, indistinct in the twilight,
> Stand like the Druids of eld, with voices sad and prophetic,
> Stand like harpers hoar, with beards that rest on their bosoms.
>
> Loud from its rocky caverns, the deep-voiced neighboring ocean
> Speaks, and in accents disconsolate answers the wail of the forest.
>
> Yet, though on certain solemn and pious occasions (the death of an old friend,

a visit to the deep woods) we can take Longfellow straight, quite clearly our world, however hungry for rhyme and sentimentality, is not his in all respects — distrusting, for instance, his gentility and bourgeois timidity and that special humorlessness which appealed to his original audience. Precisely the strength of the School of Longfellow, its ability to appeal (as Melville or even Hawthorne could not) to women and children, became its weakness, once its practising poets and novelists agreed to make "the young girl" their censor-before-the-fact and to suppress for her presumed sake not only all overt reference to sexuality but any kind of "vulgarity." Fortunately for us, however, the definition of "the young girl" (think of the collaborators who joined with me in compiling my little anthology of Pop songs) has profoundly altered, both in terms of our way of thinking about her and of her way of regarding herself, so that "Lay, lady, lay," seems not to challenge but to reinforce her tenderest sentiments. We do not, therefore, have to choose between excluding her (and relegating half of life to parody for men only) or submitting to her tyranny and denying that half of life to print entirely.

As a matter of fact, our Longfellow, the restored Longfellow of our kind of Children's Hour, must include not merely his texts but the parodies of them as well; for they, too, are genuine Pop — not the negation of all he is after, as are parodies of high art, but its completion, its worse half, as it were. It is, I am trying to suggest, not accidental that Longfellow is the most parodied of poets, his availability to travesty being an aspect of his popularity, like the proverbial role his very name plays in the world of Pop culture: "His head was in the balcony, his feet were in the orchestra, Longfellow"; or, "You're a poet and your feet show it, they're Longfellows." Most parodied of all his works is *Hiawatha,* and it is with Mark Twain's burlesque of that intended epic that we might well begin to reconstruct a Longfellow useful to us here and now, since Twain's use of that poet (in his infamous Whittier Birthday Dinner Speech of 1877) was both — as he himself saw it — a joke *inside* an honored tradition and — as his Brahmin auditors heard it — as assault on that tradition bound to alter it profoundly. In Twain's account of three scoundrels who, in order to cadge a meal and some drinks, pretend to be Longfellow and Emerson and Holmes, the pseudo-Longfellow is described as follows:

> Mr. Longfellow was built like a prize-fighter. His
> head was cropped and bristly, like as if he had a
> wig made of hairbrushes. His nose lay straight down
> his face like a finger with the end joint tilted up.
> They had been drinking, I could see that. And what
> queer talk they used! . . . and next comes Mr. Longfellow
> and he buttonholes me, and interrupts me.

Says he:
"Honor be to Mudjekeewis!
You shall hear how Pau-Puk-Keewis —"

But this constitutes the simplest kind of parody, which involves direct quotation in an absurd context and which introduces the first distortion to travesty, the transformation of the solemn to the comic, ultimately of sense to non-sense. The second, common to most of the schoolboy parodies of *Hiawatha* still being produced when I myself was a student, involves the transformation of sentimentality to pornography. And we shall, I have no doubt, be honoring in the years just ahead a kind of poetry which is at once sentimental and pornographic, quite serious and utterly absurd — a kind of surrealism of the commonplace, blended with a tender-hearted vulgarity appropriate to nineteenth-century cadences and the most banal of rhymes. In short, the most ambitious poetry of the immediate future will be faithful to the nostalgic romanticism of songs like, say, "Little Red Wing," yet always aware that behind the original lyrics echo and re-echo words of the even-better-known parody:

Now this buckaroo was wise,
He crept between her thighs,
With an old gumboot
On the end of his toot
He soon made Red Wing open up her eyes.

In any case, we shall remain true to the cliché, reverent or irreverent, pious or impious, rational or fantastic.

Such a prospect means for me personally a deliverance from a bondage too long self-imposed, from that Terror to which I have submitted proudly, *learned* to submit, persuaded that such enslavement represents final wisdom. In my fifty-third year, however, I feel free at last to evoke in public the kinds of poems which I have never ceased to love, but which I've long felt obliged to recite in the catacombs, as it were; pretending, when my own kids were young enough, that it was for their sake only I kept alive the old chestnuts; and then, as they grew older, that it was for the sake of remembering together the time when they were young — as if there were ever a time when, at the levels touched by song, we were any of us anything else.

11.
Fiction and Future:
An Extravaganza for Voice and Tape

I. Beginning Now

We can begin anywhere. Man is a generalist. Buckminster Fuller says: "Nothing seems to be more prominent about human life than its wanting to understand all and put everything together . . . . Man is going to be displaced altogether as a specialist by the computer . . . *automation* displaces *automaton*."

A generalist may find in graffiti a start. I saw a sentence on a crumbling wall the other day: "We have met the enemy and he is us. Pogo." The handwriting on the wall reminds me of Marx. History repeats itself, according to Marx, the first time as tragedy and the next time as farce.

I will come to my topic, contemporary fiction, bye and bye. I am at my topics, on various levels, now.

II. Scene: Flashback and Forward [Tape]

A desert road, the sky still and green, a bearded man in the pride of life. Though he is not given to deep knowledge of his acts, he senses the mystery now. Suddenly she is there before him, the Sphinx, monstrous, hungry, bored, managing still a metaphysical leer. She asks the usual question and he answers: "Man!"

Our hero knows how to answer! He has killed an older man at the crossroads and the strength of murder still stirs in his heart. But his strength falls outwards, outwards; the ordeal remains ahead. Oedipus, King of Thebes, will blind himself and lick the blood in his beard to see what blind Tiresias already knows.

They say that the story of Oedipus is a myth that we dream time and time again. A famous version of the story comes down to us as tragedy, and repeats itself every day as grim farce. The Sphinx endures in stone under Egyptian stars; she no longer needs to waylay or ask.

"We have met the enemy and he is us." But this is also the predicament of gods. Must we then endlessly dream the past?

[Tape Ends]

III. Dream, Ecology, and The Stars

The dream of Oedipus strikes close to home. In Greek, the study of homes is called ecology. Nowadays, we define ecology as the study of living things in relation to their environment.

But what is the environment of man, that quiddity of life in search of itself? Is it the entire universe, or the earth, or his own consciousness murmuring in the dark? The language of human dreams may vex the farthest star.

This much we know: desire shapes our fictions and our future, and dreams become fact. We create and procreate; and somehow transcend both.

Glimmers of that transcendence light the mind. Perhaps the imagination is the true teleological organ in our evolution, directing all change. Hence the larger interest of fiction and future: our life as it can be, our life now and to come.

I am at my topic now.

IV. The Large Place   [Tape]

We live as strangers in a large place where nothing—no, not even the solitary neutrino—stands apart. Light and gravity, twins of desire, bind the cosmos to our eye and foot. Here is proof:

a. Some think the universe breathes, expanding to the limit of gravity and contracting again, forever; some think that it began with time in a great bang, never to repeat itself again; and others say that it moves outwards into infinity, beyond the speed of light, fed at the center with continuous creation. The dimensions of the universe are five: three in space and one each of time and mass. What are the dimensions of mind?

b. Astronomers believe that as many galaxies swirl outside our own, the Milky Way, as stars shine within our "island universe." The Milky Way, a mere 100,000 light years across, contains red giants, white dwarfs, blue stars a million times brighter than the sun; and when a supernova explodes, in its unmentionable spaces, it may turn our noon into night. The solar system is but a mote in the cosmic plasm.

Anecdotal

When Charles Messier scanned the skies from his tower in the Hotel de Cluny, looking for comets, he noted 103 cloudy lights that obstructed his sight. He recorded them by numbers, M1, M2, M3 . . . , to avoid them in his search. The clouds proved galaxies beyond the Milky Way, and one neighbor, Andromeda, came to be known as M31.

Anecdotal Ends

c. Our sun may be no older than 5 billion years. In 5 billion years again, the process of fusion at its center—where the temperature is now 25 million °F—will quicken. The sun will swell into a red giant and consume the earth. Then, in another billion years, the sun will begin to shrink, radiating sluggishly an infrared light. Eventually, it will turn cold and black.

A Note on the Chandrasekhar Limit

A static mass 1.4 times that of the sun would, in contracting, develop a gravitational force so great as to vanish, creating a "black hole" in space.

Pulsars come close to this. When a supernova collapses, it may leave behind a neutron star, fifteen miles in diameter, weighing 10 billion tons per cubic inch. But this body spins fast, dissipating its gravitational energy in pulses.

Conceivably, then, a super supernova may collapse into a small, quiet ball, heavier than a quintillion suns. Such an object would contract till it vanishes from its place in the universe and reappears elsewhere. In the language of astrophysics, this star "has encountered a singularity."

Note Ends

d. Back into the solar system, where nine planets, thirty-two satellites, and countless asteroids circle about, Halley's Comet trails fifty million miles of dust and light. Sighted on the eve of the Norman Conquest, and at regular intervals since then, it will approach the earth in 1986. Shall we decide for life, and arrange to see it again?

e. Meanwhile, the earth, racing in its orbit, plunges every day into cosmic chaff. It adds two million tons to its mass as it completes a revolution around the sun. Unknowingly, we plough the dust of stars, blown around us by the wind, and drink the universe in a glass of rain.

V. Maps in The Mind

We live in a large place. But we also need maps of "reality" to find our way through the mind. Maps and miracles.

A Memory

As a schoolboy, I used to trace the map of Africa until I learned to draw it with colors, brown and green and blue. Though no one had seen the entire African continent, there were maps of it in all the books.

Many years after, they sent a man into space. Imagine, then, my surprise when the first man who saw the entire continent of Africa brought back a photograph identical with the maps I used to trace and draw. Maps are miracles.

Memory Ends

A map of contemporary fiction, however, is another matter; the terrain changes every day. The closer we approach the moment, the harder it is to discern any shape, and even the colors begin to pale. Suddenly, we are in the absolute present: blank. As we move still forward, we begin to fill the map again with fictive shapes which prove our future.

Question: How do we draw Atlantis before Atlantis breaks through the white surface of the sea?

Answer: We dream Atlantis so that it may hasten to rise from its sleep.

[TAPE ENDS]

VI. Categories, Categories: Old

We use certain bland categories to describe twentieth-century fiction —The Genteel Tradition, Naturalism, Symbolism — and also invoke the name of each decade — the Twenties, the Thirties, the Forties. For certain obstinate ladies who refuse the sprit of the decades — Ellen Glasgow, Sarah Orne Jewett, Willa Cather — we devise a regional label.

A regional label is among the first to adhere to the postwar novel. Here are four categories of fiction since 1945:

a. The Southern Novel. It emerged during the war years as a distinct region of sensibility, detaching itself slowly from Faulkner's Yoknapatawpha County. Eudora Welty and Robert Penn Warren helped to firm its outline.

Names: Carson McCullers, Flannery O'Connor, the early Styron or Capote, William Goyen, Peter Taylor, Walker Percy, Reynolds Price, others.

b. The Jewish Novel. Northern rather than Southern, urban rather than rural, more liberal than traditionalist in its sympathies, Jewish fiction harked back to Nathanael West, Henry Roth, and Daniel Fuchs, though its main impact began in the late forties.

Names: Saul Bellow, Bernard Malamud, J. D. Salinger, Leslie Fiedler, Herbert Gold, Bruce Jay Friedman, Edward Lewis Wallant, Stanley Elkin, others.

c. The Negro Novel (not yet Black). It began South and ended North; its geographical migration became a quest for identity. Its father, Richard Wright, is now both honored and repudiated.

Names: Ralph Ellison, James Baldwin, John A. Williams, William Melvin Kelley, Paule Marshall, others.

d. The Beat Novel. Committed to vision and apostasy, the Beats did not name a region their own; they lived subterraneanly or on the road. Like their predecessor, Henry Miller, they braved sentimentality and shared his wonder, lust, and spontaneity.

Names: Jack Kerouac, Lawrence Ferlinghetti, Gregory Corso, John Clellon Holmes, others.

How quaint these categories now seem, like a Ptolemaic map illustrated with dragons, sea serpents, and the puffy face of wind! By the late fifties, many names had begun to recede or else moved into new countries. Critics looked for other terms — "black humor," "Camp," "the nonfiction novel," "the literature of silence," "the new mutants" — to describe the changing scene. Certainly, some of the most compelling novelists of the last two decades — Mailer, Barth, Vonnegut, Nabokov, Burroughs, Purdy, Hawkes — evade the old categories.

VII. Some Queries on Current Fiction

There are still many gifted Southern writers. Why, then, has the Southern novel ceased to hold a charmed place? The decline of formalist criticism may be a factor; Brooks, Warren, Ransom, and Tate, great formalists, are Southerners. The Civil Rights movement and the Black Revolution have also qualified the myth of the South. Or is it simply that the enormous present — poverty, pollution, rebellion, Vietnam — deflects our attention from the language of the past?

❀   ❀   ❀

Both Southern and Jewish fiction depend upon the telling of tales. A story implies a society, a community of listeners. "Once upon a time": we say that in a circle. This affirms a recoverable past. In the Jewish novel, particularly, the story may bear a sacramental message as in Hassidic narratives. It is evidence of *emunah*, the holy persistence of Israel; see S. Y. Agnon's *The Bridal Canopy*, a patchwork of somber and bright tales. But the story may also bite the bitter rind of modernity; see Elie Wiesel's *A Beggar in Jerusalem*, which bears transcendent witness to past inhumanity and mortal interdebtedness beyond death, waiting, waiting always, testifying to the end.

❀   ❀   ❀

What, then, is a story? Scheherazade may have known the answer: so long as she can tell a tale, she lives. A story races against death, and in ending reminds us of the End. Hemingway states that all true stories must terminate in death. Beckett agrees: his unnamable heroes drone endlessly, seeking release from the stories they are condemned to tell, seeking the final stillness. When Nabokov cries, Speak Memory! he cries against the onrushing night. But a wild-eyed beggar in Wiesel's novel makes the best point of all: "Remember, child, remember that the day someone tells you your life, you will not have much longer to live." Perhaps stories always have two authors: Voice and Silence, the Ego and its Death.

❀   ❀   ❀

Suppose that Western man learns to unfear egoistic death. Like Orpheus, he may sing and, singing, become part of nature, bird and tree, stone and cloud. Singing Orpheus releases himself into the universe. With his electric lyre, can he wed technology to mythology? Can he define for us a new ecology? No more stories, then, no selections and arrangements of our lives; everything will be there at once, wired to eternity. Is this why some anti-novelists declare their distrust of stories? I think that I may read into them too much.

❀   ❀   ❀

We are not wired to eternity yet. We are in an age of transition. We are always in an age of transition but some transitions are more disjunctive than others. My angry students seldom read novels now. They read Malcolm X, Fanon, Cleaver,

Mao, Debray, Marcuse, Goodman, McLuhan, Brown, Buber, Fuller, Cage, Watts. They also listen to songs and rock. Has fiction failed the revolutionary imagination of our time? Or must it by its very nature so fail? Is this why Styron's *The Confessions of Nat Turner* finally grates? But when Bob Dylan sings "Subterranean Homesick Blues," he gives to the Weathermen their name. There may be more in *The Whole Earth Catalogue* to frame a new consciousness than the usual art novel contains. Mailer is the great exception.

❋   ❋   ❋

What about the new Black Novel? How revolutionary is it? Here the paradoxes thicken. William Denby's remarkable work, *The Catacombs*, breaks down Western civilization — Pirandello, Picasso, Stein, Heisenberg, McLuhan, Chardin, and Kennedy, Khrushchev, DeGaulle, the Pope — and puts it back again together in pure forms of the mind. Less subtle, Cecil Brown's *The Life and Loves of Mister Jiveass Nigger* diverts anger and truth into knowing games. LeRoi Jones's *The System of Dante's Hell*, however, devises a kaleidoscope of violence — against Others, against Self, against God, Nature, and Art. Its sounds and images burn the dross of America and purify Jones's own life in it. There is spell, curse, poetry, and exorcism in the novel. Can revolution become poetry? Perhaps the Black Novel has chosen the way of black surrealism. Yet some questions remain: carried to a certain level of complexity or intensity, what action does imagination prescribe? What is the color of the brain?

VIII. The Small Place [TAPE]

I have spoken of the large place; now for its smaller counterpart, no less prodigal or strange.

a. Whenever the human brain entered biological evolution, a million or two years ago, attending the club-clutching hand and word-wagging tongue, it is here to stay if we stay. We carry it about as a woman carries her unborn child, in a womb of bone, floating delicately in the cerebrospinal fluid, protected by the *dura mater* and the *pia mater,* with the tough *arachnoid* in between. Two mothers for the human brain, and the third is a spider web.

b. The brain devours energy. Weighing no more than a fiftieth of the body's weight, it still consumes a fifth of the body's air and blood. Yet this devourer can reverse the entropy of the universe by increasing the order of things; or as Buckminster Fuller would say, by synergetics, the art of "doing more with less." No muscle twitches in the head as ten million neurons work in their place. When their work is finally done, who knows but the universe may become pure mind, Teilhard de Chardin's "noösphere"?

c. But the brain is not yet whole or one. Like a divided flower, never exposed to the sun, it grows from an ancient stem that controls both heart and lungs. On each side, cerebellum, thalamus, and limbic system twice grasp the stem. Our muscles, our senses, our rages and fears and loves, in this double fistful of old matter stir about. The great new cortex envelops the whole, gray petals and convolutions, where will, reason, and memory strive to shape all into mind. A computer's magnetic tape would need to run several million miles to memorize what a single cortex easily recalls.

d. Now they tell us of strange foods for the brain. Peyote, belladonna, thorn apple, hemp, and henbane can alter our perceptions; psilocybin, from sacred mushrooms, and lycergic acid, from ergot, can alter them more. Molecular biology promises to change man's behavior, intelligence, and memory in drastic ways. Scientists have already cracked the molecular code of RNA. Soon, the prediction of J. B. S. Haldane, that our children will come into the world speaking perfect English, may be fulfilled. Or will they speak perfect Russian or perfect Chinese? No one yet knows how to answer the question: who decides what happens to whom?

Anecdotal

At the University of Michigan, Dr. Bernard W. Agranoff has experimented with a "memory erasure" drug called puromycin. Its effects on animals were spectacular.

"When asked by a reporter whether the Central Intelligence Agency has an interest in his work, Dr. Agranoff would only smilingly reply, 'I forget.'" (David M. Rorvick, *Avant-Garde,* March 1970.)

Anecdotal Ends

e. But what is the secret mission of the brain? Writing early in the nineteenth century, Sir Charles Sherrington describes the brain as "an enchanted loom where millions of flashing shuttles weave a dissolving pattern, always a meaningful pattern though never an abiding one." The brain creates perpetual patterns with a purpose, and among these are dreams. Neurologists now know that the brain dreams rhythmically. Night after night, with the regularity of universal motions, it gives itself to fictions and prophecies.

[TAPE ENDS]

IX. THE MAP OF VANISHING FICTION

More novels are published today than ever before, and the proportion of "good novels" among these may be the highest yet. Still, I offer this possibility: that the novel may be a vanishing form, undergoing deep mutations. I hope that the result will be something rich and strange.

Here is my Map of Vanishing Fiction:

Imagine two lines meeting at some point in the future. Call the left line the Novel of Silence, or as Barth would say, the Literature of Exhaustion. Call the right line the Fantastic Novel, or as Vonnegut would want, Science Fiction. The area between these lines is the literary domain, and it is filled with all manner of fictions. Most of these fictions acknowledge the boundaries that enclose them; that is, acknowledge their future.

Here are some recent examples, in the middle ground of fiction:

a. Close to the center, the work of Joyce Carol Oates seems to celebrate the traditional pieties of the novel and to deny, with scope, style, and perception, that the genre contemplates its own end. Let us admit that she shows, in her many novels, a certain faith in the shapeliness of experience. But let us also note that experience includes matricide, patricide, includes, above all, the experience of nothingness, *nada*, silence. Moreover, *Expensive People* begins to play with fictional forms, incorporating reviews of itself, discussing the "death of the novel," referring to Fiedler's *Waiting for the End*, etc. In her most recent pieces, "Matter and Energy" and "How I Contemplated the World . . . ," Miss Oates opens up the narrative further; she presents us with fragments of diary and reflection. The notes of a "delinquent" girl for an essay become the story.

b. Consider next Daniel Stern's novel, *The Suicide Academy*. Superficially, the work treats the confrontation of Black and Jew with insight into their complexities and complicities. But the work attempts more: it attempts, in the author's words, "to create a kind of para-reality; to give the imagination the concreteness and density of palpable truth while endowing it with as much strangeness and metaphoric reach as it will bear. In fact, just a little more than it can bear! Each element balances its opposite: an institution where you go when you wish to decide on committing suicide or not . . . this is balanced by a man's re-experienced love for his ex-wife."

c. In *Steps,* Jerzy Kosinski creates the cunning identity of Self from the discontinuum of experience. The Self slips, changes, contracts, leaving before us terrible lacunae and blank spaces. "Given the reader's experiences . . . ," Kosinski says in his notes on the novel, "the reader may perceive the work in a form of his own devising, automatically filling in its intentionally loose construction with his own formulated experiences and fantasies. . . . At the end of every consecutive incident *Steps* allows the reader to break his journey — or to continue reading. In the fissure separating these possibilities the struggle between the book (the predator) and the reader (the victim) takes place."

Now, as we move farther from the center, the double tendency implicit in these works begins to emerge: self-parody or play, irreality or surreality, autodestruction or transcendence, pull the novel toward its boundaries. At one boundary, that of Silence or Exhaustion, the novel moves toward abolition of its form. At the other, of Fantasy or Science Fiction, it moves beyond itself into vision. But these are limits, and before we reach them, we need to survey more our domain. Consider, then, these works left of center:

a. Stanley Berne and Arlene Zekowski, husband and wife, have written between them some dozen works. They call their method "Neo-Narrative." They believe that the sentence today is dead because it is founded on a dead language, Latin. In *Seasons of the Mind,* Miss Zekowski says: "Precisely just with words, a new field of perception must be created where the old elements will undergo something akin to a chemical and physical metamorphosis in order for new compounds and new substances to enter literature and vivify and extend its entire frame of reference." And in *The Unconscious Victorious,* Stanley Berne claims: "We may be coming to the end of the era for books, but not, be it noted, of the end of the need for the literary experience, for that will live on by way of other media." Both seek to recover, in a new grammar of images, the arcane continuity of life, without plot, character, or common syntax.

b. The title of Ronald Sukenick's work, *The Death of the Novel and Other Stories,* speaks jauntily for itself. Sukenick breaks up the printed page into aphorisms, news captions, simultaneous narratives, parallel columns, Dadaist collages, run-on sentences held together by zany, angry humor. He quotes

Beckett and repeats the refrain: "I can't go on / Go on." He quotes Wallace Stevens: "A violent order is disorder." He notes: "The didactic job of the modern novel is to teach people to invent themselves and their world — Robbe-Grillet." He simulates a tape recorder, a candid camera, an advanced honors seminar on "The Death of the Novel." He ends a section called "Momentum" by saying: "I'm happy, folks, and I wish you luck. I disappear around the bend." He mentions Spock, Coffin, the students of Columbia and the Sorbonne, shows us the absurd in home and street. Thus farce and slapstick blend with the obdurate and banal facts of our day in improvisations on an old question: How can the imagination take power again, pervade our lives, and alter the quality of existence?

c. Earl M. Rauch calls his book *Dirty Pictures from the Prom*. It contains pointless epigraphs, bland and crossed-out pages, a few "obscene" drawings, chapters sketched only in outline, a running dialogue between Author and Editor at the end of each chapter, as commentary on the main narrative. Throughout the novel, quotations also appear from a certain work — *Dialogue with an Unknown Black-Veiled Madame on the Coach Ride to Tours* by Creynaldo. Creynaldo is the brother of Barnaby, the narrator; Creynaldo dies at the age of seven, and he has some attributes of Christ or of Completeness. This desperate hoax of a book turns out to be a mystic pursuit of time, a quest for original freedom, a search for consciousness, completeness. Deadpan, Rauch moves from farce to degradation and sheer terror, exposing that ultimate evil: the eternal presence of man in forms of absence, or Nonbeing. Here farce and fiction strain their resources till the reader must either dismiss the work as trivial or else admit its outrage.

A Bibliographical and Reflective Footnote   [TAPE]

Other works in the same genre have appeared in the last few years, and some of them appear more exotic or extreme. Inevitably, when the imagination reaches toward the limit of a certain art form, radical changes in the expectations of the audience take place. See the following works:

Marvin Cohen, *The Self-Devoted Friend*
John Brockman, *By the Late John Brockman*
Andy Warhol, *A*

There are also "concrete novels," "shuffle novels," and "blank novels," a bound sheaf of pages to remind us that silence can also be literal and white.

Carlyle, however, celebrated the virtues of silence through thirty volumes. Why is this a joke? The language of paradox is as old as human consciousness, an integral part of its most complex functions. No animal can think or utter: "I do not exist."

FOOTNOTE ENDS   [TAPE ENDS]

Let us move on to some other works on the right of our imaginary center. Let us move toward Fantasy, though we may never have left it.

a. Richard Brautigan has written several works, poems and novelettes, evoking a simple and marvelous life. *Trout Fishing in America* and *In Watermelon Sugar* seem limpid as a mountain stream flashing metaphors in sunlight. His dislocation of language is subtle, sweet, and funny; we end by floating in another element, released from all our habits. Parody and poetry, nostalgia and satire, nature and human incongruity, death itself, dart between words rounded smooth as pebbles. Here is the outcome of intercourse in a hot spring between a gentle couple: "My sperm came out into the water, unaccustomed to the light, and instantly it became a misty, stringy kind of thing and swirled out like a falling star, and I saw a dead fish come forward and float into my sperm, bending it in the middle. His eyes were still like iron." Brautigan hurries from scene to short scene — his "chapters" are sometimes no longer than their headings — as his novels disclose within the reader some enchanted inscape of green leaves, laughter, memories, a vision of the American Garden "with real toads in it."

Digression

The toads in our visionary garden become every day more loathsome. *The New York Times:* "Dallas, March 28 (UPI) — Larry Joe Knox, 23 years old, has been sentenced to 1001 years in prison — the longest term in Texas history — for raping a young telephone operator. It was the third big prison term handed down in the Dallas-Fort Worth area this month."

Digression Ends

b. The fantasy of Rudolph Wurlitzer's *Nog* is calmly deranged and nocturnal. This "headventure," as the subtitle calls it, takes us through outer America — a land of Indians, desert rats, acid heads, outcasts — on the silent wings of Nog's madness. Indeterminacy guides both motive and perception: "delicate moment, when the line draws taut, when the lurching from wall to wall suddenly ends. I will miss the complaining and the whining . . . . Where do these words come from? There's no need for them now. But they dribble on. Nog, of course, can become clearer. Or dropped. Or simply forgotten." This will remind us of Beckett's *Watt*. But Nog, who speaks of himself in the third person — schizoids do that too — is a different breed of solipsist. He subsists on white pills, sharing his life with a couple, Lockett and Meredith, whom he finally destroys. "I don't know if I can remember anyone who is apart from me for very long," he manages to conclude. Nog's consciousness, like the rubber octopus in the novel, is not merely an artifact, nature aberrant; his author succeeds in giving it the hues of our own madness.

   c. "Patarealism," a term coined by Ishmael Reed, best describes his novel, *Yellow Back Radio Broke-Down*. The book brings together elements of the tall tale, horse opera, circus, absurd humor, and Hoo-Doo, a madcap version of African juju adapted to black fiction. Phrases like "crazy dada nigger," "far-out esoteric bullshit," "the cosmic jester," also suggest the quality of character and action, fancy and wordplay, in this work. As the hero, the Loop Garoo Kid, puts it to another: "What's your beef with me Bo Schmo, what if I write circuses? No one says a novel has to be one thing. It can be anything it wants to be, a vaudeville show, the six o'clock news, the mumblings of wild men saddled by demons." Words spark as anger and anarchy strike in Reed's imagination. Its violence and humor destroy all sham, and would destroy the whole world rather than yield in freedom.

We are rather more used to this genre of fantasy than to fictions of exhaustion. The novels of Joseph Heller, J. P. Donleavy, Thomas Pynchon, Terry Southern, Thomas Berger, Donald Barthelme, among others, have conditioned us to desperate burlesque and humor. But in responding to their extravagant ironies, we tend to ignore their hidden visionary qualities, and so convert them into Camp. Bizarre, satirical, and excessive, they still imply a world, in some undiscovered corner of the heart, where love binds the tiger and the lamb, and the child remains father to the man.

Surmise

Recent and remarkable, the works I have cited suggest that fiction moves toward subversion or transcendence of itself, and sometimes moves toward both at once.

The way down and the way up are the same. Perhaps only the transfiguration of reality, into something or nothing, matters. Anything can happen. Is the conclusion to fiction Cage?

X. THE VISIONS OF PRACTICAL MEN [TAPE]

Enclosed with my bill for the month of January 1970, *Telephone News* declares:

"The Age of Aquarius, famous from astrology and popular music, is a wonderful vision of a peaceful and happy world. . . .

But it takes interpreters and practical men to make visions come true. We in the communications industry are trying to help those dreams along. . . .

How would you like to have a phone that shops for you, locks your door and controls your stove? We're working on it.

And how about dialing a computerized library for information — in spoken and printed words, pictures or diagrams — or doing your math problems just by pushing the keys of your Touch-Tone telephone?

Handling money could be revolutionized too. A phone call to your bank's computer will take care of payments on your regular authorized bills such as rent or utilities. It could also keep track of your balance, and even figure out your income tax.

To help you stay healthy, your doctor could draw on the entire sum of medical knowledge through his telephone.

Yes, 1970 and beyond looks pretty exciting."

Pogo: "We have met the enemy and he is us."

Fuller: "So I'll say to you that man on earth is now clearly faced with the choice of Utopia or Oblivion."

[TAPE ENDS]

XI. WHERE BOUNDARIES MEET

In a universe curved positively, a beam of light radiating from a man's eye will travel to the boundaries and return to hit him, many billion years after, in the back of the skull.

But the boundaries of fiction meet within the skull. In my imaginary map, the Novel of Silence and the Fantastic Novel converge on some point in the future, and their convergence helps to draw the future in our midst.

Let me now speak of each at some length.

A. The Novel of Silence and Exhaustion

For almost two centuries now, a particular kind of literature has made itself by denying the assumptions of art, form, and language. We call the most recent expressions of this spirit anti-literature. But the tradition of silence is really deeper in reach and wider in scope. It may go back to Sterne's *Tristram Shandy* or Sade's *Justine,* include certain Romantic and Symbolist poets, notably Lautréamont and Rimbaud, who drove language berserk, and erupt finally in the modern avant-garde: 'Pataphysics, Dadaism, Futurism, Surrealism, etc.

Anecdotal

Alfred Jarry, 'Pataphysician, went about with a pair of revolvers in his belt and a lobster on the leash. His favorite expression was "Isn't it beautiful, like literature?" The Dadaists took their cue from him and wrote their manifestoes with bullet holes. As for Marcel Duchamp, alias Marchand Du Sel, alias Rrose Selavie, grand master of chess, silence, and art, he consecrated a urinal into art and gave the Mona Lisa a mustache.

Anecdotal Ends

In the novel, particularly, the exhaustion of form and consciousness becomes an explicit theme in a sequence of French works: Gide's *The Counterfeiters,* Sartre's *Nausea,* Beckett's *Watt,* and Robbe-Grillet's *The Labyrinth.* We can say about the authors of these original fictions what John Barth said in his essay "The Literature of Exhaustion" about the Argentinian Jorge Luis Borges: "His artistic victory . . . is that he confronts an intellectual dead end and employs it against itself to accomplish new human work. . . . In homelier terms, it's a matter of every moment throwing out the bath water without for a moment losing the baby."

Barth should know. Like Beckett, Borges, and Burroughs, he has turned "the death of the novel" to enormous advantage and given us in *The Sot-Weed Factor* and *Giles Goat-Boy* works which, in his own words, "imitate the form of the Novel, by an author who imitates the role of Author." *Lost in the Fun House* goes farther than self-parody: it appropriates techniques other than the novel's and thus offers itself to translation into another medium. The living voice, the printed word, and the magnetic tape constitute a kind of aural montage in the book, a generic conceit. The narrative swallows itself by the tail, as in "Anonymiad," or vanishes in a Chinese box, as in "Menelaiad." These tricks refine an old dream of Barth; they are not caprices of his muse. Fabulously inventive, Barth finds the phenomenal world odd, gratuitous: "Which snowflake triggers the avalanche?" Reality is merely "a nice place to visit." Beginning with *The Floating Opera,* his heroes emerge as ironists of history and their own flesh, without connection to the earth, yet marvelously free, funny, and lucid in the realm of ultimacy, which lies beyond fancy. The virtuosity of their author sustains them, lends them, perhaps, inverted vitality. But Barth knows that high wit no longer suffices and ultimacy may literally end in the void. In a piece called "Title," he takes up the predicament of the tale, the teller, and the told: "What is there to say at this late date? Let me think, I'm trying to think. Same old story. Or. Or? Silence." "Title" is an internal argument, with voice and tape and print, assent and skepticism and denial, playing against one another, concluding nothing. The last sentence trails in a blank space: "How in the world will it ever   "

A Digression on Tapes   [TAPE]

John Cage, Samuel Beckett, John Barth, playing with tapes and magnetism.

Cage: the tape as a voice other than one's own; as past made present in instant replay, hence simultaneity; as a different parameter of awareness, a new source of sound; as random order when several tapes play together; the sound of pantheism.

Beckett: Krapp's last tape as repetition, time that will not come to a stop; as the first person speaking on and on, forever; as static, noise, decay in communication; the sound of solipsism.

Barth: the tape as an aural mask for the narrator; as voices playing with mirrors, dispelling their identity; as language in its essence, without decaying flesh; the sound of nihilism.

There is also Heinrich Böll. The old man in his story, "Doktor Murkes" spends his life splicing the silences on the tapes of others to make his own tape.

Note, however, that the magnetic tape still depends on mechanics: reels, buttons, springs, motors. Only our familiar television, McLuhan says, is all electric, in sympathy with our brains.

[TAPE ENDS]

B. The Fantastic Novel and Science Fiction

This genre has an old and diverse history. It may go back to Plato's myth of Atlantis in the *Timaeus* and Lucian of Samosata's voyages to the moon in the *True*

Histories. It may draw on More's *Utopia* and all its ghastly sequels: Zamyatin's *We,* Orwell's *Nineteen Eighty-Four,* Huxley's *Brave New World.* It owes something to fantastic voyages and tales: *The Arabian Nights, Gulliver's Travels, The Adventures of Baron von Münchausen.* It also enriches itself from the large and disparate body of horror stories, gothic novels, allegorical narratives, and visionary literature. We know that Francis Bacon, Johannes Kepler, Francis Godwin, and Cyrano de Bergerac all wrote, before the nineteenth century, *ur*-science fictions. But we agree that Jules Verne and H. G. Wells gave the genre its modern aura and authority. After the Second World War, the gates of the technological dream seemed suddenly to open, flooding our unconscious. The creations of Ray Bradbury, Arthur Clarke, Robert Heinlein, loom hugely, in colors on our screens, and a book by the last, *Stranger in a Strange Land,* inspired the demonic commune of Charles Manson.

The genre really needs no pedantic definition. Wells thinks that it entails the ingenious use of "scientific patter," and Kingsley Amis notes that *"Idea as hero"* is the basis of science fiction. Bradbury gives an even broader view of fantasy: "To make the extraordinary seem ordinary, and cause the ordinary to seem extraordinary." The serious point to be made about science fiction is this: it offers critiques of the human condition and fashions new myths from the old; and, going further still, it offers radical alternatives to the destiny we assume to be our own. The best of science fiction, then, does not merely display "a mode of romance with a strong inherent tendency to myth," as Northrop Frye says; it brings, rather, intimations of a consciousness that has not yet found its myth. In short, the best of science fiction looms as true prophecy or vision.

A Digression on the New   [TAPE]

Prophecy is akin to madness, Cassandra raving, the Pythoness of Apollo in a trance.

Prediction is extrapolation: we simply extend the past and present into the future and project what we already know. Nothing new.

Phophecy *creates* the new. Deranged, the mind creates the future. We sometimes call this shaping derangement of things *imagination!*

Prophecy is akin to madness and the creative imagination, but in biological terms, it is also akin to mutation. Consider nature. The conservative instincts, the codes in the double helix, repeat and repeat the forms of life into eternity. Fanatic conservatism of the genes. But there are also random mutations: suddenly something incomprehensible occurs, something new. Thus certain breakthroughs in evolution: photosynthesis, the vertebrates, the cerebral cortex.

Who says nothing is new under the sun? Who says nothing is new by the light of the moon?

Digression Ends [TAPE ENDS]

Among contemporary writers, Kurt Vonnegut stands out as a gruff sentimentalist with a soft spot in his heart for science fiction. One of his characters, Eliot Rosewater, says to practitioners of the genre: "I love you sons of bitches. . . . You're all I read any more. You're the only ones who'll talk about the *really* terrific changes going on, the only ones crazy enough to know that life is a space voyage. . . . You're the only ones with guts enough to *really* care about the future. . . . " Vonnegut himself often wavers between the future and the past, the story in its slickest form and the vision of things to come, the bombings of Dresden and the destiny of the planet Tralfamadore. Furthermore, some of his science fiction — *Player Piano, Welcome to the Monkey House* — is in the old form of dystopia: an extension of the absurd or destructive tendencies of the present, a scientized homily, satire, or warning. This is understandable; Vonnegut is really a simple moralist, haunted by the reality of death. (The refrain, "So it goes," follows each mortal event in *Slaughterhouse-Five*, like water drops in Chinese torture.) Typically, his own moral confession sounds a bit cute: "And I realize now that the two main themes of my novels were stated by my siblings: 'Here I am cleaning shit off of practically everything' and 'No pain.' "

Still, prophylaxis and anesthesia do not constitute all his interests; Vonnegut has another visionary side. In *The Sirens of Titan,* for instance, destiny is not causal or temporal as we usually think; destiny embraces the sum total of love in the universe, the power of the Universal Will to Become. As for the government of Tralfamadore, Salo describes it as "hypnotic anarchy," adding: "Either you understand at once what it is . . . or there is no sense in trying to explain it to you." The nature of Tralfamadorian fiction proves especially relevant to my theme. A voice describes it in *Slaughterhouse-Five:* "Each clump of symbols is a brief, urgent message — describing a situation, a scene. We Tralfamadorians read them all at once, not one after the other. There is no beginning, no middle, no end, no suspense, no moral, no causes, no effects. What we love in our books are the depths of many marvelous moments, seen all at one time."

But time-warps, spaceships, and galactic materializations aside, Vonnegut, an earthling like all of us, can not push his vision past the ironic barrier of the mind.

He bestows on his ideal creatures, the Tralfamadorians, the supreme privilege of blowing up the universe. They blow it up, of all things, experimenting with a new fuel for their flying saucers. So much, then, for universal Time and Space, where vision and extinction finally become one.

And so the boundaries of fiction twice meet. They meet first as our map folds into a headless cone, bringing the lines of Silence and Fantasy together into a single seam. Thus Barth and Vonnegut exchange hilarious hints of oblivion. Thus also Nabokov, in *Ada*, brings together all our themes and creates, in *Pale Fire*, a vision of eternity through self-cancelling forms. William Burroughs, we also recall, transforms the galaxies of *Nova Express* into a cut-up collage of death.

But the boundaries, two sides of the cone, meet again at some future point where the apex hides. There, beyond where Silence and Fantasy exhaust themselves, a new form of art, of consciousness, lies.

Caveat

Here are works that I failed to name:
  a. Hawkes's *The Lime Twig*
  b. Malamud's *The Fixer*
  c. Cohen's *The Beautiful Losers*
  d. Bellow's *Mr. Sammler's Planet*
There are many others. Who says the novel is dying? Couldn't Mailer, for instance, keep it alive for a while?

XII. For The Humanists [TAPE]

The important questions before the human race are not literary questions. They are questions of consciousness — reason, dream, love — since consciousness affects the use of our physical means. Humanists have something to say in the matter, though most prefer to keep the Humanities in the museum stage.

But even museums change: they lose their walls. Curators and critics of art, Harold Rosenberg shows, turn their eyes on the future, and historians help to make art history rather than wait for that history to be made. Custodians of the word, however, usually have a heavier mien. This sadness is not merely in academe. Compare the Arts and Books sections in a popular magazine: their authors seem to hail from different centuries.

We need not walk as amnesiacs in history to keep the mission of the Humanities alive. John McHale writes: "To invent the future we need, in certain senses, to reinventory the past." The literary past is full of mutability; it guarantees the persistence of no genre or form. Epic, romance, ballad, sermon, pastoral, sonnet have all seen their brightest day. What piety, then, compels us to regard the novel as eternal?

New media have come into our midst since the printing press — telephone, film, comic strip, television, Xerox, computer — and it is still hard to know how these and future media will affect the literary response, will alter the needs of the imagination. The time for large speculation may have caught up with us, may soon leave us far behind.

Scientists know that modern technology does not only create a new reality for mankind; it also permits the coexistence of several realities. Coexistence takes place in a context of universal sentience, much like McLuhan's "global village" or Chardin's "noösphere." Here is McHale again: "This idea of organized human thought now covering the globe as a functional part of the overall ecological system is, to an extent, physically demonstrable in our present global communications network. . . ."

Humanists must enter the sphere of active symbols now surrounding the earth and bring to it what they know of language and the sovereign imagination. Humanists must enter the future. They must also dream.

[TAPE ENDS]

XIII. Science and Prophecy, Fiction and Future

Galileo, staring too long at the sun, turned blind, and the Inquisition trod on his tongue. Seers endure constraints on speech and sight. Nostradamus, also looking heavenward, chose to write his *Centuries* "by abstruse and twisted sentences . . . under a figure cloudy, rather than plainly prophetic." Deep in his "ecstatic work, amid prolonged calculation, and engaged in nocturnal studies of sweet odour," Nostradamus still sought a unifying concept for all his shadowy labors. "The reason is too evident," he says in a Preface, "the whole is predicated by the afflatus of divinity. . . ."

Someday, it may be possible to place both astronomy and astrology within a larger and simpler frame, some vast noetic vision of things, or as Wordsworth put it:

Characters of the great Apocalypse,
The types and symbols of Eternity.

Meantime, we do well to ponder the words of an eminent savant, Sir James Jeans: "Mind no longer appears as an accidental intruder in the realm of matter. We are beginning to suspect that we ought rather to hail it as the creator and governor of the realm of matter." Perhaps this is where science and prophecy meet: in deep fictions of the mind, still locked in emblems of our sleep.

Our view of human consciousness remains at best limited, and we limit it even more by defining it in individual terms only. Our investigations of the Freudian unconscious draw us, willy-nilly, into psychic realms larger than a single organism, longer than the life span of any man. We begin to mumble about "memory traces," "the oceanic feeling," the collective unconscious." Ira Progoff goes even further. For him, the unconscious reverses the ordinary sense of time and becomes the carrier of experiences still to come. "The unconscious," he says, "as the seed aspect of the personality, contains the possibilities for future experience. It is unconscious because it has specifically not yet been lived." Is the child, then, really father to the man, and time reversible?

We do not really know.

Anecdotal

Freud charted the mind, its surface and depths. He found his way among its terrors. He also loved to hike in spring and summer. When he went out, looking for mushrooms and wild flowers, he always got lost in the woods.

Anecdotal Ends

Yet something tells us that dream looks back to myth and forward to prophecy, sharing with both certain forms and wisdom. There are also in science certain forms that will dream us onward and extend our senses to the limits of the invisible universe. It is no longer enough for man to rely simply on his common senses. Already, he entrusts his life every day, on land and air and sea, to secret extensions. Where is the limit of sight or touch?

Man must dream himself onward: he has grown tired of the back of the primeval cave. Though he may meet at the end of his journey the same face he left behind him, he must continue his way. And who is there to say that, at the end, the face to greet him may not be a transfiguration of his own?

It is always journey-time, and new fictions may give man a map a small part of the way.

12.
Man's Changing Role in Universe

Hoping that we in our present moments of omniworld upheaval may be able to avoid inadvertent self-betrayal by our own ignorance of those fundamentals of nature operative in universe, there are aspects of change that I find myself intuitively urged to think-out-loud about at this perhaps auspicious moment in man's history. At best I can interpret history as relayed to us by others, and I find that throughout all of our documented experience, humanity has thought of reality exclusively in terms of what could be seen, smelt, heard, and touched. Some realized that their own thoughts as well as the thoughts of others, conveyed to them by the air wave propagated sounds and formulated as words and sentences, were in essence weightless. There has always been mystified human awareness of the a priori existence of unpredictably experienced forces, possibly constituting universal regularities beyond those already understood or anticipated by man. But still reality always has been thought of spontaneously as limited to the reaches of sensorial experience.

Freud disturbed and altered this socially accepted concept of reality. In such an exclusively sensorial reality, humanity held all individuals consciously responsible for their every behavior. It followed that any were at fault when they did not seem to behave in the customarily acceptable ways. Freud instilled in society a developing awareness born of actual experimental demonstration that much of human behavior was subconsciously motivated. In due course, therefore, it had to be legally recognized that normal and sane humans were not always responsible for their every act.

During World War I, the micro and macro cosmic patterns of man's experience began to change more swiftly than ever before in his history. We went from wire to wireless communications, from track to trackless transportation, and from visible muscle to invisible alloys whose increasing strength permitted ever slenderer cables to have ever greater tensile strength. "The thinner the stronger" became a truth incomprehensible to the oppositely conditioned reflexes of society. Swayed in 1917 by the vital threats of the new technical ways of waging war, the masters of both sides allowed their scientists to pursue their most powerfully pure scientific capabilities. Employing ever more powerful and incisive new instruments and tools, the scientists and engineers began to probe and operate almost exclusively in those realms of universe which are noncontactable directly by man's senses.

A century and a half ago, man began to employ a new kind of energy — steam — which you could see, and lead through a pipe into a powerful engine and control it to do work. Then, about a century ago, man discovered and developed the uses of electricity, by which vastly larger quantities of energy per pound of generating and distributing equipment could be conveyed invisibly through a seemingly solid wire in seemingly no time at all to impel an engine. When the literary men asked the scientists for a conceptual model of what was going on in electromagnetics so that the writers could explain to the everyday man in everyday visualisable experiences what was transpiring, the scientists said, "We cannot give you any model. What goes on is, to the best of our experimental knowledge, utterly invisible and non-conceptual and is only expressible in mathematical terms." Since that time, science has been flying blindly on mathematically operated instruments. For a century scientists have not sensed their responsibilities because they have been dealing only in abstract, ergo senseless, mathematics.

As a little child, my mother told me about the various extraordinary new scientific capabilities of man which most impressed her. As I heard more about those new developments from others, I found science being regarded by society as in effect employing magic. Magic as dramatized to all children by all the great legends and fairy stories was something accomplished both instantly and invisibly by a magic formula. Science was also something that could be coped with without seeing, hearing, touching, or smelling. To all non-mathematically educated humans, science was just magic. Though scientists asserted that their accomplishments were not magic but mathematics, the public simply "accepted" their incredulous assertions in the same humbly believing way that they accepted the religious dogma in which they were reared.

When in World War I, scientists penetrated the new realms of what we call today the electromagnetic spectrum, society as yet did not think about that invisible universe as constituting reality. Scientists were doing things they themselves didn't understand, or find it necessary to conceive of, in a sensible way.

Though they knew and taught that the sun was not "going down," they continued to "see" and sense it to be doing so. Thus science accomplished extraordinary results by non-conceptual and invisible means which, however, affected our reality in important and highly sensorial ways.

In 1930, the first graphic chart was published of the great electromagnetic spectrum. It presented in logarithmically proportioned array all the frequencies characterizing all the different chemical elements in our universe as ascertained by the spectroscope. Each element had its own special set of invisible colour bands or frequencies — usually four. They were analogous to four colour hat bands. The four colour hat bands are not in separate, serial order, but overlap one another. You have to be an expert to recognize, for instance, where iron's four invisible colour bands or frequencies occur. But just as iron is a great reality, so too all the rest of the invisible electromagnetic spectrum is reality.

We also discovered at that time that the portion of universal reality where man could "see" was only about one-millionth of the total range of the great physical reality. We have only a meager, narrow-band, tuning machine with which to directly apprehend about one-millionth of the known ranges of physical reality. We can amplify our knowledge of the vast ranges of reality only by use of instruments. But society has not yet achieved spontaneous and conceptual comprehension of the true nature of reality. To world society in general, what we call commonsense reality as yet — in 1970 — consists only of the sensorial.

We are always told, for example, in both euclidean and non-euclidean geometries that a plurality of lines can be run through any one point. The engineer puts a point on a paper and draws line after line (approximately) through (approximately) the same point. He assumes this to be theoretically and realistically done. But try this with knitting needles or even the thinnest line elements you can find. In fact, reduce your line to the size of a neutron's diameter. Let your "line" be the trajectory in the cloud chamber of a neutron shot into a plurality of atoms. Suddenly there is an interference of the trajectory as the neutron interferes with another nuclear component's linear trajectory, and the component separates into further subcomponents as all of the individual atomic components now diverge angularly from one another in identifiable angular directions unique to each, having failed to permit the neutrons simultaneous passage through the one point of interference. Because they cannot go through the same point at the same time, we get little angles by which cloud-chamber physicists recognize the sub-atomic particles. If lines, which experimentally are always vectors, are unable to go simultaneously through the same point, then we can't have "planes" which are absurdly thin wafers of solids. We find that we are dealing with a very different kind of universe from the one that we are told about and that the children still are "learning" about in grade schools.

Because you can't have two actions going through the same point at the same time, we have the phenomena of reflection, with which we are all familiar, or we have refraction. These two experimentally reliable interference phenomena are direct consequences of the fact that actions cannot take place through the same point at the same time.

Mathematically, there are very important concepts regarding the tetrahedron. The tetrahedron is made up of four triangles. The angles of each triangle are interstabilized. Each of the separate angles, which as such was originally amorphous — that is, unstable — becomes stable because the vector (line) opposite any angle of any triangle is always operating at and between the ends of the levers which are the sides of the angle, thus providing maximum advantage over its own angular stability with minimum effort. The triangle is the fundamental function of structure, but it always takes two functions, the positive and negative, to make any structure. The tetrahedron is the simplest structure known to man. The triangle exists operationally only as a positive or negative function of a polyhedron.

Of all the polygons, only a triangle is structurally stable. A square folds up. Try any other rubber jointed polygon: it will fold up. Try a rubber jointed triangle: it won't fold up: it is stable. If we want to have a structure, we have to have triangles and to have a structure requires a minimum of four triangles. A structural system may be symmetrical or asymmetrical, but it always has withinness and withoutness. A structure or system divides universe into two parts: all of the universe that is inside the structure or system and all the rest of universe that is outside the structure or system.

We find that there are only three types of fundamental omni-triangular symmetrical structural systems. We can have three triangles around each vertex of a symmetrical structure making a regular octahedron. We can have four triangles around each vertex of a symmetrical structure making a regular octahedron. Finally, we can have five triangles around each vertex of a symmetrical structure making the regular icosahedron. The tetrahedron, octahedron and icosahedron are made up, respectively, of one, two and five pairs of positive-negative function open triangles. We can't have six symmetrical or equilateral triangles around each vertex because the sum of the angles would be six times sixty degrees or three hundred and sixty degrees, thus forming an infinite edgeless plane. The structural system with six equilateral triangles around each vertex never comes back upon itself. It cannot be constructed with pairs of positive-negative function open triangles. A structural system must return upon itself in all directions. If the system's openings are all triangulated, it is structured with minimum effort. There are only three possible omni-symmetrical, omni-triangulated, least effort structural systems in nature: the tetrahedron, octahedron, and icosahedron. When their edges are all equal in length, the volumes of these three structures are approximately and respectively: one, four, and eighteen and two-thirds.

When I began to explore the above volume relationships and then gave the simplest, the tetrahedron, a volume value of one, I found that a cube had a volume of exactly three. That's very interesting because if you try to account in cubes for nature's energy associabilities as structural systems, you use up three times as much space as you do if you count space volumes in tetrahedronal units. The physicists have found that nature only uses those structures which are the most economical; therefore, she could not use cubes to quantitate her structurings. Cubes, as you know, represent our x, y, z coordinate system.

If you use tetrahedra as your coordinating system, something very fundamental and economical happens. A cube's angles are each ninety degrees. When you want to make a bigger cube out of littler cubes — want to double the size of the cube — you must put eight little cubes together symmetrically "closest stacked" around one point. The edges of the thus created big cube are each two units of little cube-edge long. The big cube edges are two. The face areas are four. The volume of the two linear-module edges cube is eight which is the third power of two.

When we deal in tetrahedra, we are dealing with sixty degree angle systems since in a regular tetrahedron, all of the angles are sixty degrees; they are equilateral (and equilangular) triangles. Heretofore, when the scientists found an energy relationship in the fourth power value, they were unable to make a conceptional model of it because there is no fourth perpendicular to a cube which is not in a plane parallel to one of the planes of the cube. But the scientists did not need a model to calculate fourth power problems. They were able to handle it very easily algebraically. They did it by using what they called an imaginary number, e.g., by using the square root of minus one. If that sounds complex, don't let it bother you. What they were saying was that, in effect, they had a cubical clock. Their cubical day consisted of eight little cubes around the center of the big cube. The first dimension used up one cube, the second dimension used up four cubes, and the third dimension used up all eight cubes. Their day's entire clock capacity would only take care of three dimensions. So what they did was to borrow cubes from "tomorrow" or from "yesterday." They then carried out their problem algebraically without any reference to conceptional models. After they got finished, they'd paid back the borrowed time and once again had a visual three dimensional model quantity.

When sixty degrees is used for coordination, imaginary or complex numbers are not needed to carry out fourth power calculations because there is a volume of twenty tetrahedra around one point instead of eight. Two to the fourth power is sixteen and there are twenty tetrahedra with which to work. The additional two to the second power in the model is very useful when this vectorial grouping around a common nucleus is employed to account for nuclear energy behaviors. When the nuclear group of vectors has a radial or edge module of two (as do the eight small cubes in closest packing), then the vectorial system has a volume around its center of one hundred and sixty, which is five times two to the fifth power. It is perfectly possible then, today, for a child to make fourth and fifth power models with tetrahedronal and octahedronal building blocks. Einstein was working on fifth power problems just before his death. He was trying to reconcile gravity and electromagnetics.

I have found this arithmetical-geometrical energy coordinating system to coincide rationally and comprehensively with nature's behaviors. With this system, models can be made that can handle fourth and fifth power problems. Systems on an x-y-z coordinating system using cubes cannot do this. This latter fact has accounted for the discard of models and the preoccupation of science with a completely abstract treatment of nature.

Linus Pauling received his first Nobel Prize for his contributions to the general knowledge of chemical structures. He gave me his Nobel laureate paper to read and it was the best and most concise history of chemical structures that I know. The first part of the paper is about organic chemistry.

It was in the years around 1800 that the organic chemists, while making experiments, discovered that the associating-disassociating in organic chemistry seemed to be in whole number increments of one, two, three, four. Those were the only numbers that had to be accounted for in all organic chemistry experiments. In about 1810, a man named Frankland was the first to make a written notation of this fact. Then two men, Kikule and Cooper, added a little more to the same information. In 1835, a Russian, Butlerov, was the first to use the term "chemical structure." He was the first to say that one, two, three, four seemed to have something to do with "bonding" together and he called this bonding "valence"

Then there was a gap in further fundamental discovery until 1885, when a man named Jacobus van't Hoff said that the oneness, twoness, threeness and fourness were the four vertexes of a tetrahedron. Other chemists looked at him askance. He was called an outright charlatan and a faker of every kind. Otherwise, the other chemists paid no attention to van't Hoff's research. He was greatly stunned, but still continued his experiments. He lived long enough to give experimental, optical proof of the tetrahedronal configuration of carbon, the combining master of organic chemistry. Van't Hoff was the first chemist to receive the Nobel Prize. From this time on, chemistry recognized that organic chemistry was coordinated tetrahedronally.

Two tetrahedra linked together by one vertex of each is a single bonding and is very flexible. Bonding by one vertex is like a universal joint and is the situation of gases. Many tetrahedra so linked could be stretched to fill more space than if linked mutually by two or three vertexes. Two bonds form a hinge along one edge of two tetrahedra. This is still a flexible situation as in liquids, but it is, of course, much more compact. Triple bonding or face bond between two tetrahedra is rigid as in crystals. You can get four vertexes of tetrahedra together, which means that they will be congruent and most densely compacted, possibly like diamonds.

In van't Hoff's day, the majority of the chemists were metallurgists and they had found no vertexial bondings. That was probably the reason that they became incensed at van't Hoff's hypothesis. Although there exist in nature visible crystals with the forms of octahedra, rhombic dodecahedra, etc., the other chemists found no way to account for their atomic structuring. In 1932, approximately half a century after van't Hoff, Linus Pauling began to use x-ray diffraction to probe metal structures. X-ray diffraction machines operate in ways analogous to radar: x-ray diffraction sends x-rays right into the atoms to be explored and then these same rays are bounced back giving general pattern information that can be interpreted. In this way, Pauling discovered all the metals he analyzed to be tetrahedronally coordinate, but instead of being linked vertex to vertex, they were linked mid-edge to mid-edge often with common centers of gravity. While Linus Pauling has not, to my knowledge, said that all metals are tetrahedronally coordinated, so far no exceptions have been called to my attention. Pauling's Nobel laureate discourse twenty years ago discussed no exception.

For eighty years, organic chemistry has recognized tetrahedronal coordination. Twenty years of x-ray diffraction experiments have found the metals tetrahedronally coordinate. I came to this subject in an entirely different way from that of the chemists and have found the tetrahedron to be the coordinating unit in experimental mathematics, which is what the scientists call my work. I will say to you what I have said to C.P. Snow: "All of nature's formulating is tetrahedronally coordinate." And Snow, a scientist, said, "From what you have related to me, I am inclined to agree with you. In fact, this information comes to me at a very strategic moment in my life." In the 1965 new year statements harvested by the press from world leaders, Lord Snow had quite a long piece saying that he was able to retract his "two forever unjoinable worlds" (science and the humanities) statements. He felt that he was wrong and it looked like the chasm between the two were closing. In the Nineteenth Century, the literary man had the models taken away from him. He had no model to explain science to the people. Popularization of science employed superficial romance. True science was shunned as too difficult, too dry or too obscure. Now, the bridge has been found between structural conceptuality and pure science exploration.

As conceptuality returns, the great chasm between the humanities and the sciences will be completely repaired. The power of man's thinking, his ability to deal with his universe in ways which differ completely from yesterday, will no longer be frustrated by a lack of conceptional formulation. Man will be able to handle problems with numbers. He will read the calculus and advanced mathematics: he will know what science is doing. In the next decade, you will find nuclear physics models in the kindergartens. Conceptualization of this type can help man solve one of the greatest changes that has come upon us now and which has not been realistically digested; that fact that reality, like thought, is almost entirely invisible.

And this then brings us to generalized principles which have been discovered to be operative in that great invisible realty of the electromagnetic spectrum of 99.99% untouchables, unsmellables and unhearables. Whereas in the literary world a generalization means covering too much territory too thinly to be cogent, the title *generalized principle* in science can be accorded only to relationships and behaviors which hold true in every and all special case experiences. There can be no exception. Science has found in the great realms of the invisible electromagnetic spectrum an extraordinary complex of interrelated and inter-accommodative, separately operative and uniquely definable generalized principles, all of which, like leverage, are, of course, a priori to men. They were not invented but were discovered by human intellect and are, therefore, a priori.

These inter-accommodative generalized principles seem to constitute a body of anticipatory, comprehensive, intellectual abstractions weightlessly governing universe, evolution and humanity's fate therein. Thus the great scientists are beginning to discover God at first hand, as the most comprehensive generalization of the invisibly finite reality. We have then these great generalized principles, of which the average man is unaware, operating supremely and bringing about the evolutionary rearrangements in our total experience of being aboard a planet.

There are over a quadrillion times a quadrillion atoms dynamically inter-coordinating in each of our brains, of whose successful local intercoursings within microcosmic dimensions, at seven hundred million miles an hour, we have no conscious awareness. Nor may we claim any conscious design responsibility for their fantastically successful electromagnetic performances which altogether result in our consciously-cerebrating the sensations and thoughts which integrate as our seemingly simple awareness of just being alive — here and now — and evolving and considering these self-emergent "thoughts." It is not surprising that so exquisitely designed an apparatus can be carelessly and imperfectly tuned-in by us, with superficially misleading results.

And as an example of the inadequacy of our macrocosmic apprehending I think of students who say to me, "I wonder what it would be like to be on a spaceship." (Oldsters have for so long assumed that such events were impossible that they no longer tend spontaneously to think of participating personally in space travel.) I always answer the students by saying, "What does it feel like? That's all you have ever been experiencing. You are all astronauts, for you live aboard a very little spaceship, illogically called 'Earth.' I say illogically because of the relative meagerness of its exquisitely superficial, stardust and radiation supplied, biologically photosynthesized and chemically composted 'top soil' — i.e., the very complex variety of fine particle aggregates generally identified as the substance *earth.*

Once in a while we launch a little spaceship at a velocity of fifteen thousand miles an hour from our bigger, sixty-thousand miles per hour speeding spherical Spaceship Earth which is only 8,000 miles in diameter. We launch our little ships from our bigger Spaceship Earth at only one quarter the speed of our own sun orbiting travel. Our 8,000 miles diameter may seem big to the only-one-thousandth-of-a-mile-high *you* or *me* but our spaceship's size is negligible in respect to the macro distances of the sky. The nearest space 'gas station' (or energy station) from which we get our energy to regenerate life aboard our spherical spaceship is the Sun which is flying in formation with us at 92 million miles distance. As our Spaceship Earth flies formation in annual circles around the Sun it rotates 365 times per orbit and thereby exposes all of its surface to the Sun's radiation thus permitting optimum impoundment of this prime life supporting energy. Our next nearest energy supply skyship 'Star' maintains space flight position with us at 100 thousand times greater distance than the Sun as we altogether fly formation through the vast reaches of the ever transforming Galactic Nebula."

The physical universe is entirely characterized by entropy — an ever increasing random mess, an ever increasing diffusion as all the different and non-simultaneous transformations and reorientations occur. While the entropy of and disorderliness of physical universe increases and expands, we have the metaphysical universe countering with comprehensive contraction and increasing order. In the contracting metaphysical universe we have the human mind digesting and sorting out all the special cases and therefrom generalizing commonly held characteristics of all special cases. All the fundamental principles apparently governing both physical and metaphysical universe are the experimentally derived generalizations.

While all the stars are radiantly entropic, the Planet Earth is not radiant and does represent a physically collecting local system in universe. The geophysical year disclosed that possibly a hundred thousand tons of stardust is collected daily by Planet Earth. Earth also collects star radiation, particularly the radiation from the sun star. The Earth seems to be cooling off, contracting and collecting as an anti-entropic locality in universe. Not all of the sun's radiation bounces off the Earth. Its heat is impounded in the sea, by plants through photosynthesis, until gradually the sun's energy is buried deeply in the form of fossil fuels. The biologicals act antientropically because they make orderly molecular chains and other orderly structures.

Then we have the human mind developing antientropically far beyond the biologicals by the formulation of metaphysical generalizations. From a great many special cases experiences the human mind extracts the generalized principles which are always operative in all the special cases.

The human mind can start generalizing by saying "I take a piece of rope and tense it. As I tense it more tautly, its girth contracts; therefore, it goes into compression in a plane at 90 degrees to my tensing." I now take a cigar shaped compression column and load its top end. As I do so, its girth expands and therefore goes into tension in a plane at its girth at 90 degrees to the column's compression axis. The human mind thus discovers that tension and compression always and only coexist. So too does the mind discover that concave and convex always and only coexist. So too it discovers that the proton and neutron always and only coexist. Thus, it came to the theory of functions in which any function always and only coexists with another function. Then, we can generalize still further by reducing the theory of functions to the one word "relativity."

This whole process of generalizing generalizations forms a pyramid whose base consists of all the special cases of direct physical experiences. But when we said, "We take a piece of rope and tense it," we did not in fact have a rope in our hands. We have all had so many rope experiences that we generalized the concept. This was a first degree generalization. The discovery of always and only coexisting tension and compression was a second degree generalization. Finding a whole family of always and only coexisting phenomena was third degree generalization. Developing the theory of functions was a fourth degree generalization and conceiving therefrom the theory of relativity was a fifth degree generalization.

In this pyramid of generalization, the human mind then goes way beyond the biologicals in its development of an increasing and diminishing conceptual universe. So we find the metaphysical not only balancing the physical, which should have been expected, but also encompassing the physical by one tetrahedron and thereafter reducing its myriadness to unity. The metaphysical, as with the circumferentially united great circle chord vectors of the vector equilibrium, coheres the physical.

I am convinced that the difference between animal brains and the human mind lies specifically in man's unique ability to generalize to progressively compounding degrees of abstraction. I think that this is man's unique function in universe — antientropy. The physical universe is entropic; that is, energies escape from local systems and the "fall-out" is described as the law of increase of the random element. That increase of diffuse energies brings about the expanding physical universe; in superb balance with which the human mind continually probes for and discovers order in universe and continually contracts the descriptions of the separate orderly behaviors discovered in nature and then combines these generalized observations into progressively more comprehensive generalizations. Therefore, the metaphysical universe co-functions equally with the physical universe as its contracting universe and increasing orderliness counterpart.

Man is the great antientropy of universe. The famous "second law" of thermodynamics propounds entropy. But the human mind discovered and described and harnessed in orderly fashion this disorderly propensity of nature. Einstein's mind discovered and generalized the comprehensive law of physical energy universe as $E = MC^2$ and the process of metaphysical mastery of the physical is irreversible. It is unthinkable and unexperienced that energy can and does pronounce what intellect is.

I am certain that what we speak of as human morality is a form of intuitive and tentative generalization of experiences not as yet worked out in mathematical degree of incisiveness. Man has also the unique ability to objectively employ generalized principles — once recognized — in a consciously selective variety of special case interrelationships. He is thus able to alter the inanimate environment and thereby to alter the "specialized case" patterning of human experiences and thereby to provide more opportunity to verify or discard previous generalizations and to formulate new ones.

But today we find that man, in his ignorance of being aboard a spaceship of such beautiful design and equipment as to be able to regenerate human life on board for perhaps more than two million years, and also unaware popularly of the a priori set of invisible principles inexorably governing his evolutionary success, has been carrying on only in visible and fantastically shortsighted ways. Consequently, he has been abusing all the great capabilities which lay there, potential to his use, which, if understood, could make all of humanity physically and economically successful. Instead, we find polluting and despoiling going on in such a way that man can only last for a very short time unless he makes important changes in his behavior regarding his passengership aboard Spaceship Earth.

Amongst the changes implicit to all the foregoing realizations which impress me the most, is the fact that whereas up to now in history man has been assuming that there never would be enough vital resources to support all of humanity, this is now proving to be a false premise. At the turn of the century, just before World War I, those in the know assumed that economic conditions were such that only one in one hundred would have any chance of living out his physical days, going beyond an average lifespan of 27. Although science has discovered that man can be a success, still all our great governments are organized and as yet operate on the *only-you-or-me; not-both-can-survive-basis.* Instead of having everybody carrying their own bludgeons, spears, swords or later guns, the major nations have professional soldiery developing enormous mass-killing guns against the day of reckoning when it is decided by war which side is going to survive.

Until the day before yesterday, the theory of sovereign autonomy of national ideologies held and as yet holds that only the side whose military can deliver the greatest hitting power, the greatest distance in the shortest time with the greatest accuracy and least effort will survive and prosper. Inherently shortsighted and articulate business and politics, looking only to this year's crop or profit, or next year's election, has left it to the national defense's military to look ahead and watch widely for the hopefully far ahead total war enjoinments. To attain and maintain their superior power over all comers, the military employ the scientists as masters of energy in all its 99.99% invisibly operative behaviors. Progressive reports of the opposing spy systems escalate the scientific undertakings and breakthroughs. Thus science has been employed almost exclusively for both direct and supportive military purposes. And out of their escalated scientific preoccupations has come the proposed acquisition of technology to cost many-fold what their respectively competing societies thought they could afford. When it came to the critical verge of war, however, the opposed people and their political leaders were told by their military they must either buy or die. So, unwitting how they might pay, they bought the new hardware. Out of that technological evolution has come this epochal change:

That the world can be made to work successfully is now conceded by knowledgeable scientists for the first time in man's history. When speaking only from their universal — ergo: unbiased scientific — viewpoint advantage, the scientists say Malthus is wrong. They admit, rather than assert, that there can be enough and more to permit all of humanity to enjoy all the Earth.

This is the state of affairs right now. We may check this out experimentally for ourselves by a systematic examination and interrelation of a specific family of pertinent facts and then by asking ourselves how the inter-scoring of such juxtaposed information comes out. The facts are that the metals in eighty percent of all the scrap of yesterday's obsolete mechanics and structures have been recovered, refined as "pure metals" and put to work again. But the combined rate of mining increase, scrap metal recovery, and the increased discovery of additional metal ores is slower than human population increase.

Throughout the twentieth century, therefore, the known extant metals, both mined and unmined, have been decreasing per each world man. At the present moment the cumulative total of metals — mined and refined by man throughout history — is wholly employed in machines or structures, the designed capabilities of which, operating at full limit capacity, can accommodate and serve only forty-four percent of living humanity. No exclusively political act of any political system can make the world's resources take care of more than forty-four percent of mankind.

Despite the constant increase in human population and constant decrease of metals per person, between 1900 and 1965 the number of people attaining economic and physical success by full participation in the highest standard of living progressively developed by world industrialization — a personal standard of living and health superior to that ever enjoyed by a pre-twentieth century man — rose steadily from less than one percent to forty percent of all living humanity. The forty percent of humanity thus surprisingly grown successful, despite constantly diminishing physical resources per capita, can be explained, therefore, only by the doing-more-with-less, or design science revolution.

The doing-more-with-less revolution does not accomplish this stepped-up efficiency as much by penny-pinching and progressive refinement of a given technique as by substitution of a whole new technology or a whole new industry or a completely new general systems change. For instance, the shift from wire to wireless communication systems wherein one telstar satellite weighing only one-quarter of a ton out-performs, and in due course displaces, the trans-oceanic cables systems weighing hundreds of thousands of tons and handling the same number of messages in an inferior way.

The doing-more-with-less revolution has in turn been generated almost exclusively by the technology of the world's weaponry race whose ultimate objective has always been to deliver the greatest blows the furthest, most accurately and swiftly with the least effort. The doing-more-with-less economic success of forty percent of humanity, accomplished in little more than half a century, occurred as the ultimate but inadvertent fall-out into the domestic economy of the weapons developed technological advances. The doing-more-with-less effort cannot be attributed to any political doctrine. Political doctrine undertakes only to do more with more — more security with higher, thicker and heavier walls — more and bigger guns — more and more soldiers who only consume rather than produce and conserve wealth. Fall-out of the ever-more-capability with ever-less-expenditure-of-effort,-time-and-material-per-each-unit of performance came primarily from the sea, air and space support industries. Its fall-out into domestic commonwealth affairs has flourished equally well under all the various and/or opposing ideologies.

Fortunately, the do-more-with-less invention initiative does not derive from nor depend upon political debate, bureaucratic licensing, or private economic patronage. The license comes only from the blue sky of the inventor's intellect. No one licensed the inventors of the airplane, telephone, electric light and radio to go to work. It took only five men to invent these world transforming do-vastly-more-with-exquisitely-less developments. Herein lies the potentially swift effectiveness of the world design revolution.

It is possible — and is going to be necessary, if society is to continue on Earth — for the professional scientists, engineers, and architects to satisfactorily anticipate the economic needs of not only the next generation of humanity, but of all generations of all men to come. It is going to be necessary for the scientists, engineers, and professionals in general, and for the world students in particular, to take the initiative in respect to articulating the total advantages to make the world work for all.

Science now says that the design science revolution could make possible all of humanity's enjoying all of our spherical space vehicle Earth without anyone interfering with another and without any individual being advantaged at the expense of another, but that it cannot be accomplished while maintaining protective trade restraints of the sovereign boundaries of nations. Mankind will learn that the design revolution requires universal integrity of intellectual formulations and unbiased cerebral coordination which man will inevitably come to discover and cultivate, because integrity is innate and has been frustrated in the past only postnatally and only then by the inertial paralysis of once excellent but later obsolete "good customs" of yesterday, originally adopted under conditions of overwhelming ignorance and deep-seated mortal fears, if not for self, then for one's helpless dependents.

But we can scientifically assume that by the 21st Century either humanity will not be living aboard Spaceship Earth, or, if approximately our present numbers as yet remain aboard, that they then will have recognized and organized themselves to realize effectively the fact that humanity can afford to do anything it needs and wishes to do and that it cannot afford anything else.

As a consequence, Earth-planet based humanity will be physically and economically successful and individually free in the most important sense. While all enjoy total Earth, no human will be interfering with the other and none will be profiting at the expense of the other. Humans will be free in the sense that 99.9 percent of their waking hours will be freely investible at their own discretion. They will be free in the sense that they will not struggle for survival on a "you" or "me" basis and will therefore be able to trust one another and be free to cooperate in spontaneous and logical ways.

It is also probable that during that one-third of a century of the curtain raising of the 21st Century the number of boo-boos, biased blunders, short-sighted misjudgments, opinionated self-deceits of humanity will total, at minimum, six hundred trillion errors.

Clearly, man will have backed into his future as evolution, operating as inexorably as fertilized ovaries gestate in the womb, will have brought about his success in ways that are perhaps today synergetically unforeseeable. All of this does not add up to say that man is stupidly ignorant and does not deserve to prosper. It adds up to the realization that in the design of universal evolution, man was given an enormous safety factor as an economic cushion — within which to learn by trial and error to dare to use his most sensitively intuited intellectual conceptioning and greatest vision in joining forces with all of humanity to advance into the future in full accreditation of the individual human intellect's most powerfully loving conceptions of the potential functioning of man in universe.

Eddington defined science as "The earnest attempt to set in order the facts of experience." In attempting earnestly to think about our environment we realize gradually that it is not a static stage set. It is the continually transforming sum of all our external experiences. It is omni-dynamic. It is a complex of events. Environment is all else of universe but self. Sometimes it feels superbly synchronous — at others, discordant. Ninety-nine and ninety-nine one-hundredths percent of the events which constitute the physical and metaphysical universe are undetectable directly by our senses.

Considering and reconsidering clues which may permit our setting the complexedly compounding facts of our environment in order requires (unfortunately not too obviously) that we first remind ourselves that many experiences have shown us the ease with which all our perceptual faculties can be deceived. We have also experienced the persistent and lightning-like contagion of misinformation. For instance, it is difficult to intercept and rationalize the two year old children's innocently relayed infusion of the artificial concept of "that is mine" — at first mimicked from adults but having such excitingly abrupt effect on other children as to induce attitude-forming repetition.

We are also reminded of the fact that our spontaneously developed shortsightedness and frequently deliberate exclusion from consideration of a large proportion of the environmental events have most often precluded our discovery of the fundamental evolutionary trendings implicit in the non-simultaneous continuity of our total experiences. Our vision is limited to the tiny red, orange, yellow, green, blue, and violet bands of frequency tunabilities representing far less than one-thousandth of one percent of the great electromagnetic spectrum of the thus far discovered vast range of the physical universe realities. Our after image overlapping which results in our sense of motion is even more limited in its perceptual range. We cannot see the hands of the clock move. We cannot see life growing. We cannot see either the stars or the atomic components move though they move at fantastic speeds. We can only see the ultra slow motions of the clouds, locally running waters, human beings, other creatures and their parts. No wonder that little man who within his average lifetime has seen only about one millionth of the surface of his planet and has lived but a split second of the astronomical ages does not see and cope spontaneously with the larger evolutionary patternings and life aboard planet Earth. Only through memory plus thought — greatly aided by instruments — does man discover the ultra and infra-motion effects.

Sum totally we discover that the many different and equally erroneous opinions of humanity regarding life and the world — and how to get along in it — gradually merge into often lethally divergent religions and ideologies — every one of them based on fundamental misconceptions and incomprehensions of the realities of universe — and the universally complex integrity of generalized principles, including for instance, the principles of irreversibility and entropy which together result in inexorable evolution and its myriad of constant local transformations.

The more we learn the more we realize how little we know. That little seems to say: We, humans, have been successful thus far in history only by virtue of the supreme intellectual capability manifest in the harmoniously scientific design of the *minimum perpetual motion machine* — the infinitely regenerative universe.

But humanity now everywhere around Earth is intuitively aware of the increasing threat to human survival — around our planet — that is bound to be consequent to the further promulgation of our egotistically ignorant and illogically opposed individual and group viewpoints.

Let us, therefore, be as scientifically orderly as it is at present feasible in dealing intellectually and practically with that complex scenario of transformations which is Universe. To do so, let us examine our macrocosmic and microcosmic experience apprehending processes and then our deliberate experimental-explorations toward comprehending the macro-micro-environmental event complex. Finally, let us scientifically reconsider our intuitively objective formulations for the objective employment of the generalized principles which we seem to have winnowed from our experiences with the environment which, in turn, may permit us to make life favoring alterations of Universe's environment scenario. In this way can man find his full accomplishment in Universe.

Contributors

JOHN CAGE. Born in 1912, Los Angeles, California. Composer, poet, artist, a major influence on the avant-garde imagination, Mr. Cage has received many awards and performed widely in America, Europe, and the Far East. His books include *Silence,* 1961; *A Year from Monday,* 1967; and *Notations,* 1969.

DAVID DAICHES. Born in 1912, Sunderland, England. Literary critic and scholar, Mr. Daiches has taught at Cambridge, Chicago, Cornell, and Sussex, where he has served as Dean of the School of English Studies since 1961. His numerous publications include *Literature and Society,* 1938; *The Novel and the Modern World,* 1939, 1960; *Robert Burns,* 1950; *Critical Approaches to Literature,* 1956; *Two Worlds: An Edinburgh Jewish Childhood,* 1956; and *A Critical History of English Literature,* 1970.

LESLIE A. FIEDLER. Born in 1917, Newark, New Jersey. Man of letters, Mr. Fiedler has taught at Montana, Princeton, Rome, and Sussex. He is currently Professor of English at the State University of New York, Buffalo. His works include *An End to Innocence,* 1955; *Love and Death in the American Novel,* 1960, 1966; *No! in Thunder,* 1960; *Back to China,* 1965; and *Being Busted,* 1970.

R. BUCKMINSTER FULLER. Born in 1895, Milton, Massachusetts. Architect, inventor, visionary, Mr. Fuller is the builder of many original structures, including the geodesic dome and the dymaxion house. He is a pioneer of global design science and synergetics, and the recipient of innumerable honors and awards. He is currently Professor of Generalized Design Science at the University of Southern Illinois at Carbondale. His numerous published works include *Nine Chains to the Moon,* 1938; *Education Automation,* 1962; *Untitled Epic Poem on the History of Industrialization,* 1963; and *Operating Manual for Spaceship Earth,* 1969.

IHAB HASSAN. Born in 1925, Cairo, Egypt. Literary critic and scholar, Mr. Hassan has taught at Wesleyan University, where he served in 1969–1970 as Director of the Center for the Humanities. He is currently Vilas Research Professor of English and Comparative Literature at the University of Wisconsin–Milwaukee. His works include *Radical Innocence,* 1961; *The Literature of Silence,* 1967; and *The Dismemberment of Orpheus,* 1971.

FRANK KERMODE. Born in 1919, Douglas, Isle of Man. Literary critic and scholar, Mr. Kermode has taught at Reading, Manchester, and Bristol. He is currently Lord

Northcliffe Professor of Modern English Literature at University College, London. His works include *Romantic Image*, 1957; *Wallace Stevens*, 1960; *Puzzles and Epiphanies*, 1962; *The Sense of an Ending*, 1967; and *Continuities*, 1968.

Louis Mink. Born in 1921, Ada, Ohio. Philosopher and aesthetician, Mr. Mink has taught at Yale and Wesleyan, where he is currently Professor of Philosophy and Chairman of the Department. He has edited *The Review of Metaphysics* and *History and Theory*. His publications include *Collingwood: Mind, History and Dialectic*, 1969.

Richard Poirier. Born in 1925, Gloucester, Massachusetts. Literary critic and scholar, Mr. Poirier has taught at Harvard and Rutgers, where he is currently Professor of English and Chairman of the Department. He is also an editor of *Partisan Review*. His works include *The Comic Sense in Henry James*, 1960; *In Defense of Reading*, 1962; and *A World Elsewhere*, 1966.

Harold Rosenberg. Born in 1906, Brooklyn, New York. Art and literary critic, Mr. Rosenberg has taught at the New School of Social Research, Berkeley, and Chicago, where he is currently Professor of the Committee on Social Thought. He is also on the staff of *The New Yorker*. His works include *The Tradition of the New*, 1959; *Arshile Gorky*, 1962; *The Anxious Object*, 1964; and *Artworks and Packages*, 1969.

Daniel Stern. Born in 1928, New York City. Novelist, literary critic, and cellist, Mr. Stern writes frequently for the *New York Times Book Review, Book Week, Life, Harper's*, and other periodicals. His novels include *The Girl with the Glass Heart*, 1953; *Who Shall Live, Who Shall Die*, 1963; *After the War*, 1967; and *The Suicide Academy*, 1968,

Hayden White. Born in 1928, Martin, Tennessee. Historian of culture and ideas, Mr. White has taught at Wayne State, Rochester, and U.C.L.A., where he is currently Professor of History. His works include *Emergence of Liberal Humanism*, 1967; *The Uses of History*, 1968; *Vico Tercentary Commemorative Volume* (with G. Tagliacozzo), 1969; and *Ordeal of Liberal Humanism*, 1969.

Michael Wolff. Born in 1927, London, England. Literary and cultural historian, Mr. Wolff has taught at Indiana University and is currently Professor of English and Victorian Studies at the University of Massachusetts. He is founder and editor of *Victorian Studies* and has contributed articles to *1859: Entering an Age of Crisis*, 1959, and *Editing Problems in the Nineteenth Century*, 1967.